APPLIED CRISIS COMMUNICATION AND **CRISIS MANAGEMENT**

Cases and Exercises

W. Timothy Coombs
University of Central Florida

Los Angeles | London | New Delhi
Singapore | Washington DC

Los Angeles | London | New Delhi
Singapore | Washington DC

FOR INFORMATION:

SAGE Publications, Inc.

2455 Teller Road

Thousand Oaks, California 91320

E-mail: order@sagepub.com

SAGE Publications Ltd.

1 Oliver's Yard

55 City Road

London EC1Y 1SP

United Kingdom

SAGE Publications India Pvt. Ltd.

B 1/I 1 Mohan Cooperative Industrial Area

Mathura Road, New Delhi 110 044

India

SAGE Publications Asia-Pacific Pte. Ltd.

3 Church Street

#10-04 Samsung Hub

Singapore 049483

Printed in the United States of America

Library of Congress Cataloging-in-Publication Data

Coombs, W. Timothy.
Applied crisis communication and crisis management: cases and exercises / W. Timothy Coombs, University of Central Florida.

pages cm
Includes bibliographical references and index.

ISBN 978-1-4522-1780-2

1. Crisis management. 2. Business communication. 3. Management. I. Title.

HD49.C6625 2013
658.4'056--dc23   2013001199

This book is printed on acid-free paper.

Acquisitions Editor: Matthew Byrnie

Editorial Assistant: Stephanie Palermini

Production Editor: Olivia Weber-Stenis

Copy Editor: Patrice Sutton

Typesetter: C & M Digitals (P) Ltd.

Proofreader: Sally Jaskold

Indexer: Diggs Publication Services

Cover Designer: Janet Kiesel

Graphic Designer: Cristina Kubota

Marketing Manager: Liz Thornton

13 14 15 16 17 10 9 8 7 6 5 4 3 2 1

Contents

CHAPTER 1

A Short Introduction to the Case Study Method

The term *case study* can have different meanings. For instance, Yin (1984) has a well-known book that explains the case study as a research method. That book details how case studies can be used to collect data and answer research questions. This is not a research methods book, it is a book designed for courses in crisis communication and crisis management. In this book, the term *case study* refers to a type of educational tool, the case study method to be more precise. The case study method has students learn by analyzing real-life situations. This book utilizes crisis cases as a focal point for analysis. Learning occurs as students apply theories and principles to analyze events in the case. Based upon that analysis, students evaluate the actions taken in the crisis case and recommend what they believe would be the best course of action to take in the case. The evaluations and recommendations are grounded in the theories and principles used to analyze the crisis case.

Case studies have applications beyond the classroom. Corporate trainers find case studies to be engaging tools for developing critical thinking skills. In addition, some consulting firms use case studies to evaluate potential job candidates. This first chapter is a short introduction to the case study method for students and a review of the concept for instructors. This introduction includes a history of the case study method, steps that can be used to conduct a case study, and an overview to the structure of the book.

Origins of Case Studies

In professional education, a case is a description of a real-life event. A case study is the systematic analysis of a case. The person reading the case applies some analytic tools to explain what has happened in the case and/or what actions should be taken in the case. Public relations has followed in the tradition of business by adopting the case study method as part of professional education. In the United States, the case study method originated in the Harvard Law School. Cases allowed students to draw their own conclusions about a case instead of just memorization and recall of existing law cases. Christopher Columbus Langdell is the name associated with introducing the case study methods at the Harvard Law School in the 1850s (Garvin, 2003).

Wallace P. Donham graduated from Harvard Law School, and his practice drew him into the business world. He eventually began to teach courses in corporate finance. Donham began to see a parallel between law and business. These connections led him to believe that future managers could benefit from the case study method. Donham observed that managers had to make and implement decisions. However, those decisions were often made in ambiguous situations—not all the facts would be known when it was time to act. Donham believed students should practice making decisions by analyzing real-life situations—cases. Students could practice using the theories and analytic tools of business to analyze the cases and to justify their recommended decisions. Donham convinced other faculty to write and use business cases in the early 1920s, making the Harvard Business School the birthplace of business case studies (Garvin, 2003). Case studies have since been adopted in a variety of professional disciplines as a pedagogical tool. Crisis communication is one of the professional disciplines that values the case study method for teaching the practice.

Purpose of the Casebook

Following the Harvard Business School model, this casebook places students in the shoes of the crisis managers. The casebook contains what are called *library cases*. Library cases are composed of public records about the case, not interviews with the people involved in the case. Students take the role of the crisis managers in the case. Based upon information in the case, students evaluate the crisis communication effort and make suggestions about what other actions they would recommend. A key component of the analysis is the application of theories and principles from crisis communication. Students need to explain how they reached their evaluation of the actions and why they would recommend additional actions. The analysis of the case is based upon principles and theories (analytic tools), not just opinion. Crisis communication is an applied field, meaning its principles and theories are supposed to solve real-world problems. The ultimate goal of the case analysis is to demonstrate how the various principles and theories can be used in actual crises and to provide practice in making decisions about crisis communication.

How to Work with a Case

Students are to provide an analysis and recommendations for the case or what we can call *case solutions* for short. Students execute a number of steps when developing their case solutions. This section outlines the process used to create case solutions and follows a process outlined by the Eugene D. Fanning Center for Business Communication (O'Rourke, 2000).

1. Read the case carefully. Focus on finding the relevant details in the case such as key stakeholders, actions taken by various actors in the case, and the effects of the crisis on the organization and its stakeholders. As students read the case, they should take notes on these key factors as a memory aid.

2. Identify the central crisis communication concerns. Crisis management involves a myriad of communication concerns. Students need to determine what crisis communication concerns are the most pertinent to the case. Chapter 2 provides a more detailed discussion of the various crisis communication concerns. Crises are complex, and the challenge for any crisis manager is to determine what needs their attention at a particular time. Students should isolate the most important crisis communication concerns in the case. Before managers can implement a solution, managers need to understand the problem. There may be a number of different problems. When there are multiple problems, managers need to prioritize them in order of importance—in other words, which problem is addressed first, second, and so on. Students assume the role of managers in identifying and prioritizing problems.

3. Decide on the objectives of the crisis communication effort. Crisis communication is strategic because it is designed to achieve certain outcomes. Students should determine what the objective or objectives should be for the crisis team. In other words, "What does the crisis team hope to achieve through crisis communication?" Objectives are critical to evaluating the success or failure of a crisis communication effort. Specifying what the crisis team hopes to achieve will provide a standard for evaluating its results.

4. Develop a list of solutions. For each problem, students should list a number of different crisis communication solutions. The solutions should be guided by the principles and theories of crisis communication. Research is used to develop and to test the theories and principles of crisis communication. Past research should give managers and students confidence about what theories and principles should work in this case. *Should* is an important qualifier. Crisis communication is a social science that involves how people react to situations. Social scientists, including many crisis communication researchers, can make predictions about human behavior, but people frequently act in ways that defy logic and theory. There are recommended actions in crisis communication that should work, but there are no guarantees the recommendations will work. Students will end this section with a draft of their crisis communication message and a rationale for that message or set of messages.

5. Evaluate, select, and implement a solution. Students select the one, best option from their list options. Consider the benefits and liabilities of each option before selecting the final solution. Again, theory and principles can help students to determine which solution is the best. A solution has to be implemented. Explain what actions need to be taken to implement the chosen crisis communication solution. This explanation should include identifying the stakeholders that will receive the message and the channel or channels used to reach the stakeholders. Table 1.1 provides a summary of the basic steps in a case study analysis.

Table 1.1   Summary of Steps in a Case Study Analysis

1. Carefully read and take notes on the case.
2. Identify the central crisis communication concerns.
3. Determine the objective(s) for the crisis team.
4. Use theories or principles to develop solutions for the crisis communication concerns.
5. Use theories or principles to explain which solution would be the best for the case and to implement the solution.

These five steps are not the only way to conduct a case study analysis. The steps are offered as a starting point for discussing the case analysis process. Instructors will bring their own ideas to the case study method and develop their own custom guidelines for case analysis. What will remain constant in the case analysis is the use of theories and principles to analyze the cases and to justify the actions recommended for crisis managers. Exhibit 1.1 provides a generic outline for a sample case analysis.

Exhibit 1.1   Outline for a Case Study

I. Introduction

   A. Orient the reader to the case

   B. Provide a preview of the key points in the analysis

II. Explanation of the Case

   A. Provide a summary of the case

   B. Specify the key actors in the case including their stake in the case

   C. Identify the crisis communication concerns in the case

   D. Specify the objective or objectives for the crisis team

III. Analysis of the Case

   A. Explain the analytic tools to be applied in the case—the theories and/or principles that will be applied to the case

   B. Develop and explain a list of potential solutions you developed using the analytic tools

IV. Final Solution and Discussion

   A. Justify the selection of your preferred solution using the analytic tools

   B. Describe how the solution should be implemented

   C. Review the lessons learned from the case

Structure of the Book

The previous section suggests students need two key ingredients to conduct a case study: (a) cases and (b) theories and principles they can apply to the cases. Chapter 2 provides summaries of key theories and principles from crisis communication that can be used as analytic tools. Students should not limit themselves to just these analytic devices and the information each capsule provides about the tools. Students and instructors are encouraged to explore the crisis communication literature to find additional analytic tools and to expand on the information provided in the capsules.

Chapters 3 through 19 provide case studies derived from actual crises. There are four groupings of crisis cases: (a) crises emphasizing element of the precrisis phase, (b) crises emphasizing the crisis response phase, (c) crises emphasizing the postcrisis phase, and (d) classic crisis cases. Each crisis case details what happened in the crisis. As in any case study analysis, the case provides the basics, and students are encouraged to gather additional information about the case. The first three sets of crises reflect the three phases of crisis management: (a) precrisis, (b) crisis response, and (c) postcrisis. It is important to study crises that emphasize various stages of crisis management because the crisis communication demands vary among the different crisis stages. Each case chapter includes a reading guide, additional information resources, and discussion questions. The reading guide highlights key points in each case while additional information resources provide links for gathering additional data. The discussion questions raise concerns that confront the crisis managers and stakeholders in the case. Students can utilize both the reading guides and discussion questions when preparing to discuss the case or to prepare a formal case solution.

Though the first three sections emphasize different crisis phases, students and instructors will need to decide what theories and principles to apply to each case. The goal is for students to learn how to make and to evaluate decisions about crisis communication, not simply to read what other people have done or said. The case study method has value because it helps students to develop critical thinking skills. Critical thinking requires students to understand a set of analytic tools (e.g., theories and principles) and the ability to apply them to analyze cases.

References

Garvin, D. A. (2003, September/October). Making the case: Professional education for the world of practice. *Harvard Magazine, 106*(2), 56–65, 107.

O'Rourke, J. S. (2000). Analyzing a case study. Retrieved from http://www.awpagesociety .com/images/uploads/Study_Analysis.pdf

Yin, R. (1984). Case study research: Design and methods. Beverly Hills, CA: Sage.

CHAPTER 2

Crisis Capsules

This chapter provides crisis capsules that summarize the key points from various theories and principles of crisis communication. The crisis capsules provide the analytic tools for the case study analysis and the justifications for crisis communication actions. As analytic tools, the crisis capsules can be used to dissect the cases and to explore the crisis communication actions. As justification, the crisis capsules can provide the rationale for why certain crisis communication actions should or should not be taken in a particular case. The crisis capsules are summaries of the theories and principles. Each crisis capsule lists one or more additional readings that could be helpful for executing an in-depth analysis of a case. Keep in mind that a case can be analyzed by using a variety of crisis capsules either individually or in combination with one another. It is up to the person who is creating the case analysis to decide which crisis capsule or capsules would be most appropriate for the case. Part of a strong case study is justifying your selection of critical tools for the analysis.

An Overview

I want to start the presentation of the crisis communication theories and principles with a more general discussion of crisis communication. There are two categories of crisis communication: managing information and managing meaning. Managing information involves the collection, analysis, and dissemination of information during a crisis. Managing meaning involves the messages used in attempts to shape how people perceive the crisis or the organization in crisis. The cases emphasize managing meaning because they examine the public aspect of the crisis and do not include private information from the crisis teams themselves. This focus reflects the crisis communication research itself that has a strong managing meaning focus. People need to interpret the information and actions they encounter, the symbolic behavior perspective that argues organizational reality is socially constructed through communication (Cheney & Christensen, 2000). Meaning should not be considered devoid of action or substance. The crisis communication is linked to behavior when it seeks to influence how people interpret those actions or events.

A second way of categorizing crisis communication is by the phase of crisis management: precrisis (prevention and preparation), crisis response, and postcrisis (learning) (Coombs, 2010). The vast majority of crisis communication research examines the managing of meaning during the crisis response phase (Coombs, 2010). Moreover, the crisis cases themselves all involve some form of crisis response. The crisis capsules reflect this emphasis of managing meaning during the crisis response phase. The following crisis theories and principles each have capsules: corporate apologia, image repair theory, focusing event, instructing and adjusting information, validated accepted wisdom, rhetoric of renewal or discourse of renewal, rhetorical arena, situation crisis communication theory, contingency theory, complexity theory, and paracrisis and crisis prevention. Each capsule is followed by a discussion of how the capsules can be used in combination with one another and what aspects of a crisis suggest a specific capsule might fit with that crisis.

Corporate Apologia

Corporate apologia was the earliest communication-based approach to crises. *Apologia* is a rhetorical concept involving self-defense. The origins of apologia flow from political communication and the strategies politicians employed when they would defend their public character from attacks. The essential elements of apologia were an actual attack on someone's public character, which could include accusations of wrongdoing, and a defense of that character. The four strategies that could be utilized in apologia are denial (people claim they are not involved in any wrongdoing), bolstering (the audience is reminded of the good things the people had done), differentiation (remove the action from its negative context), and transcendence (place the action in a new, broader context that is more favorable) (Ware & Linkugel, 1973).

Dionisopolous and Vibbert (1988) presented the first published work that argued corporations could engage in apologia thereby creating the concept of corporate apologia. Their position was that corporations have public characters, what we would term *reputations*, just like individuals. Reputations can be defined as how people perceive the organization. Reputations are evaluative and are created from the accumulated information a person has about an organization (Carroll & McCombs, 2003; Fombrun & van Riel, 2004; Meijer, 2004). Moreover, corporate character-reputation can be attacked and require defense the same as individual character can. A crisis is an example of wrongdoing that would threaten the corporate character-reputation and require defense. Crisis communication strategies can be used to defend the corporate character-reputation.

Hearit (1994, 1995, 2006) is the name most commonly associated with corporate apologia. Hearit's research refined and expanded our understanding of corporate apologia. Hearit argued that a crisis was a threat to an organization's social legitimacy. *Social legitimacy* is the consistency between stakeholder and organizational values.

Stakeholders will oppose organizations that they do not *believe* possess social legitimacy; hence, a crisis can be a serious threat if it erodes social legitimacy. Social legitimacy can be viewed as an element of reputation. Reputation does include expectations of how organizations should behave (Fombrun & van Riel, 2004). Corporate apologia serves to protect reputations by restoring social legitimacy.

Hearit (1995, 2006) integrated dissociations into corporate apologia. *Dissociations* occur when an idea is divided into two parts. Why should this matter to crisis communication? In crisis communication, the dissociation tries to decouple the organization and the crisis (wrongdoing). Crisis responsibility is the link between the organization and the crisis. Organizations suffer harm from a crisis because stakeholders judge them as being responsible for the crisis. A dissociation tries to redefine the crisis situation so that the organization is viewed as less responsible for the crisis. Less crisis responsibility should reduce stakeholder anger and hostility about the crisis (Hearit, 1995). Dissociations protect reputations by reducing the threat posed by the crisis. A dissociation creates the perception that the crisis is a limited threat to social legitimacy and reputation.

There are three dissociation strategies: opinion–knowledge, individual–group, and act–essence. The opinion–knowledge dissociation attempts to remove any connection between the organization and the crisis. The crisis managers claim that people only think the organization is associated with the crisis. When people examine the facts (knowledge), they realize the organization has no connection to the crisis. The individual–group dissociation seeks to reduce the crisis responsibility attributed to an organization by identifying a subset of the organization as responsible for the crisis. People should just blame one or a small group of people in the organization for the crisis, not the entire organization. The organization then takes actions to punish the bad employees and that should be enough to satisfy stakeholders—reduce stakeholder anger toward the organization. The act–essence dissociation admits the crisis did occur and that the organization is responsible. However, managers argue that the crisis was an isolated incident and does not represent the true organization. Stakeholders should forgive the overall "good" organization for a momentary lapse (Hearit, 1995).

Image Repair Theory, Image Restoration Theory, Image Repair Discourse

William Benoit (1995) created image restoration theory (IRT) (aka image repair theory and image repair discourse) by integrating ideas from corporate apologia and account giving. Account giving is an interpersonal concept that involves people supplying reasons for their actions. Others besides Benoit have adapted account giving to organizations (e.g., Allen & Caillouet, 1994). Similar to apologia, there is some attack on the organization's character in image repair. This attack must include an offensive act and claims that the organization is responsible for the offensive act. In other words, stakeholders perceive that something bad has happened and hold the organization responsible for the negative action. Corporate communication is viewed as strategic (goal-directed). IRT holds that one of the primary goals of corporate communication is to defend the organization's reputation. A crisis threatens an organization's reputation, and crisis response strategies are used to defend and to repair the reputation. Here is a list of the crisis response strategies developed by IRT, divided into the five categories of "image repair strategies":

1. Denial: sever the connection between the organization and the crisis
   - Simple denial: claim organization is not involved
   - Shift the blame: blame some other person or group for the crisis

2. Evading responsibility: reduce organizational responsibility for the crisis
   - Provocation: response to actions of others
   - Defeasibility: lack of information about or control over the situation
   - Accidental: things just happen sometimes
   - Good intentions: the organization meant well with its actions

3. Reduce offensiveness: make the crisis look "better" to stakeholders
   - Bolstering: remind stakeholders of past good work by the organization and/or praise those who are helping with the crisis
   - Minimizing offensiveness of the act: argue situation is not as bad as it seems
   - Differentiation: compare the crisis to other, more negative events
   - Transcendence: place the crisis in a new, less negative context
   - Attack the accuser: challenge those promoting the crisis
   - Compensation: offer victims money, goods, or services

4. Corrective action: restore the situation to its precrisis state and/or note how corrections will prevent similar crises in the future

5. Mortification: admit guilt, express concern, and ask for forgiveness (Benoit, 1995); IRT provides a list of recommendations for crisis communicators:
   - Admit guilt when known
   - Deny if innocent
   - Shift blame (can work)
   - Prove lack of control
   - Report corrective action
   - Minimize (may not help)

Multiple strategies can be used in combination.

Focusing Event

Fishman (1999) introduced the idea of the focusing event to crisis communication, and sociologist Thomas Birkland developed the idea further: "an event that is sudden, relatively rare, can be reasonably defined as harmful or revealing the possibility of potentially greater future harms, inflicts harms or suggests potential harms that are or could be concentrated on a definable geographical area or community of interest, and that is known to policy makers and the public virtually simultaneously" (Birkland, 1997, p. 22). The key points are that a focusing event is "sudden and unpredictable" but becomes widely known in a short period of time. Fishman (1999) argued there were two types of focusing events: Type One and Type Two. A Type One focusing event is "normal" and includes natural disasters. A Type Two focusing event is new, violates expectations, and creates uncertainty and includes chemical spills and accidents. The relative novelty of a Type Two focusing event demands public attention. Fishman posited that only some crises can qualify as Type Two focusing events because not all crises become widely known in a short period of time. Focusing events can be powerful because they can influence the public agenda, thereby potentially influencing policy decisions (Birkland, 1997; Fishman, 1999). With a focusing event, crisis communication can be a matter of policy making, not just reputation protection. The crisis creates pressure on public officials to adopt new laws or regulation to protect against the factors creating the crisis. For instance, the Bhopal disaster discussed in Chapter 16 resulted in new legislation in the United States, requiring organizations that use hazardous chemicals to engage in risk communication with their stakeholders. Effective crisis communication serves to prevent a policy action.

Instructing and Adjusting Information

Most crisis communication research addresses reputation repair in some fashion (e.g., Coombs, 2010). Sturges (1994) is among the few researchers to consider the range of stakeholder communication needs during a crisis. Sturges (1994) divided crisis communication into three areas: (a) instructing information, how to cope physically with the crisis; (b) adjusting information, how to cope psychologically with the crisis; and (c) reputation repair, attempts to ameliorate the damage a crisis inflicts on an organization. The three areas are interrelated. For instance, adjusting information should facilitate reputation repair as well.

Sturges believes instructing information is the first priority in a crisis. Most people would agree that public safety should be the top priority in a crisis. Instructing information tells people how to protect themselves from the potentially harmful effects of the crisis. Instructing information includes product recall information and warnings either to evacuate an area or to shelter-in-place (Coombs, 2012). Yet there is little research that examines instructing information (e.g., Gibson, 1997). It is assumed that crisis managers will engage in instructing information and execute it well. Failure to address public safety is likely to spawn a second crisis. Management compounds the crisis by appearing callous to the welfare of its stakeholders. Frandsen and Johansen (2008) refer to this as a "double crisis." Essentially improper crisis communication creates an additional crisis.

Sturges (1994) argued that adjusting information should be the second communication concern during a crisis. Expressions of sympathy and explanations of corrective actions (what the organization is doing to prevent a repeat of the crisis) are types of adjusting information. Researchers often consider expressions of sympathy and corrective actions as reputation repair strategies and studied them as part of that research. Researchers have found that expressions of sympathy and corrective actions do create positive reactions from stakeholders (Cohen, 2002; Fuchs-Burnett, 2002; Patel & Reinsch, 2003; Sellnow, Ulmer, & Snider, 1998). The research findings justify Sturges's (1994) argument that adjusting information is an essential part of crisis communication and is second in importance to instructing information.

Adjusting information is relevant to the postcrisis phase too. Some crises create victims by injuring or killing people. When a crisis creates victims, survivors and those close to the crisis victims need a chance to grieve and heal. The grief and healing are related to adjusting information because it helps people cope psychologically with the crisis. Crises can trigger the creation of memorials. Memorials can be physical entities but frequently are created online today. In either form, memorials serve to celebrate or honor the memory of people or events. Memorials facilitate mourning and coping with grief (Foot, Warnick, & Schneider, 2005).

Validated Accepted Wisdom

Before there was research to test theories and principles of crisis communication, we had accepted wisdom. Accepted wisdom was a list of what crisis communicators should and should not do. The lists were based on the experiences of people who had managed crises. The danger with accepted wisdom is that it is untested. People may think a certain action is responsible for a positive or negative outcome in a crisis, but they could be wrong. Some of the accepted wisdom has been validated and is being presented as one capsule.

Crisis communicators are told to avoid the statement "no comment." Guth (1995) found that when the phrase *no comment* is used, people overwhelmingly interpret it as managers saying "we are guilty." It appears the advice to avoid *no comment* is well founded.

Another piece of accepted wisdom is to respond quickly in a crisis. Research in stealing thunder, a crisis communication strategy, has proven the value of responding quickly. When an organization releases information about a crisis before some other source does, the organization suffers less reputational damage from the crisis (Arpan & Pompper, 2003; Arpan & Roskos-Ewoldsen, 2005; Claeys & Cauberghe, 2010). Stealing thunder researchers find that for the same exact crisis, more reputational damage is done when stakeholders learn about the crisis from the media than when they learn about the crisis from the organization in crisis. Stealing thunder also raises an issue about the problem of silence. Being quick implies that silence is an ineffective strategy. Silence is very passive and allows others to control the story. Crisis managers are often told to be quick so that they can tell their side of the story. The story is how the crisis is being framed and that includes the severity of the crisis and who or what is responsible for the crisis. Ferrin, Kim, Cooper, and Dirks (2007) have demonstrated that silence is an ineffective strategy for workplace trust violations. This research does have implications for crisis communication because crises are trust violations. Again, being quick and getting a response from the organization is preferable to no comment or the organization being silent.

Rhetoric of Renewal/Discourse of Renewal

Originally called the rhetoric of renewal, the discourse of renewal (DR) focuses on the future rather than the crisis event itself. The emphasis is on helping victims and projecting a positive view of the future for the organization and its stakeholders. Through the discourse of renewal, organizations learn and grow from the crisis. The discourse used by the crisis managers helps to structure reality and create an optimistic future for the organization and its stakeholders. The discourse of renewal concentrates on opportunities, is prospective rather than retrospective, is natural rather than strategic (organization automatically employs it), and is leader-based (flows from the leader) (Ulmer, Seeger, & Sellnow, 2007). It could be argued that the discourse of renewal is an extension of adjusting information because it seeks to help stakeholders cope psychologically with a crisis.

The discourse of renewal has some very specific parameters that limit when it can be used. There are four criteria that must exist if managers are to utilize the discourse of renewal: (a) The organization has a strong precrisis ethical standard, (b) the organization's precrisis relationships with constituencies are strong and favorable, (c) the organization can focus on life beyond the crisis rather than seeking to escape blame, including fixing the problem, and (d) the organization desires to engage in effective crisis communication (Ulmer et al., 2007). Not all organizations will have the requisite background and relationships with stakeholders to employ DR.

Rhetorical Arena

Frandsen and Johansen (2007, 2010a, 2010b) developed the rhetorical arena model to capture the complexity that can surround a crisis. Their applications have utilized international crises, such as the Arla Foods and the Mohammed cartoon reactions, to illustrate the value of taking a more complex view of crises and crisis communication. The rhetorical arena is a multi-vocal approach, meaning it considers the voices of any actors who try to communicate about the crisis rather than focus on a single crisis manager's voice. A rhetorical arena opens around a crisis. In fact, a rhetorical arena can begin to emerge before the crisis occurs and continue into the postcrisis phase. Various actors enter into this arena by engaging in communication about the crisis. Hence, crisis communication is composed of multiple crisis communicators and listeners. The crisis actors may communicate with, against, to, past, or about each other. The rhetorical arena provides a macro level of analysis that maps the key voices involved in crisis communication and the relationships between the voices. It should be noted that the rhetorical arena conceptualizes crisis communication as mediated strategic communication (Frandsen & Johansen, 2010b).

There is a micro level to the theory built on four parameters: context, media, genre, and text. The four parameters are filters that influence all mediated strategies. The four concepts are still being refined. Context can include situational, organizational, cultural, and societal factors that can shape the dynamic character of the crisis. Media denotes the channels used to deliver the crisis communication strategies. Genre is closely associated with communication tactics. Each tactic has its own conventions, which serve to shape and filter the crisis communication message it delivers. Text is related to the crisis response strategies, what crisis managers say and do after a crisis occurs, but is more than the strategies. Text actors or critics consider how the crisis response strategy is crafted. As Frandsen and Johansen (2010b) note, there are many different ways to express denial. Analysis of the text has the critic examine the choices made by the crisis actor when constructing his or her crisis communication messages. Any of these four parameters may be important in a crisis. The critic must examine each parameter and determine the relevance value of each to the current crisis case.

Situational Crisis Communication Theory

Situational crisis communication theory (SCCT) is driven by the belief that the nature of the crisis situation helps to determine the most effective response to that crisis. Prior to SCCT, there were lists of possible crisis situations and lists of possible crisis response strategies, but no theoretical link between the two (Benson, 1988). SCCT used attribution theory to link the crisis situation to the crisis response strategies. Attribution theory holds that people search for the reasons for events, especially negative events. People typically attribute the causes of events to internal or external factors. Internal factors are the people involved in the event and indicate that the person could control the events. External factors are environmentally based factors and indicate that the person could not control the events (Weiner, 2006). For instance, did a student miss an exam because he or she overslept or because a power outage disrupted the alarm?

A crisis is a negative event that does trigger the search for attributions of responsibility. Early work in marketing showed that when people learn about a crisis, they do make attributions about crisis responsibility—how much they perceive the organization in crisis to be responsible for that crisis (Bradford & Garrett, 1995; Jolly & Mowen, 1985; Mowen, 1980). Moreover, increased attributions of crisis responsibility have been linked to increased reputational damage, reduced purchase intention, increased anger, and increased likelihood to engage in negative word-of-mouth (Coombs & Holladay, 2005, 2007; Jorgensen, 1996). SCCT builds upon this work to connect the crisis situation and the crisis response through attributions of crisis responsibility. Based upon key factors in the crisis situation, stakeholders make attributions about crisis responsibility. Crisis response strategies vary in the degree to which the crisis managers take responsibility for the crisis. SCCT practitioners argue that the perceived acceptance of responsibility for the crisis response strategy must match the perceived crisis responsibility generated by the crisis situation. As attributions of crisis responsibility increase, the crisis managers must utilize crisis response strategies that have the requisite perceptions of taking responsibility for the crisis (Coombs, 1995, 2007).

SCCT posits that all crisis communication must begin with an ethical base composed of instructing and adjusting information. After the ethical base is used, crisis managers decide what additional crisis response strategies might be used to facilitate reputation repair. Similar to corporate apologia and IRT, SCCT has a strong focus on corporate reputation repair as one goal of crisis communication. Other outcomes identified by SCCT include reducing anger, preserving purchase intentions, and reducing the likelihood of negative word-of-mouth (Coombs, 2007). Following SCCT, practitioners recommend evaluating the threat posed by the crisis situation to determine which crisis response strategies to utilize. Again, the idea is that as the crisis threat intensifies, crisis managers will draw upon crisis response strategies that are perceived to accept greater responsibility for the crisis.

SCCT uses a two-step process to assess the crisis threat. Step 1 is to identify the basic crisis type the organization is facing. Crisis types vary in terms of the attributions of crisis responsibility they generate among stakeholders. Using survey research, SCCT analysts have identified three categories of crisis types: victim, accidental, and preventable. Table 2.1 lists and defines the crisis categories and specific types.

Table 2.1 Crisis Categories and Types
Victim Cluster: Very little attribution of crisis responsibility
Natural disasters
Rumors
Workplace violence
Malevolence
Accidental Cluster: Low attribution of crisis responsibility
Challenges
Technical-error accidents
Technical-error product harm
Preventable Cluster: Strong attribution of crisis responsibility
Human-error accidents
Human-error product harm
Organizational misdeeds

Source: Coombs (2012, p. 158).

The second step in the crisis threat assessment is to determine if any intensifying factors are present in the crisis situation. Intensifying factors increase attributions of crisis responsibility. These increases in crisis responsibility attributions result in victim crises being viewed as accidental crises and accidental crises being viewed as preventable crises (Coombs, 2004; Coombs & Holladay, 2006; Schwarz, 2008). So far, SCCT researchers have identified crisis history and prior reputation as intensifying factors. Crisis history involves whether or not an organization has had similar crises in the past. Similar crises intensify attributions of crisis responsibility (Coombs, 2004). Prior reputation refers to whether or not the organization is viewed negatively before the crisis. A negative prior reputation intensifies attributions of crisis responsibility (Coombs & Holladay, 2006). Researchers continue to find additional factors that can alter stakeholder attributions of crisis responsibility (Schwarz, 2008).

It should be noted that SCCT is a stakeholder-focused approach to crisis communication. SCCT actors try to anticipate how stakeholders will react to a crisis by predicting the strength of their crisis responsibility attributions. Crisis managers make their selection of crisis response strategies based upon the anticipated levels of crisis responsibility a crisis will generate. Crisis managers select crisis response strategies to reflect the level of crisis responsibility perceived by stakeholders. SCCT has used empirical research to array crisis response strategies along a continuum of perceived crisis acceptance. The list of crisis response strategies found in SCCT is presented in Table 2.2.

Table 2.2   Crisis Response Strategies

Denial Posture	
Attacking the Accuser	The crisis manager confronts the person or group that claims that a crisis exists. The response may include a threat to use force (e.g., a lawsuit) against the accuser.
Denial	The crisis manager states that no crisis exists. The response may include explaining why there is no crisis.
Scapegoating	Some other person or group outside of the organization is blamed for the crisis.
Diminishment Posture	
Excusing	The crisis manager tries to minimize the organization's responsibility for the crisis. The response can include denying any intention to do harm or claiming that the organization had no control of the events that led to the crisis.
Justification	The crisis manager tries to minimize the perceived damage associated with the crisis. The response can include stating that there were no serious damages or injuries or claiming that the victims deserved what they received.

	Rebuilding Posture
Compensation	The organization provides money or other gifts to the victims.
Apology	The crisis manager publicly states that the organization takes full responsibility for the crisis and asks forgiveness.
	Bolstering Posture
Reminding	The organization tells stakeholders about its past good works.
Ingratiation	The organization praises stakeholders.
Victimage	The organization explains how it too is a victim of the crisis.

Source: Coombs (2012, p. 155).

The following recommendations for crisis communication have been derived from SCCT:

- All victims or potential victims should receive instructing information, including recall information. This is one half of the base response to a crisis.

- All victims should be provided an expression of sympathy, any information about corrective actions, and trauma counseling when needed. This can be called the "care response." This is the second half of the base response to a crisis.

- For crises with minimal attributions of crisis responsibility and no intensifying factors, instructing information and care response should be sufficient.

- For crises with minimal attributions of crisis responsibility and an intensifying factor, add excuse and/or justification strategies to the instructing information and care response.

- For crises with weak attributions of crisis responsibility, and no intensifying factors, add excuse and/or justification strategies to the instructing information and care response.

- For crises with strong attributions of crisis responsibility (preventable crises and accidental crises with an intensifying factor), add compensation and/or apology strategies to the instructing information and care response.

- The compensation strategy is used any time victims suffer serious harm.

- The reminder and ingratiation strategies can be used to supplement any response.

- Denial and attack-the-accuser strategies are best used only for rumor and challenge crises.

Contingency Theory and Crisis Communication

Contingency theory can be considered a grand theory of public relations because its framers seek to understand how public relations operates across all contexts—it explains an entire discipline (Botan, 2006). Professor Glen Cameron is the name mostly strongly linked to contingency theory. Cameron has worked with a number of researchers to explicate and test the theory (e.g., Cameron, Pang, & Jin, 2008; Cancel, Cameron, Sallot, & Mitrook, 1997). Conflict between organizations and stakeholders is the driver for contingency theory. Contingency theory actors and researchers seek to understand how conflict can be strategically managed so as to benefit both organizations and their stakeholders. The organization-stakeholder relationship is treated as dynamic rather than static. The goal is to understand how various factors (variables) influence what communicative actions will result in an effective and ethical resolution to the conflict (Shin, 2005). Contingency theory actors seek to map the factors that influence how the organization responds to the conflict situation.

The term *stance* is used in contingency theory to denote how an organization responds to conflicts with stakeholders. Stances are placed on a continuum that has advocacy and accommodation as its anchor points. Advocacy involves an organization arguing for its own interests, while accommodation involves the organization making concessions to the other parties. The stance an organization should take depends on the nature of various factors that make up the conflict situation. Sometimes, an organization needs to be accommodative; at other times, it may need to favor advocacy (Cameron et al., 2008).

Jin and Cameron (2007) refined stances by establishing the degree of accommodation perceived to exist in various stance options. Their research created two categories: action-based accommodation and qualified-rhetoric-mixed accommodation. Action-based accommodation involves agreeing with the stakeholders and accepting their solutions to the conflict. Qualified-rhetorical-mixed accommodation expresses regret but does not take concrete actions related to the conflict. Below is a list of stances associated with each category:

Action-Based Accommodation

- Yield to stakeholder demands
- Agree to follow actions proposed by stakeholders
- Accept the stakeholders' propositions
- Agree with the stakeholders on future actions or procedures
- Agree to try the solution proposed by stakeholders

Qualified-Rhetoric-Mixed Accommodation

- Express regret or apologize to stakeholders
- Collaborate with stakeholders to solve the problem
- Change the organization's position toward that of the stakeholders
- Make concessions with the stakeholders
- Admit wrongdoing

Contingency theory draws on 87 factors and variables to help predict what stance should be used in a particular situation. Predisposing variables shape these stances prior to the situation and represent "predisposed" stances. In other words, an organization will have a default stance it prefers. Predisposing variables include organizational characteristics, PR department characteristics, and individual characteristics (Cancel et al., 1997; Shin, Cameron, & Cropp, 2006). Situational factors, if they are strong enough, can alter an organization's stance. The situational factors can be divided into five external factors and six internal factors (Pang, Jin, & Cameron, 2010). The external and internal factors are listed below. It is important to note that each factor in the list is actually a cluster of factors. Refer to Pang et al. (2010) for a complete list of the 87 factors. The complexity of contingency theory is drawn from trying to understand the relationships between its many variables.

Contingency Theory Factors

External Variables

Threat

Industry environment

General political and social environment and/or external culture

The external public

Issue under question

Internal variables

Organization characteristics

Public relations department characteristics

Characteristics of dominant coalition

Individual characteristics

Relationship characteristics

Internal threats

Contingency theory has been applied to crisis communication (e.g., Hwang & Cameron, 2008; Jin & Cameron, 2007; Jin, Pang, & Cameron, 2007; Pang, Jin, & Cameron, 2004) because there are conflict elements in most crises. Researchers have noted the similarity between the stances and the crisis response strategies from IRT and SCCT (e.g., Holtzhausen & Roberts, 2009; Pang et al., 2004). The integrated crisis mapping (ICM) model and the threat appraisal model are two direct modifications of contingency theory for application to crisis communication. It is helpful to explain each model when considering contingency theory's application to crisis communication.

The ICM model emphasizes the importance of emotion (affect) in crisis communication. The ICM model is a crisis matrix created by two axes. The X-axis is the public coping strategy. Publics cope by either taking action (conative coping) or by changing their interpretations of the situation (cognitive coping). The Y-axis is the level of organizational engagement. Organizational engagement is the amount of resources an organization devotes to the situation and ranges from high to low. The crisis matrix has four quadrants. Each quadrant represents different types of crises and identifies the emotions that publics are likely to experience, how publics are likely to cope, and the amount of organizational engagement. Crisis communication should be consistent with the emotions and coping strategies of the publics. Here is a summary of the quadrants:

Quadrant 1: anger, conative coping, and high engagement (e.g., technology breakdown)

Quadrant 2: sadness, cognitive coping, and high engagement (e.g., natural disaster and accidents)

Quadrant 3: fright, cognitive coping, and low engagement (e.g., rumors and terrorism)

Quadrant 4: anxiety, conative coping, and low engagement (e.g., transportation failure and human resources)

The ICM model research has shown that anxiety is the most common emotional reaction by publics during crises, followed by anger. Conative coping was the most common public response, and organizations tend to have moderate engagement (Jin & Pang, 2010). The most common communication response was a qualified-rhetoric-mixed stance. Jin and Pang (2010) argue that organizations should be using more action-based stance if they want to effectively address the emotions generated by and conative coping used by publics.

The threat appraisal model (Jin, 2009; Jin & Cameron, 2007) focuses on understanding threats in a crisis. The argument is that threat appraisal is critical to crisis management. Crisis managers react according to the perceived threat they encounter. Drawing from contingency theory, threat is conceptualized along two dimensions: threat type and threat duration. Threat types can be internal (within the organization) or external (from outside of the organization). Threat duration refers to short-term or long-term effect from the crisis.

Threats have three consequences: cognitive, affect, and conation. Cognitive effects include assessments of severity of the threat and the organizational resources needed to address the threat. Affect is the emotion generated by the crisis and includes the valence of the emotion (positive to negative) and the arousal created by the emotion (energized to calm) (Jin & Cameron, 2007). Conation is the stance the organization enacts in response to the crisis.

Long-term threats were considered more severe, required more organizational resources, created stronger negative emotions and greater arousal, and were more likely to produce an accommodative stance. Research has found that external threats show the predicted pattern of results except that there was no significant effect for valence of the emotion. There was also an interaction effect for threat type and duration on perceived situational demands (Jin & Cameron, 2007). Overall, the evidence indicates that people perceive external and long-term threats to be the strongest threats organizations can face. Understanding the perceived threat level created by a crisis helps crisis managers select their stance—crisis response strategies. In the case of an external and/or long-term threat, crisis managers need to consider utilizing accommodative crisis response strategies.

Complexity Theory

Complexity theory is related to systems theory. Complexity utilizes ideas such as systems (an organization can be a system), environment, and boundaries. There are many challenges when discussing complexity theory and trying to adapt it to crisis communication. The central challenge is that there is no single complexity theory. Rather, complexity theory is a collection of ideas. Those who work with complexity theory have identified a set of common principles shared by complexity theories. Below is a list that contains some of the common principles:

- Complexity is defined by the amount of information necessary to define it.
- Complexity relates to systems that are composed of many interacting agents. The agents may not even know they are interacting with one another.
- Complexity emerges from the interactions between agents.
- Systems coevolve with their environments.
- Boundaries are difficult to determine.
- Small disturbances can be amplified and become large disturbances.
- Systems are resilient because they can self-organize and adapt.
- Solutions need to be as complex as the problems they address (requisite variety).
- Systems exist along a continuum ranging from equilibrium (balance) to disorder (chaos).

The list could be longer, but these points provide a feel for complexity theory.

So how does complexity relate to crisis communication? Requisite variety is a good place to start. In complexity theory, not all problems are complex. Complexity is a function of the information needed to describe it. Some problems are simple and can be answered using simple models. Some problems do not require a large amount of information to solve them. Weick (1979), an organizational psychologist whose systems ideas often are used in complexity theory, notes that situations involving little equivocality (uncertainty) can be addressed by rules, stock responses for these "simple" situations. When a situation has high equivocality, a large amount of information is needed to address the situation. Managers need to apply cycles whereby they share information and discuss the situation. Translated to crisis communication, some crises are simple and some are complex. Simple crises can be managed using traditional crisis communication theories. Complex crises require a different approach inspired by complexity theory.

Complexity theory brings the notions of uncertainty and flexibility to crisis communication. If the environment influences the organization and its boundaries are blurred, managers should place a premium on vigilance—actively scanning the environment for possible threats. Moreover, managers must not become blinded by what they already know. Managers must be open to the fact that there is information they do not know and cannot know, what is called the *unknown-unknowns*. Unknown-unknowns have implications for training. The concept of the black swan helps to explain unknown-unknowns. Europeans believed swans were only white until black swans were found in Australia. The term *black swan* became a term used to describe outliers that challenge preconceived notions. Crises can be black swans—something no one thought could happen. Taleb (2010) defines a black swan as an event that is a surprise, has a major effect, and people use in hindsight to claim there was evidence to predict the event. Crisis managers face the challenge of preparing for "black swans" by being ready for an event that will be novel.

Part of crisis preparation is preparing crisis plans and training the crisis team. Crisis management plans (CMPs) are rough guidance for actions, not exact guides for what to do. People often have the mistaken view that a CMP is a step-by-step set of instructions for handling a crisis. In reality, CMPs are collections of information that might be useful in a crisis (Coombs, 2012). Teams train by practicing crisis situations. Will the crisis team see the exact same crisis in reality? The answer is no. A crisis team might face a crisis they did not even anticipate could exist—an unknown-unknown crisis. The team practices working together and honing their skills and knowledge. Smart teams know they will need to adapt those skills and knowledge to whatever crisis they might face in the real world. It is a mistake to think that training is for a specific crisis—it is for the process. By emphasizing the unknown-unknown, complexity highlights the need to be flexible and adaptable in a crisis. Complex crises can morph and change rapidly; crisis managers must be able to adapt to those changes. The need to be flexible is why some crisis training now includes improvisation skills. Improvisation skills teach flexibility for reacting when the unknown-unknown occurs. The essence of improvisation is reacting to the moment. The key is to have a set of skills that can be used when reacting to the moment. For example, jazz musicians improvise a song but have an extensive knowledge and skill of music to support that improvisation. Improvisation is not for unskilled amateurs.

The need to be flexible and to adjust to the unknown extends through the crisis response and postcrisis stages. It should be noted that complexity theory dislikes stages because it is difficult to distinguish when a crisis moves from one phase to the next. Traditional crisis communication experts would agree with that assessment (e.g., Coombs, 2012). In a complex crisis, the crisis manager and even the victims responding to the crisis will self-organize in ways no one could have predicted before the complex crisis event occurred. Traditional crisis communication is based on equilibrium in a system—the organization moving toward "normal" operations. Complex crises are at the edge of chaos—far from equilibrium. Therefore, it is difficult and even unwise to predict what crisis communication strategies might be needed in a complex crisis (Gilpin & Murphy, 2008). However, crisis managers can draw upon other crisis communication theories to help them react to the ever-evolving reality of the crisis.

The greatest strength of complexity theory is the postcrisis phase. Complexity theory places a premium on learning from crises. Crises, in fact, can be transformative for an organization. Crises can be caused by the existing way of thinking and acting in an organization. A crisis allows managers to see the flaws and to create a new and better organization built upon a different way of thinking and acting. The existing assumptions that precipitated the crisis are questioned and replaced (Gilpin & Murphy, 2008, 2010). The learning transforms the organization rather than being incremental. Incremental learning from crises occurs when organizations make minor changes but seek to return the organization to the way it existed prior to the crisis. Traditional crisis management does emphasize returning to business as usual. To be fair, returning to normal generally refers to keeping the business running, not necessarily to how the business should operate. Still, there is an emphasis on adding some new knowledge to the status quo in traditional crisis management rather than improving the organization through transformation.

Note that the complexity theory discussion does not provide specific guidance for crisis communicators. Complex crises are too unknown to provide such guidance. Complexity theory is more of a mind-set to prepare crisis communicators. That mind-set emphasizes flexibility and adaptability and a willingness to change an organization after a crisis and not just learn to manage the crisis. One way to build flexibility is to understand the various approaches to crisis communication and when each can be employed effectively in a crisis.

Paracrisis and Crisis Prevention

Part of crisis management is the effort to prevent a crisis from occurring. Crisis prevention is a difficult task, and many crises cannot be prevented. Unfortunately, there is a lack of crisis communication theories or principles for crisis prevention. The basic crisis prevention process is to identify the crisis threat or warning sign and take action designed to reduce the likelihood of that risk becoming manifest into a crisis (Coombs, 2012). Paracrisis is a crisis communication–based principle for crisis prevention. A paracrisis is a crisis threat or warning sign that appears and must be managed in public view (Coombs & Holladay, 2012). It is a paracrisis because it looks like a crisis, and people often refer to it as a crisis, but it is not a crisis. Social media allows people outside of an organization to see how the organization handles a threat. Most paracrises involve a challenge crisis whereby some stakeholders challenge the responsibility of organizational behavior. The charges of irresponsible behavior are a crisis threat and warning sign because, if the charge sticks and is embraced by other stakeholders, the threat becomes a crisis as it damages an organization's reputation (Coombs, 2012).

Paracrises require crisis managers to make important decisions. First, crisis managers must decide whether or not to take action on the crisis threat or warning sign. Second, if action is warranted, crisis managers decide what their response should be. The crisis managers may respond by refuting the charges or modifying organizational behavior to "fix" the behavior. The modification can involve simply making and announcing the changes or involve working with the challengers to create the necessary corrections. Crisis managers need to determine the financial cost of the change and the impact that change might have on their organizational strategy (Coombs & Holladay, 2012). The paracrisis process reflects the crisis warning process, assesses the threat and takes preventative action when necessary, and integrates crisis communication into crisis prevention.

Application Suggestions and Relationships Between the Theories and Principles

The theories and principles can be used individually or in combination with one another. Their application depends upon the nature of the crisis and what seems to be the critical factors in the crisis. As noted earlier, the theories and principles reflect the emphasis on crisis communication for responding to a crisis. However, some theories and principles offer insights into precrisis and postcrisis phases of crisis management as well. This final section identifies the critical factors for the various theories and principles and suggests how they might be combined with one another for an analysis.

Corporate apologia, image repair theory, and SCCT all examine various response options that crisis communicators might employ. Corporate apologia's discussion of dissociations specifies how certain crisis response strategies can be combined. Corporate apologia would be relevant if crisis communicators used one of the three dissociations or if a case seems to indicate one of the three dissociations would be appropriate. Image repair theory provides the widest array of crisis response strategies and is ideal for identifying specific crisis response strategies. SCCT provides a prescriptive framework of crisis response strategies. SCCT identifies key variables in a crisis (e.g., crisis history and prior reputation) and how those variables should affect the selection and utilization of crisis response strategies. SCCT can be used in conjunction with either corporate apologia or image repair theory by helping to explain whether or not the crisis response strategies from those theories were appropriate in a given crisis. SCCT is helpful when either prior reputation or crisis history is a factor in the crisis. Moreover, SCCT can be useful when anger is a factor in the crisis.

Contingency theory is useful when threats are an important aspect of crisis. Contingency theory can help to evaluate threats (e.g., type and duration) and how the threat should affect the crisis response. Contingency theory does make prescriptive recommendations for crisis communication that are derived from evaluations of the crisis threat. Also, contingency theory can be helpful when anxiety is a key aspect of the crisis or in understanding when a crisis generates high levels of anxiety. Contingency theory fits well with instructing and adjusting information. Both instructing and adjusting information can reduce anxiety. Hence, contingency theory can predict when anxiety will be high and there is a strong need for instructing and adjusting information. Instructing information is critical whenever public safety is a concern in the crisis. Adjusting information is relevant whenever a memorial is created in memory of the victims or the event.

Focusing events denote very high profile crises and suggest that the crisis will trigger an issue for policy makers. Its application is to a very narrow set of high profile crises. Similarly, the discourse of renewal is limited to crisis situations that fit with the ability to engage in renewal. The rhetorical arena is ideal when there are multiple crisis communicators. The rhetorical arena can be used to identify and map the multiple crisis communicators while theories such as corporate apologia, image repair, or SCCT can be used to analyze use of various crisis response strategies utilized by the crisis communicators. The rhetorical arena is very amenable to use with other crisis communication theories and principles because those other theories aid in the micro-level analysis of the rhetorical arena.

Complexity theory demonstrates the strongest concern for learning (postcrisis phase). If learning, including the need for learning, is a key element of the crisis case, complexity theory is appropriate. Moreover, complexity theory can be combined with other crisis communication theories and principles. Complexity theory is more descriptive; thus, other theories that are more prescriptive serve as a compliment to its analytical value. Paracrises, in contrast, is designed for the precrisis phase of crisis management. A crisis that has an element related to prevention or the possibility to prevent a crisis fits well with the paracrisis principles.

Each of the validated, accepted wisdom ideas addresses very specific aspects of a crisis. Stealing thunder is concerned with the timing of the release of the crisis information. Stealing thunder is appropriate when the organization seeks to be the first to release information about the crisis or timing is important to the case. If an organization uses silence or *no comment*, there is evidence to explain the problematic nature of those responses. Any of the validated, accepted wisdom ideas can be used with other theories as well. Stealing thunder is about timing, not the nature of the crisis response strategies that were used. Other crisis communication theories or principles could be used to explain what more effective alternatives the crisis managers could have used instead of silence or *no comment*.

Additional Readings

Complexity Theory

Gilpin, D., & Murphy, P. J. (2008). *Crisis management in a complex world.* New York, NY: Oxford University Press.

Gilpin, D., & Murphy, P. J. (2010). Complexity and crises: A new paradigm. In W. T. Coombs & S. J. Holladay (Eds.), *The handbook of crisis communication* (pp. 683–690). Malden, MA: Blackwell.

Murphy, P. (2000). Symmetry, contingency, complexity: Accommodating uncertainty in public relations theory. *Public Relations Review, 22*(2), 95–113.

Roux-Dufort, C. (2000). Why organizations don't learn from crises: The perverse power of normalization. *Review of Business, 21*(3/4), 25–30.

Contingency Theory

Cancel, A. E., Cameron, G. T., Sallot, L. M., & Mitrook, M. A. (1997). It depends: A contingency theory of accommodation in public relations. *Journal of Public Relations Research, 9*(1), 31–63.

Cameron, G. T., Pang, A., & Jin, Y. (2008). Contingency theory. In T. L. Hansen-Horn & B. D. Neff (Eds.), *Public relations: From theory to practice* (134–157). New York, NY: Pearson.

Jin, Y. (2009). The effects of public's cognitive appraisal of emotions in crises on crisis coping and strategy assessment. *Public Relations Review, 35*(3), 310–313.

Jin, Y., & Cameron, G. T. (2007). The effects of threat type and duration on public relations practitioner's cognitive, affective, and conative responses to crisis situations. *Journal of Public Relations Research, 19,* 255–281.

Jin, Y., & Pang, A. (2010). Future directions of crisis communication research: Emotions in crisis—The next frontier. In W. T. Coombs & S. J. Holladay (Eds.), *The handbook of crisis communication* (pp. 677–682). Malden, MA: Blackwell.

Pang, A., Jin, Y., & Cameron, G. T. (2004). *"If we can learn some lessons in the process": A contingency approach to analyzing the Chinese government's management of the perception and emotion of its multiple publics during the severe acute respiratory syndrome (SARS) crisis.* Miami, FL: IPRRC.

Pang, A., Jin, Y., & Cameron, G. T. (2010). Contingency theory conflict management: Directions for the practice of crisis communication from a decade of theory development, discovery, and dialogue. In W. T. Coombs & S. J. Holladay (Eds.), *The handbook of crisis communication* (pp. 527–549). Malden, MA: Blackwell.

Shin, J. H., Cameron, G. T., & Cropp, F. (2006). Occam's razor in the contingency theory: A national survey of 86 contingent variables. *Public Relations Review, 32,* 282–286.

Corporate Apologia

Dionisopolous, G. N., & Vibbert, S. L. (1988). CBS vs Mobil Oil: Charges of creative bookkeeping in 1979. In H. R. Ryan (Ed.), *Oratorical encounters: Selected studies and sources of 20th century political accusation and apologies* (pp. 241–252). Westport, CT: Greenwood.

Hearit, K. M. (1995). "Mistakes were made": Organizations, apologia, and crises of social legitimacy. *Communication Studies, 46,* 1–17.

Hearit, K. M. (2001). Corporate apologia: When an organization speaks in defense of itself. In R. L. Heath (Ed.), *Handbook of public relations* (pp. 501–511). Thousand Oaks, CA: Sage.

Hearit, K. M. (2006). *Crisis management by apology: Corporate response to allegations of wrongdoing.* Mahwah, NJ: Erlbaum.

Discourse or Renewal

Ulmer, R. R., Seeger, M. W., & Sellnow, T. L. (2007). Post-crisis communication and renewal: Expanding the parameters of post-crisis discourse. *Public Relations Review, 33*(2), 130–134.

Ulmer, R. R., Seeger, M. W., & Sellnow, T. L. (2010). Considering the future of crisis communication research: Understanding the opportunities inherent to crisis events through the discourse of renewal. In W. T. Coombs & S. J. Holladay (Eds.), *The handbook of crisis communication* (pp. 691–697). Malden, MA: Blackwell.

Focusing Event

Fishman, D. A. (1999). ValuJet flight 592: Crisis communication theory blended and extended. *Communication Quarterly, 47*(4), 345–375.

Image Repair Theory

Benoit, W. L. (1995). Accounts, excuses, and apologies: A theory of image restoration. Albany: State University of New York Press.

Benoit, W. L. (2005). In R. L. Heath (Ed.), *Encyclopedia of public relations* (Vol. 1, pp. 407–410). Thousand Oaks, CA: Sage.

Benoit, W. L., & Brinson, S. (1994). AT&T: Apologies are not enough. *Communication Quarterly, 42,* 75–88.

Benoit, W. L., & Czerwinski, A. (1997). A critical analysis of USAir's image repair discourse. *Business Communication Quarterly, 60,* 38–57.

Benoit, W. L., & Pang, A. (2008). Crisis communication and image repair discourse. In T. L. Hansen-Horn & B. D. Neff (Eds.), *Public relations: From theory to practice* (pp. 243–261). New York, NY: Pearson.

Instructing and Adjusting Information

Holladay, S. J. (2009). Crisis communication strategies in the media coverage of chemical accidents. *Journal of Public Relations Research, 21*(2), 208–217.

Sturges, D. L. (1994). Communicating through crisis: A strategy for organizational survival. *Management Communication Quarterly, 7*(3), 297–316.

Paracrisis and Crisis Prevention

Coombs, W. T. (2012). *Ongoing crisis communication: Planning, managing, and responding* (3rd ed.). Thousand Oaks, CA: Sage.

Coombs, W.T., & Holladay, S. J. (2012). The paracrisis: The challenges of publicly managing crisis prevention. *Public Relations Review, 38*(3), 408–415.

Rhetorical Arena

Frandsen, F., & Johansen, W. (2010a). Apologizing in a globalizing world: Crisis communication and apologetic ethics. *Corporate Communications: An International Journal, 15*(4), 350–364.

Frandsen, F., & Johansen, W. (2010b). Crisis communication, complexity, and the cartoon affair: A case study. In W. T. Coombs & S. J. Holladay (Eds.), *The handbook of crisis communication* (pp. 425–448). Malden, MA: Blackwell.

Situational Crisis Communication Theory

Coombs, W. T. (2004). Impact of past crises on current crisis communications: Insights from situational crisis communication theory. *Journal of Business Communication, 41,* 265–289.

Coombs, W. T. (2006). The protective powers of crisis response strategies: Managing reputational assets during a crisis. *Journal of Promotion Management, 12*, 241–260.

Coombs, W. T. (2007). Protecting organization reputations during a crisis: The development and application of situational crisis communication theory. *Corporate Reputation Review, 10*(3), 163–177.

Coombs, W. T., & Holladay, S. J. (1996). Communication and attributions in a crisis: An experimental study of crisis communication. *Journal of Public Relations Research, 8*(4), 279–295.

Coombs, W. T., & Holladay, S. J. (2001). An extended examination of the crisis situation: A fusion of the relational management and symbolic approaches. *Journal of Public Relations Research, 13*, 321–340.

Coombs, W. T., & Holladay, S. J. (2002). Helping crisis managers protect reputational assets: Initial tests of the situational crisis communication theory. *Management Communication Quarterly, 16*, 165–186.

Coombs, W. T., & Holladay, S. J. (2005). Exploratory study of stakeholder emotions: Affect and crisis. In N. M. Ashkanasy, W. J. Zerbe, & C. E. J Hartel (Eds.), *Research on emotion in organizations: Vol. 1. The effect of affect in organizational settings* (pp. 271–288). New York, NY: Elsevier.

Coombs, W. T., & Holladay, S. J. (2006). Unpacking the halo effect: Reputation and crisis management. *Journal of Communication Management, 10*(2), 123–137.

Coombs, W. T., & Holladay, S. J. (2007). The negative communication dynamic: Exploring the impact of stakeholder affect on behavioral intentions. *Journal of Communication Management, 11*, 300–312.

Schwarz, A. (2008). Covariation-based causal attributions during organizational crises: Suggestions for extending situational crisis communication theory. *International Journal of Strategic Communication, 2*, 31–53.

Validated Accepted Wisdom

Arpan, L. M., & Pompper, D. (2003). Stormy weather: Testing "stealing thunder" as a crisis communication strategy to improve communication flow between organizations and journalists. *Public Relations Review, 29*, 291–308.

Arpan, L. M., & Roskos-Ewoldsen, D. R. (2005). Stealing thunder: Analysis of the effects of proactive disclosure of crisis information. *Public Relations Review, 31*, 425–433.

Claeys, A. S., & Cauberghe, V. (2010). Crisis response and crisis timing strategies: Two sides of the same coin. *Public Relations Review, 38*(1), 83–88.

Guth, D. W. (1995). Organizational crisis experience and public relations roles. *Public Relations Review, 21*(2), 123–136.

References

Allen, M. W., & Caillouet, R. H. (1994). Legitimation endeavors: Impression management strategies used by an organization in crisis. *Communication Monographs, 61*, 44–62.

Arpan, L. M., & Pompper, D. (2003). Stormy weather: Testing "stealing thunder" as a crisis communication strategy to improve communication flow between organizations and journalists. *Public Relations Review, 29*, 291–308.

Arpan, L. M., & Roskos-Ewoldsen, D. R. (2005). Stealing thunder: An analysis of the effects of proactive disclosure of crisis information. *Public Relations Review, 31*(3), 425–433.

Benoit, W. L. (1995). *Accounts, excuses, and apologies: A theory of image restoration*. Albany: State University of New York Press.

Benson, J. A. (1988). Crisis revisited: An analysis of strategies used by Tylenol in the second tampering episode. *Central States Speech Journal, 39*, 49–66.

Birkland, T. (1997). *After disaster: Agenda setting, public policy, and focusing events*. Washington, DC: Georgetown University Press.

Botan, C. (2006). Grand strategy, strategy, and tactics in public relations. In C. H. Botan & V. Hazelton (Eds.), *Public relations theory II* (pp. 223–248). Mahwah, NJ: Erlbaum.

Bradford, J. L., & Garrett, D. E. (1995). The effectiveness of corporate communicative responses to accusations of unethical behavior. *Journal of Business Ethics, 14*, 875–892.

Cameron, G. T., Pang, A., & Jin, Y. (2008). Contingency theory. In T. L. Hansen-Horn & B. D. Neff (Eds.), *Public relations: From theory to practice* (134–157). New York, NY: Pearson.

Cancel, A. E., Cameron, G. T., Sallot, L. M., & Mitrook, M. A. (1997). It depends: A contingency theory of accommodation in public relations. *Journal of Public Relations Research, 9*(1), 31–63.

Carroll, C. E., & McCombs, M. E. (2003). Agenda-setting effects of business news on the public's images and opinions about major corporations. *Corporate Reputation Review, 6*, 36–46.

Cheney, G., & Christensen, L. T. (2000). Identity as issue: Linkages between "internal" and "external" organizational communication. In F. M. Jablin & L. L. Putnam (Eds.), *New handbook of organizational communication* (pp. 231–269). Thousands Oaks, CA: Sage.

Claeys, A. S., & Cauberghe, V. (2010). Crisis response and crisis timing strategies: Two sides of the same coin. *Public Relations Review, 38*(1), 83–88.

Cohen, J. R. (2002). Legislating apology: The pros and cons. *University of Cincinnati Law Review, 70*, 819–895.

Coombs, W. T. (1995). Choosing the right words: The development of guidelines for the selection of the "appropriate" crisis response strategies. *Management Communication Quarterly, 8*, 447–476.

Coombs, W. T. (2004). Impact of past crises on current crisis communications: Insights from situational crisis communication theory. *Journal of Business Communication, 41*, 265–289.

Coombs, W. T. (2007). Protecting organization reputations during a crisis: The development and application of situational crisis communication theory. *Corporate Reputation Review, 10*(3), 163–177.

Coombs, W. T. (2010). Pursuing evidence-based crisis communication. In W. T. Coombs & S. J. Holladay (Eds.), *The handbook of crisis communication* (pp. 719–725). Malden, MA: Blackwell.

Coombs, W. T. (2012). *Ongoing crisis communication: Planning, managing, and responding* (3rd ed.). Thousand Oaks, CA: Sage.

Coombs, W. T., & Holladay, S. J. (2005). Exploratory study of stakeholder emotions: Affect and crisis. In N. M. Ashkanasy, W. J. Zerbe, & C. E. J Hartel (Eds.), *Research on emotion in organizations: Vol. 1. The effect of affect in organizational settings* (pp. 271–288). New York, NY: Elsevier.

Coombs, W. T., & Holladay, S. J. (2006). Unpacking the halo effect: Reputation and crisis management. *Journal of Communication Management, 10*(2): 123–137.

Coombs, W. T., & Holladay, S. J. (2007). The negative communication dynamic: Exploring the impact of stakeholder affect on behavioral intentions. *Journal of Communication Management, 11*, 300–312.

Dionisopolous, G. N., & Vibbert, S. L. (1988). CBS vs Mobil Oil: Charges of creative bookkeeping. In H. R. Ryan (Ed.), *Oratorical encounters: Selected studies and sources of 20th century political accusation and apologies* (pp. 214–252). Westport, CT: Greenwood.

Ferrin, D. L., Kim, P. H., Cooper, C. D., & Dirks, K. T. (2007). Silence speaks volumes: The effectiveness of reticence in comparison to apology and denial for responding to integrity- and competence-based trust violations. *Journal of Applied Psychology, 92*(4), 893–908.

Fishman, D. A. (1999). ValuJet flight 592: Crisis communication theory blended and extended. *Communication Quarterly, 47*(4), 345–375.

Fombrun, C. J., & van Riel, C. B. M. (2004). *Fame and fortune: How successful companies build winning reputations.* New York, NY: Prentice Hall.

Foot, K., Warnick, B., & Schneider, S. M. (2005). Web-based memorializing after September 11: Toward a conceptual framework. *Journal of Computer-Mediated Communication, 11*(1), article 4. http://jcmc.indiana.edu/vol11/issue1/foot.html

Frandsen, F., & Johansen, W. (2007). The apology of a sports icon: Crisis communication and apologetic ethics. *Hermes: Journal of Language and Communication Studies, 38*, 85–104.

Frandsen, F., & Johansen, W. (2008): *Krisekommunikation.* Frederiksberg, Denmark: Forlaget Samfundslitteratur.

Frandsen, F., & Johansen, W. (2010a). Apologizing in a globalizing world: Crisis communication and apologetic ethics. Corporate Communications: An International Journal, 15(4), 350–364.

Frandsen, F., & Johansen, W. (2010b). Crisis communication, complexity, and the cartoon affair: A case study. In W. T. Coombs & S. J. Holladay (Eds.), *The handbook of crisis communication* (pp. 425–448). Boston, MA: Blackwell.

Fuchs-Burnett, T. (2002, May/July). Mass public corporate apology. *Dispute Resolution Journal, 57*, 26–32.

Gibson, D. C. (1997). Print communication tactics for consumer product recalls: A prescriptive taxonomy. *Public Relations Quarterly, 42*(2), 42–46.

Gilpin, D., & Murphy, P. J. (2008). *Crisis management in a complex world.* New York, NY: Oxford University Press.

Gilpin, D., & Murphy, P. J. (2010). Complexity and crises: A new paradigm. In W. T. Coombs & S. J. Holladay (Eds.), *The handbook of crisis communication* (pp. 683–690). Malden, MA: Blackwell.

Guth, D. W. (1995, Summer). Organizational crisis experience and public relations roles. *Public Relations Review, 21*(2), 123–136.

Hearit, K. M. (1994, Summer). Apologies and public relations crises at Chrysler, Toshiba, and Volvo. *Public Relations Review, 20*(2), 113–125.

Hearit, K. M. (1995). "Mistakes were made": Organizations, apologia, and crises of social legitimacy. *Communication Studies, 46*, 1–17.

Hearit, K. M. (2006). *Crisis management by apology: Corporate response to allegations of wrongdoing.* Mahwah, NJ: Erlbaum.

Holtzhausen, D. R., & Roberts, G. F. (2009). An investigation into the role of image repair theory in strategic conflict management. *Journal of Public Relations Research, 21*, 165–186.

Hwang, S., & Cameron, G. T. (2008). Public's expectation about an organization's stance in crisis communication based on perceived leadership and perceived severity of threats. *Public Relations Review, 34*, 70–73.

Jin, Y. (2009). The effects of public's cognitive appraisal of emotions in crises on crisis coping and strategy assessment. *Public Relations Review, 35*(3), 310–313.

Jin, Y., & Cameron, G. T. (2007). The effects of threat type and duration on public relations practitioner's cognitive, affective, and conative responses to crisis situations. *Journal of Public Relations Research, 19*, 255–281.

Jin, Y., & Pang, A. (2010). Future directions of crisis communication research: Emotions in crisis—The next frontier. In W. T. Coombs & S. J. Holladay (Eds.), *The handbook of crisis communication* (pp. 677–682). Malden, MA: Blackwell.

Jolly, D. W., & Mowen, J. C. (1985). Product recall communications: The effects of source, media, and social responsibility information. *Advances in Consumer Research, 12,* 471–475.

Jorgensen, B. K. (1996). Components of consumer reaction to company-related mishaps: A structural equation model approach. *Advances in Consumer Research, 23,* 346–351.

Meijer, M. M. (2004). *Does success breed success? Effects of news and advertising on corporate reputation.* Amsterdam, Netherlands: Aksant Academic.

Mowen, J. C. (1980). Further information on consumer perceptions of product recalls. *Advances in Consumer Research, 8,* 519–523.

Pang, A., Jin, Y., & Cameron, G. T. (2004). *"If we can learn some lessons in the process": A contingency approach to analyzing the Chinese government's management of the perception and emotion of its multiple publics during the severe acute respiratory syndrome (SARS) crisis.* Miami, FL: IPRRC.

Pang, A., Jin, Y., & Cameron, G. T. (2010). Contingency theory conflict management: Directions for the practice of crisis communication from a decade of theory development, discovery, and dialogue. In W. T. Coombs & S. J. Holladay (Eds.), *The handbook of crisis communication* (pp. 527–549). Malden, MA: Blackwell.

Patel, A., & Reinsch, L. (2003). Companies can apologize: Corporate apologies and legal liability. *Business Communication Quarterly, 66,* 17–26.

Schwarz, A. (2008). Covariation-based causal attributions during organizational crises: Suggestions for extending situational crisis communication theory. *International Journal of Strategic Communication, 2,* 31–53.

Sellnow, T. L., Ulmer, R. R., & Snider, M. (1998). The compatibility of corrective action in organizational crisis communication. *Communication Quarterly, 46,* 60–74.

Shin, J. (2005). Contingency theory. In R. L. Heath (Ed.), *Encyclopedia of public relations: Volume 1* (pp. 191–193). Thousand Oaks, CA: Sage.

Shin, J. H., Cameron, G. T., & Cropp, F. (2006). Occam's razor in the contingency theory: A national survey of 86 contingent variables. *Public Relations Review, 32,* 282–286.

Sturges, D. L. (1994). Communicating through crisis: A strategy for organizational survival. *Management Communication Quarterly, 7*(3), 297–316.

Taleb, N. N. (2010). *The black swan: The impact of the highly improbable* (2nd ed.). New York, NY: Random House.

Ulmer, R. R., Seeger, M. W., & Sellnow, T. L. (2007). Post-crisis communication and renewal: Expanding the parameters of post-crisis discourse. *Public Relations Review, 33*(2), 130–134.

Ware, B. L., & Linkugel, W. A. (1973). They spoke in defense of themselves: On the generic criticism of apologia. *Quarterly Journal of Speech, 59,* 273–283.

Weick, K. E. (1979). *Social psychology of organizing* (2nd ed.). Reading, MA: Addison Wesley.

Weiner, B. (2006). *Social motivation, justice, and the moral emotions: An attributional approach.* Mahwah, NJ: Erlbaum.

CHAPTER 3

Pampers and Dry Max Chemical Burn Rumor

Companies that sell products to customers—business-to-consumer, or B2C, organizations—must be concerned about product harm crises. Product harm occurs when people are made aware that a product can be defective or dangerous (Siomokos & Kurzbard, 1994). There are two elements to the definition. First, the product has to be defective or dangerous in some way to the customer. Second, the customers and other stakeholders must know about the problem. The second point is important because there are instances where companies engage in "stealth recalls." In a stealth recall, the company seeks to remove a product from the market while drawing as little attention as possible to their actions. Stealth recalls are executed in hopes of avoiding the many ways product harm crises can hurt a company. Potential damages from product harm crises include decline in revenues, drop in share price, decreased profitability, damage to reputation, loss of market share, and decreased brand equity. Product harm crises are among the most serious situations a company can face (Siomokos & Kurzbard, 1994).

If product harm crises are so damaging, it is logical that a company would try to prevent being in a product harm situation when their product was actually safe. This seems like an odd situation but is exactly the predicament Procter & Gamble (P&G) faced in May of 2010. In 2010, P&G had released a new version of its Dry Max diapers. In April, stories began appearing in various social media outlets that said the new Dry Max diapers were causing chemical burns on babies. Facebook was the center of this social media storm with a page titled "Recall Pampers Dry Max Diapers!" The 3,000 plus people who "like" the page argued that the new Dry Max diapers caused burns and diaper rash, that P&G ignored the problem, and that P&G should recall the product ("About," n.d.). On the site, people published their problems with Dry Max. Of course, there were occasional posts from people supporting P&G. Here is an exchange from October 2011:

I tried Pampers Cruisers 2x this year on my daughter. . [.] both times rash with red almost bloody looking soars!!! put huggies on. . [.] no problem!!

What is going on with Pampers? we used them with our first child in 2007 and didn't have a problem.

I'm sorry people are having negative results with these diapers but I must share my experience as well. I've used these diapers for a year and a half and I have loved them. They fit my tiny daughter perfectly and she has never had any diaper rash and she has never leaked out of her diaper. I loved the product. It has been difficult to find the dry max lately and I am bummed because I felt they worked so well for us. It's a bummer that others haven't had the same results. (Since switching diapers, she leaks out of almost everyone.) ugh!

Jenny, will all do [sic] respect, how can you call other parents stupid and ignorant because they are having a problem with these diapers when you aren't? I can tell you that my 4 month old has had a severe reaction to these diapers. [. . .] am positive it is the diapers seeing as how all he eats is formula, applesauce and bananas, and his diet hasn't changed at all, yet his diapers have. Does this mean I am stupid and ignorant? If your child had the severe rashes and boils that my son, and other people's children have had, you surely wouldn't be calling anyone ignorant or stupid. Your comments make it quite clear that you are the only one that is stupid and ignorant.

Calling her stupid and ignorant is putting it nicely, Kelly. I hate people who like a page even though they disagree with it, just to be an underhanded little punk, nice and safe behind their computer screen. . . . brand you like, you can do that without being a turd, like Michelle has done. It's one thing for a kiddo to be sensitive to certain brands, but a product that causes diaper rash that is similar to chemical burns is ridiculous. I'm SOO happy for Jenny that her kid does fine with them but that doesn't change the fact that these diapers BURN some babies butts horribly bad. Michelle, if you haven't tried already, try finding them online like at diapers. com or amazon. Both have loyalty programs where you get discounts. Good luck!

Can we just shut down pampers already? Come on, nothing should go on this long with so many issues . . . really? really?, and w[h]ere are these test results at? and who ran them? lol what a joke. . [. .] We should do tests of our own? That way in court nothing can stop the people. . [. .] CHEAP DOES NOT WORK>>> NO CHEMICALS . . . You will fail every time. . . ., and now it is just a matter of time. Chemical free everything parents even your water. ("Recall," 2011)

We can see emotion emerging on both sides of the Dry Max concern. The emotion is to be expected given the nature of the product. People are naturally more involved with products they consume or place on their bodies. Now factor in babies, and the level of involvement spikes even further. No parent wants to harm his or her baby with the diapers they are using. This is a volatile crisis threat for P&G. Who will buy Dry Max diapers if they hurt babies?

P&G probably has more experience combating rumors than any other company in the world. P&G fought a rumor over its old man on the moon symbol being linked to satanism for over two decades (Emery, n.d.). P&G saw the Dry Max situation as a rumor (a crisis risk) that posed the potential to escalate into a substantial crisis. The reason P&G considered Dry Max a rumor was that research did not support the claims of chemical burns. Hence, P&G defined the situation as untrue information about their product—a rumor. P&G mobilized a variety of communication resources and third-party endorsements to help fight the rumor. Third-party endorsements are from people not affiliated with the organization who support the organization's position in some way. There were earlier signs that a problem was brewing, but the situation escalated for P&G when its monitoring found the term "chemical burns" appearing in the social media posts about Dry Max. The social media concerns began attracting some traditional or legacy media attention, so P&G determined now was the time to combat the rumor ("How," 2010). The first statement by P&G was a news release on May 6, 2010 titled "Pampers Calls Rumor Completely False." Here is the text of the news release:

"For a number of weeks, Pampers has been a subject of growing but completely false rumors fueled by social media that its new Dry Max diaper causes rashes and other skin . . ."

Pampers (NYSE: PG) today described rumors about its new Dry Max diaper as "completely false."

Jodi Allen, Vice President for Pampers, said, "For a number of weeks, Pampers has been a subject of growing but completely false rumors fueled by social media that its new Dry Max diaper causes rashes and other skin irritations. These rumors are being perpetuated by a small number of parents, some of whom are unhappy that we replaced our older Cruisers and Swaddlers products while others support competitive products and the use of cloth diapers. Some have specifically sought to promote the myth that our product causes 'chemical burns.' We have comprehensively and thoroughly investigated these and other claims and have found no evidence whatsoever that the reported conditions were in any way caused by materials in our product. Independent physicians, highly respected in the field, have analyzed our data and have confirmed our conclusions. This week we have shared these findings, and other detailed safety information, with the Consumer Product Safety Commission, and we welcome its involvement in reviewing these claims and helping to educate parents on the true causes of diaper rash.

At Pampers, we want to reassure all parents that the materials used in the new diaper are not new—they are the same type used in our previous products—and do not and cannot cause so-called chemical burns or other serious skin conditions. We have encouraged these parents who have contacted us to speak with their own pediatricians about the true nature and cause of these problems.

To date, there have been in excess of two billion diaper changes using the new product, with only a handful of rash complaints, none of which were shown to be caused by the type of materials in our product. In fact, we have received fewer than two complaints about diaper rash for every one million diapers sold, which is average for our business and does not deviate from the number of calls we received prior to Dry Max. The majority of our consumers are telling us that they prefer the Dry Max product over the ones it replaced because it is 20% thinner than before.

Unfortunately, diaper rash is very common, and sometimes severe, regardless of the diaper used. At any given moment, more than 250,000 babies will experience a serious rash. Disposable diapers in fact have helped reduce the incidence of rash by more than 50 percent since they were first introduced in the 1960s because they pull wetness away from a baby's skin. It is very common for parents to correlate a change in our products with the sudden appearance of a rash. Pampers routinely sees a temporary increase in calls whenever we introduce a modification to our products.

We will continue to work hard to educate parents on the facts surrounding this story, as well as defend the integrity of our product from false and misleading information." ("Pampers," 2010)

The news release reflects the core of P&G's response strategy—deny the claims and provide supporting evidence that Dry Max is safe while still respecting the concerns of parents. P&G had statistical evidence to support the safety of Dry Max and was beginning to use third-party endorsements, in this case a New York City pediatrician. But P&G showed respect for those parents concerned about diaper rash. They recognized the seriousness of the problem while explaining how Dry Max was designed to prevent the problem. P&G also noted that a temporary spike in diaper rash reports occur any time they introduce a new product. We see this respect for parental concerns in a posting to the Recall Pampers Dry Max Diapers Facebook page by a mother who had contacted P&G about the problem:

I emailed P&G on Friday after 5 and got a reply before noon the next morning. Here was the reply to my complaint:

"Dear Natasha,

Thank you for contacting us regarding your experience with Pampers.

I'm very sorry you had this experience. I'm sure it was upsetting and we certainly share your concern about the irritation your baby had while wearing our diapers. We hope your baby is feeling better.

Many of us on the Pampers team are parents, and we share your deep commitment to the health and safety of babies. We want to understand any negative experiences about our products as thoroughly as we can. In order to gather additional information, a member of our Health and Safety Team will be following up with you via postal mail. Our goal is to understand more about your unique experience, your baby, and the products you typically use on your baby. Once you receive our mailing, we would greatly appreciate a few additional minutes of your time to complete the information requested. Please hold on to the package and any remaining product for two weeks in the event our Health and Safety Team needs to get them back.

Again, on behalf of Pampers I want to apologize for the experience you had, but I also want to assure you that Pampers with Dry Max is one of the most mom-and-baby tested diapers in our history. Before the launch of any new product, it is extensively tested to ensure we have a broad understanding of what parents will experience. In addition, we sample products regularly throughout the manufacturing process to ensure our quality standards are met at every step of production. However, at Pampers, we also know every baby is unique and a baby's skin can be especially delicate. Therefore, we greatly appreciate your taking the time to contact us so we can continue to gather data on as many babies as possible. We are closely monitoring and reporting all comments we receive and take each comment seriously.

If interested, there is more information about Dry Max posted on Pampers.com. There is both a video from Kerri Hailey and an FAQ link. Kerri not only helped create Dry Max, she did it while her youngest was in diapers so she saw the product in action at work, and at home. To view these, click on the link below:

http://www.pampers.com/en_US/Vote-Cruisers-DryMax

In addition to our request for more information, I'm also following up by postal mail with coupons good for any Pampers. Along with Swaddlers and Cruisers with Dry Max we also offer two versions of diapers that don't contain Dry Max: Pampers Baby Dry and Pampers Extra Protection without Dry Max. (Extra Protection is only available in the U.S.) Please allow 2–3 weeks for delivery." (Natashia, 2010)

Again, P&G recognized the parent's concern over the diaper rash while stating the evidence shows that Dry Max is safe. P&G shows they are willing to help investigate the problem further. While over 2 billion diaper changes went well, there is always the possibility that a child could be having an allergic reaction to the product. An allergic reaction is possible with any product that is consumed or touches the skin.

Exhibit 3.1 Pampers Dry Max Explained: FAQ

Is Dry Max safe for my baby?

At Pampers, nothing is more important to our people than ensuring the safety of our diapers for babies. We evaluate the safety of all ingredients used in our products, including specific testing for problems such as skin irritation and skin allergies. In addition, we constantly monitor consumer health comments to ensure product safety in real consumer use conditions.

Because of this commitment to safety, we made Pampers with Dry Max one of the most mom- and baby-tested diapers in our history. Hundreds of thousands of diapers were tested before they were ever placed on retailer shelves. Our Dry Max diapers use the same type of ingredients as Pampers' other trusted products and, in fact, many other disposable diapers on the market. The key difference is simply in how we applied those materials and produced the diaper itself. To date, more than a million U.S. families have used more than two billion Pampers with Dry Max diapers.

For even more information about P&G's commitment to product safety, visit http://www.pgproductsafety.com/productsafety/index.shtml

Was there ever a recall of diapers with Dry Max?

No, there was no recall of Dry Max products. In September 2010, the CPSC and Health Canada announced that they did not find a link between Pampers' Dry Max design and diaper rash. To read the complete Dry Max announcement, please click here:

http://www.cpsc.gov/cpscpub/prerel/prhtm110/10331.html

What are Pampers with Dry Max? How does the Dry Max design work?

Pampers Swaddlers and Cruisers with Dry Max are our high performance diapers and the biggest innovation to Pampers in 25 years. The development of the Dry Max design is the result of more than a decade of research and careful testing involving more than 20,000 babies—including many "tests" in our own homes. Utilizing an innovative diaper core, these hard-working Pampers with Dry Max diapers are thinner than before, and are Pampers' driest diaper ever as they help lock in wetness.

The Dry Max design refers to the absorbent part of Swaddlers and Cruisers diapers, where our innovative manufacturing process makes the product thinner than before while locking in wetness to make it our driest diaper ever. This allows us to get rid of bulky fluff material, and to put the high-powered absorbent gel exactly where you need it to help lock the wetness away.

What are the materials in Pampers with Dry Max diapers?

Pampers with Dry Max diapers are made of the same types of materials that have been used in diapers for many years. The absorbent core is primarily composed of an acquisition layer containing pulp-based fibers and a storage core containing a super absorbent gelling material. This super-absorbent gel, which is used in most disposable diapers, is made into small beads that turn into a gel-like material in order to hold the large amount of liquid. This gel has been shown to be non-irritating, safe for skin and even safe if ingested. The absorbent core also includes a touch of fragrance inside, to help mask the smell of urine and BM.

The rest of the diaper is primarily composed of soft synthetic materials (Polypropylene and Polyethylene), which are commonly used in applications ranging from clothing to housewares to food packaging, as well as Lycra (a latex-free elastic). In addition, the diaper contains lotion, a cosmetic ingredient to help maintain the baby's skin health. For a complete list of ingredients in Pampers Dry Max diapers, please visit:

http://www.pampers.com/en_US/Pampers-DryMax-Ingredients

What diapers feature the Dry Max design?

Pampers' Dry Max is a design feature included in Pampers Swaddlers (sizes N-3), Swaddlers Sensitive (sizes 3 and 4), and Cruisers (sizes 3–6) products. The Dry Max design is not featured in our Baby Dry products, or in our pants products (Easy Ups, UnderJams, and Splashers).

Who do I contact if I have any questions or need more information about Pampers with Dry Max?

We value your input, and want hear from you! If you have any questions or concerns, please give us a call at 1–800-PAMPERS (726–7377), Monday-Friday from 9:00 am to 6:00 pm ET. You can also contact us via email by clicking here:

http://babycare.custhelp.com/app/ask

http://www.pampers.com/en_US/dry-max/pampers-dry-max.

("Pampers Dry Max Explained: FAQ," 2009)

Exhibit 3.2   Pampers Is Committed

Pampers Is Committed To Your Baby's Health, Happiness, and Safety

Pampers has always created products with your baby's happiness and well-being in mind. As parents ourselves, we know that nothing could be more important. Responding to recent rumors, Jodi Allen, Vice President of Pampers North America, reaffirms the safety of our products and our steadfast commitment to earn your trust every single day.

TRUST

To those of us who work at Pampers, trust is more than a word. It's our mission. Parents trust us with their babies, and that is a responsibility that we take to heart. For nearly 50 years, we've worked with parents and babies to continually improve the way our diapers wrap babies in comfort and protect them as they grow. We're humbled by the trust parents place in us, and we work hard each day to earn and keep it.

PRODUCT SAFETY

You may have heard some concerns expressed about diaper rash, and even "chemical burns," and whether there is any correlation to our new Dry Max diaper. As you might imagine, we take these concerns very seriously. We want to let you know that, following the launch of our new Pampers Swaddlers and Cruisers with Dry Max, eight of the nation's leading pediatricians and dermatologists completed comprehensive reviews of clinical and consumer data involving the Dry Max diaper. Leading pediatric and general dermatologists also conducted face-to-face examinations of babies and reviewed photos of reported skin conditions.

We're pleased to reassure you that these experts unanimously confirmed that the cases they've seen are classic diaper rash, and are not related to the diaper.

After a comprehensive review, the U.S. Consumer Product Safety Commission (CPSC) has found no link between Pampers Dry Max diapers and diaper rash or other skin conditions.

YOUR BABIES COME FIRST

Our first and foremost responsibility is to protect the well-being of your baby. As moms and dads who work at Pampers, we're parents too. Your babies are our babies.

Our priorities are the same. Our own babies wear these diapers. Please know that we would never put a product on the market that didn't meet comprehensive safety requirements, which are even more stringent at Pampers than the government requires. As parents, if we had any doubt at all about product safety, we'd be the first to take action.

Dry Max was created by a team of scientists—many of whom are parents. One of our lead researchers used it on her own child for two years as she was developing the diaper.

Many Pampers moms and dads have babies in diapers and are using Dry Max.

Pampers Dry Max may be a new product, but it uses the same type of ingredients used safely in diapers for many years. What's new is the design which allowed us to carefully place the absorbent material exactly where your baby needs it, making it thinner than before.

To date, more than 2.5 billion Dry Max diapers have been used in the US, and we've received only two complaints per one million diapers.

Unfortunately, no diaper is perfect in preventing diaper rash. At any point in time, about one in four babies will be experiencing those unavoidable rashes.

Cruisers with Dry Max diapers are 20 percent thinner than before, more flexible for baby, and incredibly good at protecting babies from the very wetness that contributes to rashes in the first place.

OUR PROMISE

There's nothing more important to us than your baby. That's why you can absolutely count on us to provide you with safe, high quality products to help you protect and care for your child. We hope you will continue to choose Pampers, and we'll work hard every day to earn and keep your trust. As always, feel free to give us a call at 800/PAMPERS if you have any questions, comments or ideas. If you'd like to try Dry Max, please visit pampers.com.

("Pampers Is Committed," 2009)

Clearly, a news release is not enough when the story is breaking in social media. Exhibit 3.1 contains a number of the online messages provided by P&G. Pampers has its own Facebook page with over 800,000 people who "like" it. P&G responded to concerns that were posted to its Facebook page. There is an "Ask Pampers" section where customers post questions and employees of P&G respond to those questions. But to combat the rumor more effectively in social media, P&G turned to the very powerful mommy bloggers. Many mothers who blog have become influential among other mothers who depend upon them for information and advice. In fact, the first true Internet communities were formed by mothers on discussion boards. Here is part of a news story about P&G and the mommy bloggers:

Among the bloggers visiting Thursday was Kate Marsh Lord of Niceville, Fla., whose 18-month-old daughter developed a severe rash wearing a Dry Max diaper. She said her pediatrician assured her the diaper didn't cause the rash, and she has continued to use Dry Max without incident.

"We're walking the fine line of communicating that the diaper is not causing the rash and still being sympathetic to the fact that they're really having a rash, and our heart goes out to them," said Jodi Allen, a P&G Baby Care vice president. "First and foremost, we care about babies' health."

P&G says Pampers sales remain strong and it has found no evidence Dry Max, billed as 20 percent thinner than earlier versions, is more likely to cause rashes. P&G was getting fewer than two complaints of rashes per million diapers sold until this month, said officials who noted that occasional diaper rashes are common. (Sewell, 2010)

Note how P&G maintains the need to refute the rumor with concern and sympathy for parents facing diaper rash. The mommy blogger summit was designed as an informational meeting where P&G presented information about why Dry Max was safe and not linked to the rumored diaper rash outbreaks.

P&G did seem to get its points across as the bloggers agreed they now had greater confidence in P&G and the Dry Max Diapers (Sewell, 2010). The following post is typical of the comments the four mommy bloggers made after visiting P&G:

Pampers Dry Max Controversy: My Opinion

May 30, 2010

As I told you all, I was asked to travel to Pampers Baby Center to listen to their side of the Pampers Dry Max Debate. Since Blake is still in diapers, I reviewed the Dry Max Cruisers back in February and have purchased these diapers ever[y] time I had to buy diapers since then. To date, I have not had any issues with the diapers.

Contrary to popular belief, I was not compensated for this trip other than my travel expenses. And, unless you consider getting on 3 planes all within 36 hours is my idea of a good time, th[e]n THINK AGAIN! I will report to you what I learned from the Pampers team. I will state now that this is my opinion and what I learned.

1) **Pamper Dry Max contains chemicals**: The Dry Max Diapers contain the same ingredients that were present in the old Swaddlers and Cruisers. The difference in the Dry Max is that the[y] found a way to fix the adsorbent gel with using less pulp, which results in the slimmer diaper. Since the gel is more adsorbent, there is only an increase of about 5% in gel put into the diaper. The adsorbent gel used is an inert polyacrylate, which is non-toxic. For a full list of ingredients used in the Dry Max Diapers, click here.

2) **The Dry Max Diaper Causes Chemical Burns**: There has been no evidence that the new Dry Max causes chemical burns. 95% of hospitals use Pampers Swaddlers with Dry Max, and not one has reported any issue with the diapers. Pampers also reached out to the American Pediatric Association and the American Association of Dermatology and neither are seeing any complaints or increase in diaper rash. If you feel that your child is having an issue with the diapers, first see your pediatrician to make sure that you are properly treating your child's ailment, and then call Pampers at 1–800-PAMPERS to let them know.

3) **Chemical Burn vs. Diaper Rash**: The term chemical burn is very severe. I work with strong acids on a daily basis and have had small chemical burns on my arms. It is very different from a diaper rash. A chemical burn would be on every area touched by the diaper and would take months to heal. A diaper rash can clear up in 2 to 4 days with proper treatment. If you feel that your child has a chemical burn, you should immediately bring him/her to the emergency room, as you would not be able to wait to see your pediatrician.

4) **Does Pampers Care**: From what I witnessed, YES they do care! They are parents, just like us, and have been spending many extra hours at work to try and solve these issues. Since the new Dry Max Diaper complaints started they have gone back through their research an[d] re-checked everything. They have put outside eyes on the problem and have been actively addressing the issue. They have added extra staff to their call centers and tried to reach out to as many parents as possible. Keep in mind when you read media statements, they are not always released as they are stated. Have they made some media mistakes, yes, but when you are attacked you tend to go on the defensive. They are now taking a step at trying to reach out to moms and let them know that they are their [sic] to listen.

5) **Did Pampers Use Your Baby For Testing**: NO!! The Dry Max Diaper has been in the development for the last 10 years! This gave them plenty of time to test the product before it was released. In this time, the diaper went through extensive testing, including over 300,000 diaper changes on over 20,000 babies, including one of the developer of Dry Max's baby. They have used this product on their own children, and would continue to do so.

6) **Dry Max is Being Investigated By the CPSC**: The CPSC investigates every complaint that it receives, so yes they are investigating Pampers Dry Max. Pampers traveled to Washington D.C. and met with the CPSC to make sure that they have all the necessary information for this investigation. Results have not been released as of today.

7) **Why Were the Dry Max Diapers Released in Old Cruiser Packaging**: As with most new products, the Dry Max diapers were released in the old Cruiser packages. We were told that this is normal with most products, but they would reconsider this method next time. The new Dry Max diapers started hitting stores 20 months ago in the old Cruiser packaging. The complaints about the new Dry Max did not start until January and did not spike over the normal complaint line until April 2010!

I have not seen any evidence that will cause me to stop using Pampers Dry Max. I have read a lot of the articles available online and visited the Facebook page. I would be happy to try and answer any other questions that you have, but will not tolerate being attacked.

To see what the other moms who traveled to Pampers with me thought visit: Kate at The Shopping Mama, Tiffany at Babes and Kids Reviews, and Stephanie at And Twins Make 5.

If you feel that you are having issues with Dry Max Diapers, consult your pediatrician and contact Pampers. (Renee, 2010)

The bloggers presented the information they learned from P&G that indicated there is no chemical burn nor increased diaper rash risk from the new Dry Max diapers. They also noted their attendance at the event and that there was no additional compensation, just travel expenses. Such disclosures are important to maintaining transparency and an authentic voice for the bloggers. In the end, bloggers became another channel for the presentation of P&G's case for the safety of Dry Max as they repeated the evidence P&G was presenting. The blogs reflect reasoned arguments based on evidence, not mindless fan support for P&G. Notice that the sample blog provided earlier did include the fact that Dry Max was being investigated by the Consumer Safety Product Commission (CSPC). This indicates there are still some questions about safety.

The CSPC eventually found no problem with the Dry Max diapers. One of the four bloggers included a post about that announcement. Here is the statement from P&G:

No Pampers Recall: CPSC finds no cause that links Pampers Dry Max to diaper rash—from Jodi Allen, Vice President of Pampers

We cannot say enough that our mission at Pampers is to do our small part to help keep your baby happy and healthy. We want you to know that everything we do is motivated by a desire to help make life a little easier and more comfortable for you and your baby. As such, safety always has been and always will be our number one priority.

Some of you might have heard some concerns expressed earlier this year about our new Dry Max diapers and a possible link to diaper rash or other serious skin irritations. We were pleased to hear that after their very comprehensive review, the U.S. Consumer Product Safety Commission (CPSC) and Health Canada have released a Dry Max announcement that they have found no link between Pampers Dry Max diapers and diaper rash or other skin conditions.

While we know most of you and your babies have had a wonderful experience with the new Dry Max diapers, we do understand that some babies have experienced a real diaper rash over the last few months while using Dry Max. We truly and deeply sympathize with any parent who has to see their baby suffer, which is why we spent the last several months reevaluating and retesting every aspect of the product, reevaluating every material we use as well as thoroughly researching specific cases that were brought to our attention.

While all of this testing reaffirmed the safety of the product, we also learned even more about diaper rash directly from parents and pediatricians. According to the American Academy of Pediatrics (the AAP), a healthy child can be expected to experience about four diaper rashes per year. To do what we can to help parents dealing with diaper rash, we are sponsoring the distribution of comprehensive educational materials produced by the AAP that provide detailed information on the care and treatment of infant skin conditions, including diaper rash. These AAP materials are now available as free brochures and in the summer issue of AAP Healthy Children Magazine through many pediatrician offices, online at www.healthychildren.org, and at pampers.com.

> We hope that this Dry Max announcement will reassure the millions of moms, dads and child caregivers who place their trust in Pampers and Dry Max every day. We want to sincerely thank you and want you to know that you can absolutely count on us to always put your baby first. ("No," 2010)

P&G now had a third-party endorsement from the primary U.S. government organization responsible for product safety.

P&G linked its traditional or legacy media and social media relations efforts to a webpage devoted to the new Dry Max. The webpage had FAQs about the new diaper, information on fighting diaper rash, testimonials from pediatricians, and a video supporting the safety of the diaper from public health expert Dr. Kimberly Thompson of Harvard University.

The Facebook page calling for the boycott of Dry Max was still active as of the writing of this case in February of 2013. There is speculation that the social media rumor was an effort to pull consumers away from disposable diapers to cloth diapers. Many of those actively posting about the "chemical burns" were advocating the use of cloth diapers. Such comments appear on the boycott site, the Pampers site, and one of the four mommy blogger's sites. The pro-cloth diaper idea was simply speculation because there was no hard evidence of a conspiracy. P&G seemed to weather the storm as sales of Pampers remained strong. The sales figures were positive information for P&G since Pampers is its top-selling product line ("Procter," 2010).

Reading Guide

1. If this situation is a crisis, what type of crisis is it?

2. What is the problem and the source(s) of the problem in this case?

3. What stakeholders should be interested in this case?

4. How does the crisis begin?

5. Why did P&G consider the situation to be a rumor?

6. What role did the Internet play in P&G's crisis response?

7. Who are mommy bloggers, and what role did they play in this case?

8. What conspiracy arose about the reason for the crisis starting?

Discussion Questions

1. Does visiting P&G headquarters compromise the integrity of the bloggers and erode their value as third-party endorsers? Why or why not?

2. Why might third-party endorsements serve to enhance P&G's crisis response?

3. How did social media work for and against P&G in this case?

4. Why does the inclusion of babies in the case make the crisis more challenging?

5. Did defining the crisis as a rumor hurt or help P&G's crisis response effort? Why?

6. What is the relevance of the speculation about the "conspiracy?"

7. What communicative action might P&G have engaged in earlier to prevent the escalation of this situation?

8. How would you classify the crisis response strategies used by P&G? Do these strategies fit with corporate apologia, Image Repair theory, or SCCT?

9. How might including the idea of third-party endorsements improve any of the crisis response theories or principles?

Websites

Pampers Facebook page: https://www.facebook.com/Pampers

Recall Pampers Dry Max!: http://www.facebook.com/search/results.php?q=boycott%20pampers&init=quick&tas=0.13310803586962433#!/pages/RECALL-PAMPERS-DRY-MAX-DIAPERS/124714717540863

Mommy bloggers blogs about visit to P&G: http://andtwinsmake5.blogspot.com/2010/05/my-visit-to-p-pampers-baby-care.html and http://whatmommiesneed.com/2010/05/30/pampers-dry-max-controversy-my-opinion/

Pampers References

About. (n.d.). Retrieved from http://www.facebook.com/pages/recall-pampers-dry.max-diapers/124714717540863#!/pages/recall-pampers-dry-max-diapers/124714717540863?sk=info

Dry Max diaper rash experts opinions. (2009). Retrieved from http://www.pampers.com/en_US/dry-max/dry-max-diaper-rash-experts

Emery, D. (n.d.). Trademark of the beast. Retrieved from http://urbanlegends.about.com/od/business/a/procter_gamble.htm

How Pampers battled diaper debacle. (2010). Retrieved from http://gabrielcatalano.com/2010/05/10/how-pampers-battled-diaper-debacle/

Natashia. (2010). Retrieved from http://www.facebook.com/topic.php?uid=124714717540863&topic=132

No Pampers recall. (2010). Retrieved from http://www.pampers.com/en_US/drymax/pampers-recall

Pampers calls rumors completely false. (2010). Retrieved from http://news.pg.com/press release/pg-corporate-announcements/pampers-calls-rumors-completely-false

Pampers Dry Max explained: FAQs. (2009). Retrieved from http://www.pampers.com/en_US/dry-max/pampers-rash-evaluation

Pampers is committed to your baby's health, happiness, and safety. (2009). Retrieved from http://www.pampers.com/en_US/dry-max/dry-max-video#seeinaction6

Procter & Gamble's Dry Max efforts include mommy bloggers, phone lines. (2010). Retrieved from http://law.gaeatimes.com/2010/05/20/procter-gambles-dry-max-efforts-include-mommy-bloggers-phone-lines-22442/

Recall Pampers Dry Max diapers! (2011). Retrieved from http://www.facebook.com/pages/RECALL-PAMPERS-DRY-MAX-DIAPERS/124714717540863

Renee. (2010). Pampers Dry Max controversy: My opinion. Retrieved from http://whatmommiesneed.com/2010/05/30/pampers-dry-max-controversy-my-opinion/

Sewell, D. (2010). P&G hosts bloggers in defense of Pampers Dry Max. Retrieved from http://www.signonsandiego.com/news/2010/may/20/pg-hosts-bloggers-in-defense-of-pampers-dry-max/

Siomkos, G., & Kurzbard, G. (1994). The hidden crisis in product-harm crisis management. *European Journal of Marketing, 28*(2), 30–41.

CHAPTER 4

Hershey, Cocoa, and Child Slavery/Labor Abuse

In 1894, Milton Hershey decided to make chocolate to cover his caramels. From that choice, the Hershey Chocolate Company was born in Lancaster, Pennsylvania. The enterprise has grown over the years with the Hershey Company becoming the largest chocolate confectionary in North America. Hershey's is a global brand with operations in over 90 countries. When people hear the name Hershey's, they think chocolate. The Hershey's Kisses are an iconic candy known around the world.

Chocolate is derived from the seeds of the cacao tree known as cocoa beans and originated in Mexico, Central America, and South America. The beans grow in pods with each pod containing 20 to 60 beans. The cacao tree grows only in tropical climates within a 10 degree north to 20 degree south range of the Equator. According to the International Cocoa Organization, the leading producers of cocoa beans are Brazil, Ghana, the Ivory Coast (Côte d'Ivoire), Cameroon, Ecuador, Indonesia, Malaysia, and Nigeria. West Africa accounts for about two thirds of all cocoa bean production in the world. The Ivory Coast alone produces over 40% of the world's cocoa bean ("Production," n.d.).

Chocolate is a delicious treat enjoyed worldwide. However, there is a sinister problem that plagues chocolate production—the exploitation of children. Children are exploited as forced labor and many are actually slaves (child trafficking) sold to the cocoa bean producers. The problem is rooted in poverty and the exploitation of the many small farms that grow cocoa. Children are sent to the cocoa plantations in hopes of earning money for their families. Intermediaries even help to smuggle children across the border from neighboring countries. Instead of finding paying jobs, the children find themselves forced to work for no wages. The plantation owners will even sell the children to other plantations in need of workers—it is slavery and child trafficking. In 2000 and 2001, some high profile media exposure drew attention to the child exploitation in the cocoa industry yet the problems still plague the cocoa industry to this day (Boaz, 2010; "Human Cost," 2011).

In the United States, two members of Congress proposed legislation to address the child slavery-labor problem in the cocoa industry in light of the news media exposés. Senator Tom Harkin (D-Iowa) and Representative Eliot Engel (D-NY) created legislation (a rider to an agriculture bill) that would require chocolate manufacturers to certify and label their products as "slave free" ("News," 2005). The legislation passed the House of Representatives, but intense lobbying from the chocolate industry created an alternative to the legislation, and no laws were passed for "slave free" certification for U.S. chocolate. The alternative was a voluntary system whereby the chocolate industry would self-regulate the child slavery-labor problem. The compromise was known as the Harkin-Engel Protocol. The chocolate industry vowed to clean up the problem on its own. The industry pledged to have certification of cocoa beans as free of the major child labor problems by 2005. In 2005, the chocolate industry admitted it had not achieved its objective and set a new deadline for 2008 with a goal of 50% of cocoa being certified as free of major child labor problems. Experts dispute whether or not that goal was met. Some estimations are that 70% of the cocoa used in 2008 was connected to child slave labor (Ensbey, 2009).

Exhibit 4.1	Descriptions of the Four Non-Governmental Organizations

1. Global Exchange

"Global Exchange is an international human rights organization dedicated to promoting social, economic and environmental justice since 1988. We are a 501 c3 registered non-profit.

We're changing the rules across the globe from a profit-centered global economy to thriving people-centered local economies; from the politics of greed to a living democracy that respects the rights of workers and nature; and from currency to community."

("About Global," n.d., para. 1–2)

2. International Labor Rights Forum

"Millions of workers around the world toil under inhumane working conditions. In a globalized economy, corporations from developed countries produce consumer goods ranging from coffee to cellphones in poor developing countries, where they can take advantage of cheap labor and lack of environmental or community protections. Workers, including child workers, must toil extremely long hours for wages that are barely subsistence wages, and often under unsanitary and unsafe conditions. In many countries there is little or no labor law enforcement, and many workers are prevented from joining organizations to advance their interests.

Alarmingly, an estimated 211 million children between the ages of 5 and 14 are compelled to work around the world. These children produce rubber, cotton, coffee and work in mines to produce goods that are traded to the United States and other developed countries. Unable to go to school, these children face little hope of escaping poverty in their future.

Advocacy for these workers is essential to ensuring their protection, strengthening their voice, and ending abuses that violate their rights and dignity. ILRF is an advocacy organization dedicated to achieving just and humane treatment for workers worldwide. ILRF serves a unique role among human rights organizations as advocates for and with working poor around the world. We believe that all workers have the right to a safe working environment where they are treated with dignity and respect, and where they can organize freely to defend and promote their rights and interests. We are committed to ending the problems of child labor, forced labor, and other abusive practices. We promote enforcement of labor rights internationally through public education and mobilization, research, litigation, legislation, and collaboration with labor, government and business groups."

("About ILRF," n.d.)

3. Green America

"Green America is a not-for-profit membership organization founded in 1982. (We went by the name 'Co-op America' until January 1, 2009.)

Our mission is to harness economic power—the strength of consumers, investors, businesses, and the marketplace—to create a socially just and environmentally sustainable society."

("About Green," n.d., para. 1–2)

4. Oasis USA

"Our vision is for community—a place where everyone is included, making a contribution and reaching their God-given potential. Oasis is committed to working in an inclusive, integrated, empowering and comprehensive way so that all people experience wholeness and fullness of life."

("Vision," n.d., para. 5–6)

Four non-governmental organizations (NGOs) have collaborated to pressure Hershey into ending exploitive child slavery-labor in its supply chain. The campaign's title is "It's Time to Raise the Bar Hershey" or "Raise the Bar, Hershey" for short. The logo for the campaign is the distinctive Hershey chocolate bar with "Raise the Bar" instead of "Hershey's" on the wrapper. The group is led by Green America and includes Oasis USA, the International Labor Rights Forum, and the Global Exchange. Exhibit 4.1 provides descriptions of the four NGOs. When activists seek reform in an industry, they typically target a market leader. Hershey has over 40% of the U.S. chocolate market. Moreover, Hershey has been aware of the child slavery-labor problem since 2001. Table 4.1 lists the reasons the coalition has focused on Hershey.

According to a study conducted at Tulane University, many other chocolate-related companies have made the changes necessary to reduce child slavery-labor from their supply chains, including Mars, Kraft, Nestlé, and Cargill. Hershey was identified in the Tulane University report as still having abusive child labor practices in its supply chain (Newman, 2011a).

Table 4.1   Why Hershey?

Sourcing	Much of Hershey's cocoa is sourced from West Africa, a region plagued by forced labor, human trafficking, and abusive child labor. Hershey does not have a system in place to ensure that its cocoa purchases from this region are not tainted by labor rights abuses.
Transparency	Hershey continuously refuses to identify its cocoa suppliers; therefore, it is impossible to verify that its chocolate was not made under conditions of abusive child labor.
Certification	A reputable, independent, third-party certification can ensure that a process is in place to identify and remediate labor rights abuses. For cocoa, the strongest certification system currently available is Fair Trade. Unlike many of its competitors, Hershey's has not embraced certification. Only one of Hershey's chocolate bars, in its Dagoba line, is Fair Trade Certified.
Laggard	Hershey lags behind its competitors when it comes to purchasing cocoa that has been certified to meet certain labor, social, and environmental standards. Most major chocolate companies offer Fair Trade options now, and many smaller companies have been 100% Fair Trade for years.
Greenwashing	Hershey points to various charitable donations to children in the United States and programs in West Africa as examples of its social responsibility, yet it has no policies in place to ensure that the cocoa used in its products is not produced with forced, trafficked, or child labor.

Source: "Why" (2011).

The "Raise the Bar" campaign has very specific changes it wants Hershey to execute in order to end the problem with child slavery-labor. Here are the demands the campaign has made on Hershey:

1. To make an agreement to take immediate action to eliminate forced and child labor in violation of [International Labor Organization] ILO conventions 29, 105, 138, and 182 from Hershey's cocoa supply chain through

   - tracing its supply chain to the farm level

   - sourcing from farmers who can show through independent verification that they do not use forced labor or child labor

   - asking suppliers to end such practices at the farms from which they source.

2. To make a commitment to sourcing cocoa that has been 100% certified by an independent third party certification system that meets or goes beyond the fair trade standard for at least one of its top-five-selling chocolate bars that prominently displays the Hershey name by 2012.

3. Additionally, a commitment to sourcing certified cocoa for at least one additional top-five-selling bar every two years thereafter, so that Hershey's top-five-selling cocoa bars will all be 100% certified by an independent third

party certification system that meets or goes beyond the fair trade standard within 10 years or that the majority of Hershey's cocoa across all products will be certified by 2022. ("Our Demands," 2012)

The Raise the Bar, Hershey! campaign is anchored by its website that provides information about child slavery and labor abuse in the chocolate supply chain, explains why Hershey is the target, and provides various ways to get involved with the effort. The website serves as a hub that connects social media, traditional media relations, and activist actions. The social media efforts include Flickr and YouTube. These media content sharing sites are used to display the winners from competitions to create mock commercials (print and video) held by Raise the Bar, Hershey! The competition creates attention for the campaign to end child labor abuse, involves followers, and develops new materials to use in the effort. Here is the description of the contest:

The "Raise the Bar, Hershey" campaign organized a "brand jamming" contest which invited campaign supporters to create mock taglines, print advertisements and commercial videos that reveal the reality behind Hershey chocolate products. ("Contest," n.d.)

Raise the Bar, Hershey! campaign uses traditional media relations to garner traditional or legacy media coverage. The campaign sends out news releases, including the PRNewswire, and stages pseudo-events designed to attract media attention to the child labor problems in the cocoa industry. The pseudo-events merge traditional media relations with activist actions. Raise the Bar, Hershey! uses a variety of activist pressure tactics including e-mail action alerts to followers, online petitions, boycotts of products, in-store actions, online actions, and calls urging people to send e-mails and to call Hershey about the child slavery-labor issue. Exhibit 4.2 contains information about a version of the online petition that appeared on change.org. The online petition was a modest success as Hershey committed to using Rainforest Alliance Certified cocoa for its Bliss chocolate products after the petition appeared. The certification does require the chocolate to be slave free. It is a minor victory because Bliss is a small line within Hershey. While Raise the Bar, Hershey! lauded the change, it also noted it would continue to press Hershey for an even greater commitment to end child labor abuse in its supply chain. Exhibit 4.3 contains comments from the Raise the Bar, Hershey! campaign and from Hershey about the Bliss change.

Exhibit 4.2   Online Petition

Change.org Petition

Hershey: Time to Raise the Bar!

Greetings,

I am deeply concerned about child labor, forced labor and trafficking in the products that I buy. I am disappointed to learn that a decade after chocolate companies committed to ending these abuses in their cocoa supply chains, that the exploitation continues.

I believe that Hershey should be a leader in ensuring that the rights of workers and farmers are respected in the production of chocolate—from bean to bar. Hershey must do more to ensure an end to child labor, forced labor and trafficking in its chocolate products by supporting the demands of the "Raise the Bar" campaign.

It's time for Hershey to Raise the Bar by tracing the sources of its cocoa and shifting toward Fairtrade Certified cocoa. By purchasing Fairtrade Certified cocoa, Hershey can truly fulfill its mission to bring sweet moments of Hershey happiness to workers, farmers, children, consumers and shareholders worldwide every day!

[Your name]

http://www.change.org/petitions/hershey-raise-the-bar

("Hershey: Raise," 2012)

Exhibit 4.3   Victory

How We Won

January 30, 2012

On January 30th, The Hershey Company announced that it would make a commitment to purchasing Rainforest Alliance Certified cocoa for all of its Bliss Chocolate products, starting later this year.

This commitment is a welcome first step for Hershey to improve its supply chain accountability. This is the first commitment that Hershey has made to using an independent, third-party certification system to ensure that its cocoa is grown sustainably, including the monitoring of forced and child labor.

This commitment also demonstrates that The Hershey Company acknowledges the severity of the labor abuses that taint the West African cocoa sector, from where Hershey sources the majority of its cocoa.

The members of the Raise the Bar, Hershey! Campaign congratulate Hershey on this first step to achieve greater supply chain accountability and hope that it will be the beginning of comprehensive supply chain traceability and certified child-labor free Hershey chocolate products.

We declare partial victory today because of this announcement. We achieved this through sustained, consistent consumer-based advocacy targeted at Hershey. We collected over 100,000 petition signatures, through Change.org and other sources, and organized petition deliveries, brandjamming contests, protests and Facebook rallies to blanket Hershey's wall with messages.

Hershey made its announcement less than one week after we announced that an ad would run during the Super Bowl that would highlight the company's use of child slavery in cocoa production.

While this is a tremendous step, the Raise the Bar, Hershey! Coalition will not end our advocacy here. We will continue to work to end child labor and exploitation in the cocoa industry and to push Hershey to increase traceability and justice throughout its chocolate supply chain.

Why This Is Important

It has been ten years since major chocolate companies, including Hershey, committed to ending child labor, forced labor and trafficking in their cocoa supply chains; these egregious labor rights abuses continue. A decade later, hundreds of thousands of children continue to labor in hazardous conditions in West Africa, particularly in the Ivory Coast and Ghana, and the US Department of Labor has noted five West African nations whose cocoa may be tainted by forced and/or child labor.

While many chocolate companies have taken steps to trace their cocoa supply chains and implement labor rights standards among their suppliers, Hershey lags behind its competitors in responsibly sourcing its cocoa. Unlike other companies, Hershey has not committed to sourcing cocoa for its main product lines that has been independently certified to comply with international labor rights standards. Tell Hershey to raise the bar and be a leader in sustainable chocolate and shift toward Fairtrade Certified cocoa!

For more information and action ideas, please visit the Raise the Bar Hershey campaign.

("How We Won," 2012)

Exhibit 4.4   Excerpts From Hershey's News Release 1/30/12

Bliss Change in Cocoa Sourcing

The Hershey Company (NYSE: HSY) today announced its plan to reinforce cocoa sustainability efforts by accelerating farmer and family development in West Africa, where 70 percent of the world's cocoa is grown.

Over the next five years, Hershey will expand and accelerate programs to improve cocoa communities by investing $10 million in West Africa and continuing to work with experts in agriculture, community development and government to achieve progress with cocoa farmers and their families. By 2017, Hershey's public and private partnerships will directly benefit 750,000 African cocoa farmers and over two million people in cocoa communities across the region. Because cocoa farms are family farms, improving farming increases family income. Today, West African farmers can increase their cocoa output by 50 percent through modern methods. Doing so will increase school attendance and improve community health.

Later this year, U.S. consumers will be able to purchase Hershey's Bliss® products with 100 percent cocoa from Rainforest Alliance Certified farms. Rainforest Alliance Certified farms have met comprehensive sustainability standards that protect the environment and ensure the safety and well-being of workers, their families and communities. Hershey's Bliss® chocolates are available to U.S. consumers at more than 35,000 retail outlets. In addition, Hershey is working with the Rainforest Alliance to source cocoa from certified farms in Latin America and Africa for Hershey's premium brand, Dagoba®.

("Hershey Expands," 2012)

Exhibit 4.5   Hershey's Updated Press Release (10/03/12)

The Hershey Company (NYSE: HSY) today said it will source 100 percent certified cocoa for its global chocolate product lines by 2020 and accelerate its programs to help eliminate child labor on the ground in West Africa.

Certified cocoa will be verified through independent auditors [who will] assure that it is grown in line with the highest internationally recognized standards for labor, environmental and better farming practices. As Hershey increases its use of certified cocoa, the company will also continue to support community-based programs with local African partners, national governments and development agencies. These projects include village school construction, mobile phone farmer messaging, literacy and health programs and training in modern farming techniques.

Currently, certified cocoa accounts for less than five percent of the world's cocoa supply. As the largest chocolate manufacturer in North America, Hershey believes its 2020 purchasing commitment will help significantly expand the global supply of certified cocoa, particularly from West Africa, which produces about 70 percent of the world's cocoa.

"Consistent with Hershey's values, we are directly addressing the economic and social issues that impact West Africa's two million cocoa farmers and families," said J.P. Bilbrey, president and chief executive officer, The Hershey Company. "Expanding the use of certified cocoa across our iconic chocolate brands and working with public and private partners, demonstrates Hershey's responsible sourcing practices. I am confident that we can make a substantial difference in West Africa by 2020."

Today, the company also announced that the *Scharffen Berger* brand will source 100 percent certified cocoa by the end of 2013. *Scharffen Berger* joins Hershey's *Dagoba* organic chocolate, which is currently certified by the Rainforest Alliance. Hershey is also bringing certified *Hershey Bliss* brand products to U.S. consumers by the end of 2012, which the company announced earlier this year.

Hershey has set a target to reach more than two million West Africans in cocoa villages through its public/private partnerships and programs, including:

The U.S. Department of Labor's Framework of Action to eliminate the worst forms of child labor in the cocoa industry in Ghana and Cote d'Ivoire

United Nations International Labor Organization

World Cocoa Foundation projects, including Cocoa Livelihoods Program with the Bill and Melinda Gates Foundation and other companies

United States Agency for International Development

Development of the world's first mobile phone network—**CocoaLink**—for cocoa farmers in West Africa. The program is already successfully operating in Ghana and Hershey will launch CocoaLink in Ivory Coast in 2013.

The **HERSHEY LEARN TO GROW** farmer and family development center is assisting 25 community-based farmer organizations in central Ghana.

"Hershey to Source" (2012)

Exhibit 4.6   The "Raise the Bar, Hershey" Response to Bliss Announcement

On January 30th, The Hershey Company announced that it would make a commitment to purchasing Rainforest Alliance Certified cocoa for all of its Bliss Chocolate products, starting later this year.

This commitment is a welcome first step for Hershey to improve its supply chain accountability. This is the first commitment that Hershey has made to using an independent, third-party certification system to ensure that its cocoa is grown sustainably, including the monitoring of forced and child labor.

This commitment also demonstrates that The Hershey Company acknowledges the severity of the labor abuses that taint the West African cocoa sector, from where Hershey sources the majority of its cocoa.

Hershey made its announcement less than one week after we announced that an ad would run during the Super Bowl that would highlight the company's use of child slavery in cocoa production. This ad, coupled with sustained, consistent consumer-based advocacy towards Hershey, contributed to Hershey's announcement today. Because of Hershey's commitment we have decided not to run the ad, however, we will continue to press Hershey for greater commitments to end child labor throughout its supply chain.

The members of the Raise the Bar, Hershey! Campaign congratulate Hershey on this first step to achieve greater supply chain accountability and hope that it will be the beginning of comprehensive supply chain traceability and certified child-labor free Hershey chocolate products.

("Response," 2012)

Raise the Bar, Hershey! uses holidays to help create public and media awareness of child slavery-labor issue. The three big chocolate holidays in the United States are Halloween, Valentine's Day, and Easter. Here is some text from the 2012 Easter news release that appeared on PRNewswire:

The "Raise the Bar, Hershey!" Coalition which has called on The Hershey Company to remove forced child labor from its products has an additional target this Easter: Cadbury/Kraft.

While Cadbury has demonstrated its commitment to ending forced child labor in the West African cocoa industry by selling Fair Trade certified chocolates in the UK, Canada, Ireland, Japan, South Africa, Australia and New Zealand—the same cannot be said of Cadbury products sold in the United States.

Why?

In 1988, Hershey purchased Cadbury's U.S. chocolate business, including the exclusive rights to make and sell well-known brands like Cadbury Creme Eggs, and Cadbury Solid Milk Chocolate Bunnies.

The petition, launched last week, has already generated more than 5,000 signatures to the CEOs of Hershey and Kraft/Cadbury.

Steven Waters, a supporter of the campaign in North Carolina, stated: "I was shocked to learn that Cadbury's products in the U.S. are made by Hershey. Learning that forced child labor was an ingredient in their seemingly innocent Easter chocolates made it easy to persuade my girlfriend's family to discontinue their large quantity purchases of Chocolate Creme Eggs this year."

"Unfortunately, Hershey refuses to meet the standard set by Cadbury overseas of offering at least one major fair trade product, despite almost two years of mounting consumer pressure," said Green America Fair Trade Campaigns Director Elizabeth O'Connell. "With Easter around the corner, the third most popular chocolate-consuming holiday in the U.S., consumers want to be able to buy Easter treats for their families that align with their values."

The petition is coordinated by Raise the Bar, Hershey!, a coalition of organizations fighting ongoing labor abuses such as child labor, forced labor, and human trafficking in the West African cocoa industry. ("Raise," 2012)

The "chocolate holidays" prove a natural hook for news stories and a reason to remind followers about the need to take action.

The "We Want More From Our S'mores" action in the Raise the Bar, Hershey! campaign illustrates the way various communication tactics are integrated around a website. The s'mores action was a page on the larger Raise the Bar, Hershey! website. The s'mores campaign was designed to dovetail with Hershey having created a national holiday for s'mores. As part of its own publicity effort, Hershey's had the holiday displays in grocery stores throughout the summer months for s'mores. S'mores are associated with campfires, so summer is a natural time to promote s'mores, a snack that historically includes Hershey chocolate as a primary ingredient along with marshmallows melted together over a fire (Newman, 2011b).

The s'mores webpage urged people to take a number of actions against Hershey for its failure to address the child slavery-labor issue. People were urged and did take a picture of themselves, protesting Hershey's child labor issues and posted them to the "Say S'mores" website. Hershey had created the site for people to upload their pictures celebrating National S'mores Day (Bryce, 2011). People were encouraged and did upload their s'mores pictures along with information about child labor abuse on Hershey's Facebook page. People could download fliers about child labor from the website that they then placed on the Hershey's s'mores displays in their local supermarkets. A sample of the flier is shown in Exhibit 4.7. Note the flier includes a quick response (QR) code so that people can quickly retrieve additional information about the campaign via their smart phones. The s'mores webpage asked people to circulate petitions locally, asking Hershey to change its cocoa sourcing. There was also a link to a YouTube video that explained how to engage in various protest actions related to s'mores ("We Want . . . S'mores," 2011).

Exhibit 4.7	"We Want More From Our S'Mores" Flier

ACROSS THE COUNTRY, CONSUMERS ARE LETTING HERSHEY KNOW THEY WANT HERSHEY BARS FREE OF LABOR ABUSES.

- -

Join us today! Visit www.RaiseTheBarHershey.org

1. Make Your S'mores Fair Trade!

2. Collect petition signatures in your community;

3. Look for Fair Trade Certified chocolate for your summer campfire treats!

Fair Trade certification ensures that farmers are paid better prices and prohibits the use of forced and child labor on cocoa farms.

CONSUMER ALERT:
*HERSHEY'S CHOCOLATE
IS TAINTED

- -

*WE WANT MORE FROM OUR S'MORES!
Hershey's chocolate is tainted by forced and child labor.
Make your s'mores with Fair Trade chocolate this summer!
Across the country, consumers are letting Hershey know
they want Hershey bars free of labor abuses. Join us today!
Visit www.RaiseTheBarHershey.org

("Consumer Alert," 2011)

A unique point in the s'mores effort and the Raise the Bar, Hershey! campaign as a whole is the 2010 documentary the *Dark Side of Chocolate* filmed by U. Roberto Romano. The *Dark Side of Chocolate* is an exposé of child trafficking that occurs in the Ivory Coast cocoa industry. Raise the Bar, Hershey! encourages people to buy the documentary and to host viewing events in their communities. The viewing events are designed to raise awareness of the abusive child labor practices in the chocolate industry. Copies of the documentary can be purchased for $6, and a 16-page set of guidelines for screening the film is free from the websites of various

Raise the Bar, Hershey! coalition members. The s'mores efforts, similar to the larger Raise the Bar, Hershey! campaign, used various social media (e.g., Facebook and YouTube) along with in-person actions (in-store actions and viewing parties) centered around a webpage to build pressure on Hershey to reform its child labor problems.

Hershey has done little to engage with or respond to the Raise the Bar, Hershey! efforts. In 2012, Hershey spokesperson Kirk Saville said he had no knowledge of the Raise the Bar, Hershey! action. Hershey's response to questions about child labor abuse in the cocoa supply has been to refer people to its corporate social responsibility report and its work with the World Cocoa Foundation and the International Cocoa Initiative (Stoddard & Geller, 2011). The Bliss announcement did note that the Rainforest Alliance certification will involve inspections designed to prevent child labor abuse ("Hershey Expands," 2012). However, no mention is ever made of Raise the Bar, Hershey! As of February 2013, there is no public documentation of Hershey engaging with the members of the Raise the Bar, Hershey! coalition.

In October 2012, Hershey took additional action to address child labor abuse-slavery in its supply chain. Hershey announced it would have all cocoa from certified Fair Trade sources by 2020. Again, the Fair Trade certification requires that suppliers not use exploited child labor, or slave labor. This action came after Whole Foods announced it would ban Hershey's Scharffen Berger chocolates until the company could prove no child slave labor was used in its production (Antoniades, 2012). The supporters of Raise the Bar, Hershey! were cautiously optimistic but still wondered why it would take 8 more years to remove child slavery-labor from the Hershey supply chain. The Raise the Bar, Hershey! response to the Hershey Company can be found in Exhibit 4.8.

Exhibit 4.8   Response to Hershey October 2012 Announcement

Thank you, Hershey! Please keep your promise to address child labor in your supply chain.

For more than two years, our Raise the Bar, Hershey! Coalition and 150,000 people have called on Hershey to address child labor in its cocoa supply chain, as so many of its competitors have already done.

Now, we have reason to celebrate! Hershey announced that by 2020 it will transition all its chocolate products to certified cocoa sources that will address labor and environmental issues. While we welcome this announcement, the Raise the Bar, Hershey! Coalition is asking Hershey CEO John Bilbrey and other Hershey executives to detail what this commitment means.

Particularly, we are asking Hershey to specify:

Which certifier(s) will Hershey work with to meet this goal? We want the strictest standards that will protect children, and third-party verification that the standards are met. (Not all certification systems are equal; fair trade goes furthest on the ground to identify and remediate child laborers, especially in sensitive industries like cocoa and cotton.)

The timeline for transitioning the entire Hershey product line to third-party certification. We want an aggressive time line, certifying progressively more cocoa each year, demonstrating by product line and percent of product certified each year.

How it will report to the public, providing complete transparency on how it is meeting its transition goals.

The Raise the Bar, Hershey! Coalition will continue to hold Hershey accountable for the treatment of cocoa laborers, especially the youngest of them, with the smallest of voices. We will also continue to pressure major corporations, working in chocolate and other sectors to address the issues of forced labor, child labor, and human trafficking in their supply chains, as the International Labor Organization (ILO) estimates that roughly 6 million children work in forced labor conditions.

Please join us in thanking Hershey for this important step forward, and urge them to make a clear commitment to fair trade certification as fast as possible. Eight years may seem like nothing to a more than 120-year-old company, but it's an excruciatingly long time for a child working on a cocoa farms through the day and night in the Ivory Coast or Ghana.

Please send Hershey an email today!

("Thank You," 2012)

Reading Guide

1. If this is a crisis, what type of crisis is this?

2. What are the labor issues that plague the chocolate industry?

3. How organized is the campaign and why?

4. What role did social media play in the crisis?

5. What role did holidays play in the crisis?

6. What was Hershey's response to the situation?

Discussion Questions

1. Why should Hershey have anticipated this crisis, and what actions could they have taken to avoid it?

2. How would you evaluate Hershey's choice to not engage with their critics? How can Contingency Theory be used to assess the threat posed by the critics?

3. Why was the Harkin-Engel Protocol so ineffective?

4. What allows this crisis to be tracked so easily by Hershey?

5. How are the groups challenging Hershey trying to put pressure on Hershey? How would you assess their effectiveness?

6. What do the reactions to Hershey's efforts to modify their behavior say about the effectiveness of their crisis management efforts? What theory or principles can explain their reactions?

7. What crisis response strategies are being used by Hershey? How could SCCT or contingency theory be used to evaluate the effectiveness of these crisis response strategies?

Websites

Hershey's CSR information: http://www.thehersheycompany.com/social-responsibility.aspx
"It's Time to Raise the Bar" Campaign home page: http://www.raisethebarhershey.org/
Slave Free Chocolate home page: http://slavefreechocolate.org/

References

About Global Exchange. (n.d.). Retrieved from http://www.globalexchange.org/about

About Green America. (n.d.). Retrieved from http://www.greenamerica.org/about/

About ILRF. (n.d.). Retrieved from http://www.laborrights.org/about-ilrf

Antoniades, A. (2012). Hershey slave labor will end with switch to Fair Trade cocoa. Retrieved from http://www.takepart.com/article/2012/10/06/hershey-vows-stop-using-child-slave-labor-eight-more-years

Boaz, P. (2010, September 17). Hershey chocolate linked to child labour. Retrieved from http://www.ipsnews.net/news.asp?idnews=52871

Bryce. (2011, August 11). Raise the bar submits protest photos to Hershey's contest. Retrieved from http://www.fairtradevancouver.ca/blog/2011-08-11/raise-bar-submits-protest-photos-hersheys-contest

Consumer alert. (2011). Retrieved from http://www.raisethebarhershey.org/wp content/uploads/2011/07/SmoresAlertColorJPG.jpg

Contest. (n.d.). Retrieved from http://www.raisethebarhershey.org/brandjamwinners/

Ensbey, J. (2009, January 2). Acquiescence in slavery must end: The appalling state of the chocolate industry. Retrieved from http://www.thecommentfactory.com/acquiescence-in-slavery-must-end-%e2%80%93-the-appalling-state-of-the-chocolate-industry-1188/

Hershey expands responsible cocoa community programs in West Africa. (2012, January 30). Retrieved from http://www.thehersheycompany.com/newsroom/news-release.aspx?id=1653877

Hershey: Raise the bar! (2012). Retrieved from http://www.change.org/petitions/hershey-raise-the-bar

Hershey to source 100% certified cocoa by 2020. (2012). Retrieved from http://www.thehersheycompany.com/newsroom/news-release.aspx?id=1741328

How we won. (2012). Retrieved from http://www.change.org/petitions/hershey-raise-the-bar

Human cost of chocolate. (2011). Retrieved from http://thecnnfreedomproject.blogs.cnn.com/2011/09/19/the-human-cost-of-chocolate/

Newman, T. (2011a, February 11). Hershey says it doesn't know about your campaign. Retrieved from http://news.change.org/stories/hershey-says-it-doesn-t-know-about -your-campaign

Newman, T. (2011b, July 14). Take action in your supermarket to stop Hershey from profiting from child labor. Retrieved from http://news.change.org/stories/take -action-in-your-supermarket-to-stop-hershey-profiting-from-child-labor

News on chocolate is bittersweet: No progress on child labor, but Fair Trade chocolate is on the rise. (2005). Retrieved from http://www.globalexchange.org/sites/default/files/ chocolatereport2005.pdf

Our demands of Hershey. (2012). Retrieved from http://www.raisethebarhershey.org/ ourdemands-of-hershey/

Production and net export of cocoa beans. (n.d.). Retrieved from http://www.icco.org/ statistics/cocoamap.pdf

Raise the bar coalition to Hershey and Cadbury: Get child slave labor out of our Easter baskets. (2012, April 5). Retrieved from http://www.raisethebarhershey.org/raise-the-bar -coalition-to-hershey-and-cadbury-get-child-slave-labor-out-of-our-easter-baskets/

Response to Hershey's Rainforest Alliance certified Bliss announcement. (2012). Retrieved from http://www.raisethebarhershey.org/response-to-hershey%E2%80%99s-rainforest -alliance-certified-bliss-announcement/

Stoddard, E., & Geller, G. (2011, February 13). Valentines chocolate may become new blood diamonds. Retrieved from http://uk.reuters.com/article/2011/02/09/uk-cocoa-chocolate -labor-idUKTRE71850K20110209

Thank you Hershey. (2012). Retrieved from http://www.greenamerica.org/takeaction/ hershey/

Vision and mission. (n.d.). Retrieved from http://oasisusa.org/our-mission-and-vision

We want more from our s'mores. (2011). Retrieved from http://www.raisethebarhershey.org/ smores/

Why Hershey. (2011). Retrieved from http://www.raisethebarhershey.org/why-hershey/

CHAPTER 5

Cadbury Salmonella Recall

I n many parts of the world, the name Cadbury is synonymous with chocolate. Cadbury can trace its history back to 1824 when John Cadbury began selling drinking chocolate, cocoa, tea, and coffee from a shop in Birmingham, England. Cadbury was a Quaker, and he viewed these drinks as an alternative to alcohol. The Quakers, the Religious Society of Friends to be more precise, opposed alcohol and have a history of supporting social causes. According to Cadbury family historian and award winning documentarian Deborah Cadbury,

> The original founders were Quakers, and they were trying to come up with something that they thought would be a nutritious alternative to alcohol, which was the ruin of many poor families. They were trying to come up with a business idea that was actually going to help people, and cocoa was this amazing new commodity and they thought they could make a business out of this nutritious drink. ("Bittersweet," 2010, para. 11)

The Quaker religion also helped to establish Cadbury's as an early advocate of corporate social responsibility (CSR) by demonstrating a concern for addressing social issues (L'Etang, 2006). "Quaker capitalism" was about philanthropy and using businesses to benefit others ("Sweet," 2010). Chocolate came to dominate Cadbury sales in the 1870s and became their focal product. In 1969, Cadbury merged with Schweppes to form Cadbury Schweppes ("History," n.d.). In 2010, Kraft Foods purchased Cadbury after tense negotiations and a failed hostile takeover for just under $20 billion (Kennedy, 2010). There were fears that the Cadbury legacy of CSR would be lost under Kraft Food's management ("Bittersweet," 2010). In the United States, Cadbury's is distributed by Hershey.

Their quality chocolate and reputation for social responsibility helped to establish Cadbury's as dominant in the U.K.'s list of "Most Trusted Chocolate Brand" for most of the 2000s ("Cadbury and Tesco," 2007). Cadbury was even the most trusted chocolate brand in 2007, the year after it had to recall over a million chocolate products due to salmonella contamination. The 2006, recall from Cadbury was contentious because Cadbury and a number of government-related agencies had conflicting views over the need for the recall. Moreover, Cadbury was eventually fined for their actions involving the recalled chocolates ("Cadbury Fined," 2007).

On June 23, 2006, Cadbury announced a recall for seven of its chocolate products for *Salmonella* Montevideo contamination. The products were Cadbury Dairy Milk Turkish 250g, Cadbury Dairy Milk Caramel 250g, Cadbury Dairy Milk Mint 250g, Cadbury Dairy Milk 8 Chunk, Cadbury Dairy Milk 1kg, Cadbury Dairy Milk Button Easter Egg-105g, and Cadbury Freddo 10p. A series of statements about the recall by the Food Standards Agency (FSA), an independent government department in the United Kingdom created in 2000 to protect the public health and consumer concerns related to food, are located in Exhibit 5.1. The statements include the initial announcement and two updates from the FSA.

Exhibit 5.1   Food Standards Agency Announcements

Initial Statement by Food Standards Agency

Cadbury Schweppes plc recalls a range of its own brand chocolate products due to possible contamination with salmonella

Friday 23 June 2006

Food Alert: for Action

Ref: 36/2006 (38/2006 Scotland)

Heads of Environmental Health and Directors of Trading Standards will wish to be aware that Cadbury Schweppes Plc has recalled seven different own brand chocolate products due to possible contamination with *Salmonella* Montevideo.

Cadbury Schweppes Plc has undertaken a full product recall and will be issuing a press notice on 23 June to alert consumers to the reasons for the recall and the actions they can take if they have purchased the affected products.

The products recalled are:

Cadbury Dairy Milk Turkish 250g

Cadbury Dairy Milk Caramel 250g

Cadbury Dairy Milk Mint 250g

Cadbury Dairy Milk 8 Chunk

Cadbury Dairy Milk 1kg

Cadbury Dairy Milk Button Easter Egg-105g

Cadbury Freddo 10p

All Lots and Best Before Date codes

A copy of the press notice issued by Cadbury Schweppes Plc is attached to this food alert.

Action to be taken by local authorities:

These products do not comply with the food safety requirements due to possible contamination with *Salmonella* Montevideo. As these products will be on sale in a variety of outlets dealing with confectionery goods, local authorities are requested to contact

the relevant food business operators to ensure that they are removed from sale, if necessary using the powers under the Food Safety Act to ensure that this is achieved. Cadbury
Schweppes Plc has made arrangements for return of these products through trade.

("Cadbury Schweppes Plc Recalls," 2006)

Recalling a product for a food-borne illness is never pleasant for a food producer
but is not a shock either. Companies in the food industry should be prepared for a
food-borne illness recall because that is a crisis with a high likelihood of occurrence
and serious impact. Food-borne illnesses, such as *Salmonella* Montevideo, cause
unpleasant symptoms and can be life threatening for children and people with weak
immune systems. People expect joy from eating chocolates, not vomiting and diarrhea. Cadbury was facing a product harm crisis that should have been a part of its
crisis portfolio (crises an organization should anticipate) because salmonella is the
most common food-borne illness. Cadbury quickly moved to corrective action by
providing instructing information on how to identify the potentially dangerous
chocolates—and provided the recall information. Moreover, Cadbury worked with
the government to locate the source of the contamination and then took action to
eliminate the source of contamination. Exhibit 5.2 provides information about the
government's search for the cause of the outbreak. The source of the contamination
was a leaky pipe at its Marlbrook plant in Herefordshire. The source was located by
June 24, 2006. The Marlbrook plant makes chocolate crumb that is then used to
make the milk chocolate for the Cadbury products (Morgan, 2006).

Exhibit 5.2   HPA Final Report Graphics

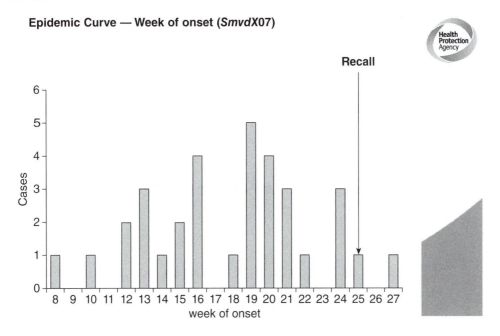

(Continued)

Interview results

Food groups reported by >60% of cases

Exposure	Yes	(%)	No	(%)
Poultry	11	73.3	4	26.7
Beef	9	60.0	6	40.0
Pork	10	66.7	5	33.3
Fish	13	86.7	2	13.3
Milk	10	66.7	5	33.3
Cheese	9	60.0	6	40.0
Other dairy	12	80.0	3	20.0
Sauces	9	60.0	6	40.0
Fruit	12	80.0	3	20.0
Infant food	3	20.0	12	80.0
Spices	3	20.0	12	80.0
Confection	14	93.3	1	6.7
Drinks	11	73.3	4	26.7
Miscellaneous	13	86.7	2	13.3

- With the exception of confectionery products, detailed examination of other food groups did not reveal a common food or brand.

Epidemiological evidence considered by the OCT in reaching its conclusion

- The dates of onset of illness for the cases (February to March) followed known contamination of products.
- The geographical disatribution of cases suggested that the outbreak was caused by nationally distributed food.
- The food histories taken from the cases.
- The frequency of cases of S. Montevideo PFGE SmvdX07 decreased following the product recall.

Conclusion

- Consumption of Cadbury's products was the most credible explantion for the outbreak
- Experts acting on behalf of Cadbury's disagreed with this, however. . .

Birmingham City Council and Herefordshire council prosecuted Cadbury's in June 2007. Cadbury Ltd pleaded guilty to nine food safety offences including:

- placing unsafe chocolate on the market;
- failing to inform the competent authority;
- failing to identify hazards from contaminated chocolate and critical controls to ensure food safety.

Mangement decisions (cont.)
Project Ivan

Between January and February 2006:

- Salmonella (including S.Montevideo) was discovered on at least 36 occasions in various plants, in crumb, liquid chocolate and finish products.
- There were 5 internal meetings regarding Project Ivan—Reflected that the company realised it had serious problem
- There was 1 visit by an environmental health officer

Nobody mentioned the problem to the EHO and . . .

Conclusion

- Fined 1,000,000 plus 1,582,000 costs for the offences
- This doesn't take into account recall cost, brand damage, loss in sponsorship, cost incurred by individual and group compensation action
- More importantly, it doesn't reflect that people were seriously ill and that this outcome was entirely preventable.

What the company said:

'Mistakenly, we did not believe that there was a threat to health and thus any requirement to report the incident to the authorities — we accept that this approach was correct . . . We offer our sincere regrets and apologies to anyone who was made ill as a result of this failure,'

- Read carefully — there is no admission that contaminated products were produced or sold by the company.

("National Outbreak of Salmonella Montevideo," 2006)

But the Cadbury recall of 2006 was not your typical product harm crisis. Notice in the third document from the FSA (Exhibit 5.3) that Cadbury had discovered salmonella contamination in January of 2006 at the Marlbrook. However, the FSA was not aware of the contamination until June 21st and convinced Cadbury to execute the recall. Moreover, there had been a similar contamination in 2002. In 2002, the product was destroyed, but the incident was not reported to the government or the public. In 2006, the news media began to focus on the time lag between when Cadbury knew there was contamination (January) and when the government knew there was contamination and the recall occurred. There was speculation that Cadbury purposely waited until after Easter for the recall. A recall at Easter, a peak time for chocolate sales, would have hurt Cadbury profits. However, the Easter allegation was never proven, just speculation in the media. The only fact was the nearly 6 month gap between the detection and the reporting of the salmonella contamination.

Exhibit 5.3 FSA Update to Recall Information

On 30 June the company issued some clarification about the Freddo product. The product being recalled was the one where '10p' is printed onto the foil that each product is wrapped in.

Some boxes have '10p' printed on the box and not on the individual foil. These are not being recalled.

The Agency's Food Alert update of 30 June made clear that the following Freddo products are not affected by the recall:

Freddo unflashed (without 10p marked on wrapping): unit number (SKU) 11000482
Freddo Caramel 10p: unit number (SKU) 11000483

In addition, the Cadbury Dairy Milk Mint 250g bar, which has been recalled, is also available, with 33% extra free, printed onto the foil. These are also being recalled.

Salmonella can cause sickness and diarrhoea and the Agency is advising people not to eat any of the affected products listed below. If you have any of these products, you can return them to: Cadbury Recall, Freepost MID20061, Birmingham B30 2QZ for a voucher. For more details you can ring the Cadbury Schweppes helpline number on 0800 818181.

Cadbury Schweppes plc recalls a range of its own brand chocolate products due to possible contamination with salmonella: Read the Food Alert issued on 23 June 2006

Further update on incident involving Cadbury Schweppes plc recalling a range of chocolate products: Read the Food Alert Update on incident involving Cadbury Schweppes Plc recalling a range of its own brand chocolate products. Read the updated Food Alert issued on 30 June 2006

("Update on Incident Involving Cadbury," 2006)

Exhibit 5.4 FSA Update August 1, 2006

Monday 31 July 2006

The Food Standards Agency has issued an updated Food Alert for Information after being notified by Cadbury Schweppes that it intends to restock five of the product lines that were recalled on 23 June 2006 due to possible contamination with salmonella.

Background information. Previous food alerts Agency advice. It is expected that the restocked products will reach shelves on Wednesday 2 August.

The products to be restocked are:

Cadbury Dairy Milk Turkish 250g, Lot Code L6152 or greater, best before end date (BBE) 05 2007, or later

Cadbury Dairy Milk Caramel 250g, Lot Code L6152 or greater, BBE 03 2007 or later
Cadbury Dairy Milk Mint 250g, Lot Code L6152 or greater, BBE 05 2007 or later
Cadbury Dairy Milk 8 Chunk, Lot Code L6152 or greater, BBE 05 2007 or later
Cadbury Dairy Milk 1 kg, Lot Code L6152 or greater, BBE 05 2007 or later
Cadbury Dairy Milk Buttons Easter Egg 105g will return to sale in 2007. Cadbury Freddo 10p will not be restocked.

Food alerts

Food alerts are the FSA's way of letting local authorities and consumers know about problems associated with food and, in some cases, providing details of specific action to be taken. They are issued under two categories:

Food Alerts: for Action

Food Alerts: for Information

Background information. Cadbury Schweppes plc first told the Food Standards Agency on Monday 19 June 2006 that it had detected salmonella contamination of products from its plant in Marlbrook, Herefordshire, in January 2006.

The Agency obtained further details from Cadbury Schweppes that led, on Wednesday 21 June, to the Agency advising the company to recall the affected products, which the company initiated on Friday 23 June.

Investigations continued with the company and a number of local authorities were involved. Information subsequently provided by the company indicated that contamination of its products with *Salmonella* Montevideo had been identified in April 2002, but these products were destroyed.

Cadbury told the Agency that it tested the "crumb"—the ingredient that forms the basis for chocolate products—and some samples of the crumb tested positive for salmonella.

The company then tested its chocolate products made from the crumb, which revealed the contamination of the seven products withdrawn on Friday 23 June.

The company has withdrawn those products where samples tested positive and increased testing on all other products. On the basis of the information supplied by the company to the Agency in the week beginning Monday 19 June, the Agency believes that proportionate action was taken by recalling the seven products.

ACMSF meeting 30 June 2006

As part of its investigation into salmonella contamination that led to Cadbury Schweppes' recall, the Food Standards Agency sought the views of the independent Advisory Committee on the Microbiological Safety of Food (ACMSF).

The Salmonella Contact Group of the ACMSF met in Oxford on Friday 30 June to discuss the issue. It concluded:

- the presence of salmonella in ready-to-eat foods such as chocolate is unacceptable at any level.
- end-product testing is not a suitable instrument for guaranteeing the safety of the food and a robust HACCP (Hazard Analysis Critical Control Point) needs to be in place.
- in order to give assurance about the absence of salmonella or any other pathogen in food, a prohibitively large amount of product would need to be tested. However, even this would not guarantee absence of the micro-organism.

Cadbury's risk assessment assumes that a threshold for infection can be estimated from previous outbreak data on levels of micro-organisms in chocolate. Such a threshold is not the same as the minimum infectious dose for salmonella in chocolate; no minimum infectious dose can be defined and infections may occur in consumers exposed to significantly lower levels than that seen in previous outbreaks.

Cadbury's risk assessment does not address the risk of salmonella in chocolate in a way which the ACMSF would regard as a modern approach to risk assessment

Based on the information provided, Cadbury appears to have used methods for product testing which the committee considered would underestimate the level and likelihood of salmonella contamination. Sample heterogeneity including clumping of bacteria will influence the MPN (most probable number) estimate and therefore the approach cannot be relied upon in foods such as chocolate

In the ACMSF's view, using the MPN approach to assess the risk of small levels of salmonella contamination in a product like chocolate is unreliable

The committee also commented that where contaminated chocolate crumb was used in the manufacture of products other than those recalled, there could also be a cause for concern. However, the committee acknowledged that it was difficult to quantify the risk.

("Cadbury Recall Update 1 August 2006," 2006)

Part of Cadbury's recall announcement appears in Exhibit 5.5. Note how Cadbury reminded stakeholders of their 100 years of quality chocolate and how it was engaging in the recall out of concern for its customers. However, some customers were unsure about just how much Cadbury cared about their safety because of how the recall transpired. The revelation about the salmonella in Cadbury chocolate took an unusual route. The outbreak was not immediately traced to Cadbury. Instead, an independent laboratory asked the Health Protection Agency (HPA) to review some samples. The HPA found those samples contained the *Salmonella* Montevideo strain that was currently being investigated. Working with the FSA, the HPA forced the independent lab to reveal the source of the samples. That source was Cadbury. Some of the samples were from February, prior to the outbreak of *Salmonella* Montevideo ("Cadbury Linked," 2006; ElAmin, 2006).

Exhibit 5.5   Part of Cadbury's Recall Announcement

This is being done purely as a precautionary measure, as some of these products may contain minute traces of salmonella. Cadbury has identified the source of the problem and rectified it, and is taking steps to ensure these particular products are no longer available for sale.

"We've been making chocolate for over 100 years and quality has always come first," said Simon Baldry, the UK Managing Director of Cadbury, "We have taken this precautionary step because our consumers are our highest priority. We apologise for any inconvenience caused."

Cadbury is inviting consumers to return the products to: Cadbury Recall, Freepost MID20061, Birmingham, B30 2QZ for a full refund or ring our helpline number 0800 818181.

("Cadbury Is Conducting," 2006)

Between March 1st and July 31st 2006, the HPA had isolated 55 cases of *Salmonella* Montevideo. Three cases required hospitalization, and the median age was 4 years. On June, 22, 2006, the HPA began interviewing the infected people. Interviews are used to help pinpoint the source of the food-borne illness. On June 23, 2006, Cadbury was identified as a potential source for the *Salmonella* Montevideo, but confirmation was still needed. The interviews showed confectionary products were the only link between the victims. However, the increased media coverage that speculated Cadbury's as the cause could have "contaminated" the victims' memories. However, the start of the outbreak is consistent with when Cadbury knew they had contamination, and the cases decreased after the recall. This fact, along with the lab tests on the *Salmonella* Montevideo samples, led the HPA to conclude, "Consumption of Cadbury's products was the most credible explanation for the outbreak" ("National," 2006, p. 28). Some of the tables from the HPA's final report on the 2006 *Salmonella* Montevideo outbreak are included in Exhibit 5.2.

According to article 19 (3) of the European Union (EU) General Food Law, companies must immediately report a situation to the government when their product poses a risk to public health (Watson, 2006). Cadbury management argued that the levels of salmonella they detected in January were so small that it did not pose a public health risk. In fact, Cadbury told consumers not to worry even if they had eaten the chocolate on the recall list. A Cadbury spokesperson noted:

> The levels are significantly below the standard that would be any health problem, but we are taking this measure as a precaution. If there are people who have eaten one of these chocolate bars today they should not worry, but they can get in touch with us if they are concerned for a full refund. (Hardie, 2006, p. 7)

Cadbury believed it was in compliance with the EU General Food Act because management did not perceive the salmonella levels as a public health risk.

The FSA's Advisory Committee on Microbiological Safety for Food disagreed with Cadbury. Here are its statements on the situation:

> Cadbury's risk assessment assumes that a threshold for infection can be estimated from previous outbreak data on levels of micro-organisms in chocolate. Such a threshold is not the same as the minimum infectious dose for salmonella in chocolate; no minimum infectious dose can be defined and infections may occur in consumers exposed to significantly lower levels than that seen in previous outbreaks. ("Cadbury Recall Update 1 August," 2006, para. 12)

> Cadbury's risk assessment does not address the risk of salmonella in chocolate in a way which the ACMSF would regard as a modern approach to risk assessment. . . . The presence of salmonella in a ready-to-eat product such as a chocolate bar is unacceptable at any level. ("Cadbury Recall Update July," 2006)

The FSA believed the situation posed a serious health threat and should have been reported immediately to the government. Cadbury responded with the following comments:

> We have acted in good faith and we do not challenge the views of the expert committee advising the FSA or the EHOs. We agree that it's the job of the FSA and EHOs to provide guidance on these matters and we welcome their advice. We'll continue our dialogue with the regulators and will be improving our procedures in the light of their advice. However, we welcome the confirmation by the FSA that they believe "proportionate action was taken by recalling the seven products." ("Chocs," 2006)

Exhibit 5.3 provides the text of the two FSA updates related to the Cadbury recall. Cadbury remained popular, but the crisis did raise concerns about the company's views on product safety.

Reading Guide

1. If this was a crisis, what type of crisis was it?

2. What is the problem and the source(s) of the problem in this case?

3. What stakeholders should be interested in this case?

4. What holiday was involved in the situation?

5. What was the time lag issue in the case?

6. What government agencies were involved in the case?

7. Who sent the sample to the HPA?

Discussion Questions

1. Why is it important that Cadbury and the HPA disagreed?

2. What does this case say about Cadbury's crisis scanning? The HPA's crisis scanning?

3. What was the possible role of the media in influencing the case? What actions could be taken to offset the influence?

4. How might the unusual origins of the situation affect stakeholder perceptions of Cadbury? What effect might that have on Cadbury's crisis communication response?

5. Why would Cadbury discount the threat? What would the crisis theories or principles recommend about discounting the threat and why?

6. What credibility do you give to the belief Cadbury withheld the safety information in favor of profits and why? What accounts for that level of credibility?

7. How would you characterize Cadbury's response, and which theory or theories can explain its success or failure?

Websites

Cadbury home page: http://home.cadbury.co.uk/
CSR-to-Quakers web link connection: http://www.qcea.org/work/economic-justice/csr/
BBC news story about the outbreak: http://news.bbc.co.uk/2/hi/5112470.stm

References

Bittersweet: How Kraft's acquisition of Cadbury ended the dynasty of a CSR luminary. (2010). Retrieved from http://www.justmeans.com/Bittersweet-How-Kraft-s-Acquisition-of-Cadbury-Ended-Dynasty-of-a-CSR-Luminary/46939.html

Cadbury and Tesco come top in Most Trusted Brands survey. (2007). Retrieved from http://www.talkingretail.com/news/industry-news/cadbury-and-tesco-come-top-in-most-trusted-brands-survey

Cadbury fined £1m over salmonella. (2007, July 16). Retrieved from http://news.bbc.co.uk/2/hi/uk_news/england/6900467.stm

Cadbury is conducting a recall of seven of its products in the UK. (2006). Retrieved from http://www.food.gov.uk/multimedia/pdfs/cadburypr.pdf

Cadbury linked to salmonella outbreak. (2006, July 24). Retrieved from http://www.which.co.uk/news/2006/07/cadbury-linked-to-salmonella-outbreak-89786

Cadbury recall update 1 August 2006. (2006). Retrieved from http://www.food.gov.uk/news/newsarchive/2006/aug/cadbury

Cadbury recall update 4 July 2006. (2006). Retrieved from http://www.food.gov.uk/news/newsarchive/2006/jul/cadbury

Cadbury recall update. (2012). Retrieved from http://autoserver.info/2012/08/cadbury-recall update/

Cadbury Schweppes plc recalls a range of its own brand chocolate products due to possible contamination with salmonella. (2006). Retrieved from http://www.food.gov.uk/enforcement/alerts/2006/jun/cadburychoc

Chocs giant popped. (2006). *Daily Record*, p. 12.

ElAmin, A. (2006, July 24). Authorities pinpoint Cadbury as source of salmonella outbreak. Retrieved from http://www.foodproductiondaily.com/Quality-Safety/Authorities-pinpoint-Cadbury-as-source-of-Salmonella-outbreak

Hardie, A. (2006, June 24). Cadbury's huge recall over bug fear. *The Scotsman*, p. 7.

History (n.d). Retrieved from http://www.superbrands.com.au/BrandDetails.aspx?id=55

Kennedy, S. (2010, Jan 19). Kraft to buy Cadbury in friendly $19.5 billion deal. Retrieved from http://www.marketwatch.com/story/cadbury-kraft-finalizing-terms-of-friendly-deal-2010-01-19

L'Etang, J. (2006). Corporate responsibility and public relations. In J. L'Etang & M. Pieczka (Eds.), *Public relations: Critical debates and contemporary practice* (pp. 405–422). Mahwah, NJ: Erlbaum.

Morgan, G. (2006, June 25). Cadbury recalls 1 millions bars in salmonella scare. *Western Mail,* p. 1.

National outbreak of *Salmonella* Montevideo infection June 2006. (2006). Retrieved from http://www.hpa.org.uk/webc/HPAwebFile/HPAweb_C/1207293973143

The sweet, social legacy of Cadbury chocolate. (2010). Retrieved from http://www.npr.org/templates/story/story.php?storyId=130558647

Update on incident involving Cadbury Schweppes Plc recalling a range of its own brand chocolate products due to possible contamination with salmonella. (2006). Retrieved from http://www.food.gov.uk/enforcement/alerts/2006/jun/cadburyupdate

CHAPTER 6

Peanut Butter
Paste Recall of 2009

Peanuts have a strong association with U.S. society. Children, except those with peanut allergies, typically love peanut butter and other peanut products. The peanut butter industry alone is an $800 million dollar a year industry in the United States (O'Brien, 2009). Dr. George Washington Carver's peanut research was a catalyst for making the peanut such a valuable cash crop and popular food item in the United States. Internationally, the United States is the third leading peanut grower and one of the leading peanut exporters in the world ("About," n.d.). But in 2009, peanut butter transformed from comfort food into frightening food due to a Salmonella outbreak associated with peanut butter paste.

What started as a small recall by the relatively unknown Peanut Corporation of America (PCA) in Blakely, Georgia, soon escalated into a major business and public health crisis in the United States. The recall cost the peanut growers over $1 billion, included over 3,900 products, and sickened over 700 people while potentially contributing to the death of nine. Even companies that did not have products in the recall suffered a drop in sales due to guilt by association. It is estimated that the recall cost the peanut industry $1 billion (Mohr, 2012).

Salmonella is a common bacteria connected with food poisoning. People infected with Salmonella can experience vomiting, diarrhea, fever, and abdominal cramps. The effects can last from 4 to 7 days. Like most forms of food poisoning, people generally recover without needing special treatment. Self-treatment includes drinking plenty of fluids. However, older people, infants, and people with compromised immune systems can become seriously ill and even die from salmonella without proper treatment. People who are at risk should seek medical attention if they suspect they have salmonella ("Frequently," 2009).

The potential negative effects of salmonella demand that it be taken seriously as a threat when it is believed to be in the food supply. In September of 2009, the Centers for Disease Control (CDC) began to receive the first reports of salmonella illness that would be linked to the peanut butter paste outbreak. In November of

2008, the CDC began assessing clusters of salmonella illness in 12 different states. It was determined that the Salmonella had the same source. The CDC uses DNA fingerprinting to determine if the infections came from the same source. In December of 2008, Shirley Mae Almer, 72, of Brainerd, Minnesota, died. Her death is believed to have been the first associated with the peanut butter paste outbreak.

When a food-borne illness outbreak occurs, the CDC works diligently to track its source. By finding the source, the CDC can help to end the spread of the disease. Victims are interviewed to determine what they have eaten. Non-victims may be interviewed as well and the data used to locate the source of the outbreak (Bettencourt, 2010). The Food and Drug Administration (FDA) became involved in the investigation and initial indicators pointed toward peanut butter paste from the Peanut Corporation of America. On January 9, 2009, the Peanut Corporation of America agreed to stop production at its Blakely, Georgia facility, the suspected source of the outbreak. On January 10, 2009, the first name brand product that used the Peanut Corporation of America peanut paste was recalled by King Nut. Shortly thereafter, the Peanut Corporation of America's Blakely facility was confirmed as the source of the Salmonella outbreak. The Peanut Corporation of America issued a series of recalls between January 13 and 18 involving products made at the Blakely facility on or after July 1, 2008 ("Timeline," 2009).

You have probably never heard of the Peanut Corporation of America, a company that processed peanuts. It is not a name brand consumers would know. The company is a supplier of peanut paste, peanut butter, and other peanut products to food processors and institutions such as schools and nursing homes. This is where the recall becomes more complex and confusing. The Peanut Corporation of America recall affected a wide number of products because so many food processors used their product. Here are some names involved in the recall that might sound familiar: Hershey, Kellogg, Little Debbie, Keebler, Archer Farms, Goo Goo, Famous Amos, and Brach's. The Peanut Corporation of America product was used in candies, crackers, cookies, ice cream, dog treats, cereal, and snack bars, and the list goes on and on. In the end, over 3,900 different products had to be recalled because of the salmonella traced to the Peanut Corporation of America ("Peanut," 2009).

Exhibit 6.1   Statement by Peanut Corporation of America for Immediate Release: January 16, 2009

Peanut Corporation of America Expands Nationwide Recall of Peanut Butter

Company Announces the Voluntary Recall of Peanut Paste Produced in Georgia Plant

Lynchburg, Va. (January 16, 2009) Peanut Corporation of America (PCA), a peanut processing company and maker of peanut butter for bulk distribution to institutions, food service industries, and private label food companies, today announced an expanded recall of peanut butter produced in its Blakely, Georgia processing facility as well as the voluntary recall of peanut paste produced in the same plant because these products have the potential to be contaminated with Salmonella. The company on January 13, 2009 previously announced the recall of 21 lots of peanut butter produced on or after July 1, 2008.

Today's announcement and voluntary recall affect all peanut butter produced on or after August 8, 2008 and peanut paste produced on or after September 26, 2008 at the Georgia facility. The peanut butter being recalled is sold by PCA in bulk packaging in containers ranging in size from five to 1,700 pounds. The peanut paste is sold in sizes ranging from 35 pound containers to tanker containers.

PCA is notifying customers who received the recalled product by telephone or in writing, as well as through the news media and a toll-free 24/7 hotline number. None of the peanut butter or peanut paste being recalled is sold directly by PCA to consumers through retail stores.

"Today, the FDA informed PCA that new product samples in unopened containers tested positive for Salmonella," said Stewart Parnell, President of Peanut Corporation of America.

The FDA has not yet confirmed the DNA fingerprints of these positive samples to match the strains causing the outbreaks of food borne illness in several states.

PCA is immediately stopping all production at the Blakely, Georgia facility and notifying its customers to recall and retain all affected product produced during these dates at this plant.

"We deeply regret that this product recall is expanding and our first priority is to protect the health of our customers. Our company has worked around the clock for the last week with federal regulators to help identify any potential problems. Our Blakely facility is currently not operating as we continue to work with federal food safety investigators," Parnell said.

Customers should call 1-877-564-7080 for further instructions on what to do with the product or visit the company website at www.peanutcorp.com.

Eating food contaminated with Salmonella can result in abdominal cramping, diarrhea, and fever. Most people infected with Salmonella develop the symptoms 12 to 72 hours after infection. The illness usually lasts 4 to 7 days, and most people recover with treatment. However, in some persons, the diarrhea may be so severe that the patient needs to be hospitalized. For more information on Salmonella bacteria, please visit the Centers for Disease Control and Prevention's website at http://www.cdc.gov.

("PCA," 2009)

Exhibit 6.2   Official Press Release

Peanut Corporation of America Expands Nationwide Recall of Peanut Butter

Company Announces the Voluntary Recall of Peanut Paste Produced in Georgia Plant

Contact: Peanut Corporation of America, 1-877-564-7080

FOR IMMEDIATE RELEASE—Lynchburg, Va. (January 18, 2009)—Peanut Corporation of America (PCA), is expanding the recall of peanut butter and voluntarily recalling peanut paste made at its Blakely, Georgia facility because the products have the potential to be contaminated with Salmonella. Salmonella is an organism that can cause serious and sometimes fatal infections in young children, frail or elderly people, and others with weakened immune systems. Healthy persons infected with Salmonella often experience fever, diarrhea (which may be bloody), nausea, vomiting and abdominal pain. In rare circumstances, infection with Salmonella can result in the organism getting into the bloodstream and producing more severe illnesses such as arterial infections (i.e., infected aneurysms), endocarditis and arthritis.

The recalled peanut butter and peanut paste were distributed to institutions, food service industries, and private label food companies in 24 states, the province of Saskatchewan in Canada, Korea and Haiti. The U.S. states are the following: Arkansas, California, Colorado, Florida, Georgia, Illinois, Indiana, Iowa, Maryland, Michigan, Minnesota, Missouri, Nevada, New Hampshire, New Jersey, New York, North Carolina, Ohio, Pennsylvania, South Carolina, Tennessee, Texas, Utah and Virginia. In addition, affected product was used as an ingredient in other products that may have been distributed in other states.

None of the peanut butter being recalled is sold directly to consumers through retail stores by PCA.

The recalled peanut butter in the expanded recall is sold by PCA in bulk packaging in containers ranging in size from five to 1,700 pounds. The peanut paste is sold in sizes ranging from 35-pound containers to tanker containers. The lot numbers for all recalled products are at the end of this news release. All of the peanut butter and peanut paste in the expanded recall was made on or after July 1, 2008, and only at the Georgia facility. The potential for contamination was noted after a small number of samples from unopened containers and environmental samples from the Blakely, Georgia facility tested positive for Salmonella. The U.S. Food and Drug Administration has said the investigation is "very active and dynamic," and PCA continues to work closely with the FDA and the Centers for Disease Control and Prevention as they continue their investigation into the nationwide outbreak of Salmonella.

The Blakely, Georgia facility has currently stopped producing all products as the FDA and CDC continue their investigation, but some PCA staff remain to assist in the on-going investigation.

PCA is notifying customers that may have received the recalled product by phone and/or in writing. Customers should segregate and hold the product and call PCA at 1–877–564–7080 for further instructions. "We deeply regret that this product recall has expanded, and our first priority is to protect the health of our customers," said Stewart Parnell, President of Peanut Corporation of America.

("PCA," 2009)

Exhibit 6.3   Sample News Release

Government Salmonella News Release

Salmonella Model Press Release (all serotypes)

FOR IMMEDIATE RELEASE DATE

COMPANY CONTACT AND PHONE NUMBER

FOOD CO. RECALLS PRODUCT BECAUSE OF POSSIBLE HEALTH RISK

Company Name of City, State is recalling Quantity and/or type of Product, because it has the potential to be contaminated with *Salmonella*, an organism which can cause serious and sometimes fatal infections in young children, frail or elderly people, and others with weakened immune systems. Healthy persons infected with *Salmonella* often experience fever, diarrhea (which may be bloody), nausea, vomiting and abdominal pain. In rare circumstances, infection with *Salmonella* can result in the organism getting into the bloodstream and producing more severe illnesses such as arterial infections (i.e., infected aneurysms), endocarditis and arthritis.

Product was distributed. Listing of states and areas where the product was distributed and how it reached consumers (e.g., through retail stores, mail order, direct delivery).

Specific information on how to identify the product (e.g., the type of container [plastic, metal, glass], size and appearance of the product, the product's brand name, flavor, code and expiration date, etc.).

Status of the number of and types of related illnesses that have been CONFIRMED to date (e.g., "No illnesses have been reported to date.").

Brief explanation about what is known about the problem, such as how it was revealed, and what is known about its source. An example of such a description—"the recall was as the result of a routine sampling program by the company which revealed that the finished products contained the bacteria. The company has ceased the production and distribution of the product as FDA and the company continue their investigation as to what caused the problem."

Information on what consumers should do with the product and where they can get additional information (e.g., consumers who have purchased Brand X are urged to return it to the place of purchase for a full refund. Consumers with questions may contact the company at 1–800-XXX-XXXX.)

####

(SAMPLE PRESS RELEASE)

XYZ Inc.

123 Smith Lane

Anywhere, MS

("Salmonella Model," 2009)

Exhibit 6.4 Sample News Release

FOR IMMEDIATE RELEASE DATE

Sam Smith /555–555–5555

XYZ RECALLS "SNACKIES" BECAUSE OF POSSIBLE HEALTH RISK

XYZ Inc. of Anywhere, MS, is recalling its 5 ounce packages of "Snackies" food treats because they have the potential to be contaminated with *Salmonella,* an organism which can cause serious and sometimes fatal infections in young children, frail or elderly people, and others with weakened immune systems. Healthy persons infected with *Salmonella* often experience fever, diarrhea (which may be bloody), nausea, vomiting and abdominal pain. In rare circumstances, infection with *Salmonella* can result in the organism getting into the bloodstream and producing more severe illnesses such as arterial infections (i.e., infected aneurysms), endocarditis and arthritis.

The recalled "Snackies" were distributed nationwide in retail stores and through mail orders.

The product comes in a 5 ounce, clear plastic package marked with lot # 666666 on the top and with an expiration date of 12/12/99 stamped on the side.

No illnesses have been reported to date in connection with this problem.

The potential for contamination was noted after routine testing by the company revealed the presence of *Salmonella* in some 5 ounce packages of "Snackies."

Production of the product has been suspended while FDA and the company continue their investigation as to the source of the problem.

Consumers who have purchased 5 ounce packages of "Snackies" are urged to return them to the place of purchase for a full refund. Consumers with questions may contact the company at 1–800-XXX-XXXX.

####

("Salmonella Model," 2009)

The Peanut Corporation of America did little besides issue the news releases provided in Exhibit 6.2. A company initiating a voluntary product recall is required, by law, only to issue a news release. That news release must conform to governmental guidelines. Exhibit 6.2 provides the model salmonella recall news release format provided by the FDA. (More recently, a government agency and the recalling company issue a joint statement release through governmental channels). By February 13, 2009, the Peanut Corporation of America had filed for Chapter 7 bankruptcy liquidation and permanently closed its facilities (McCarty, 2009). Researchers need to look more closely at the investigation to understand why the crisis became a corporate death sentence. Exhibit 6.5 provides a summary of key events in the investigation of the outbreak.

Exhibit 6.5   Timeline for Investigation

Sept. 8, 2008	CDS receives first reports of salmonella
Oct. 23, 2008	Georgia Department of Agriculture finds minor violations at PCA's Blakely facility
Nov. 25, 2008	CDC begins assessing salmonella cluster from 12 states

Dec. 3, 2008	FDA and CDC coordinate their investigation of peanut products
Jan. 7, 2009	CDC reports 388 people in 42 states are infected with link to peanut products
Jan. 8, 2009	FDA begins to identify link to King Nut peanut butter
Jan. 9, 2009	FDA collects samples from PCA's Blakely facility
Jan. 10, 2009	King Nut recalls peanut butter, Minnesota Department of Agriculture Laboratory links outbreak to 5-pound container of King Nut brand creamy peanut butter
Jan. 12, 2009	FDA begins posting information about the outbreak to its web site
Jan. 13, 2009	PCA announces voluntary recall of peanut butter and peanut paste produced at Blakely facility after July 1, 2008
Jan. 16, 2009	PCA expands its recall
Jan. 17, 2009	FDA announces it found the samples from Blakely facility tested positive for salmonella
Jan. 18, 2009	PCA expands recall again
Jan. 19, 2009	FDA creates searchable database so that consumers can identify products in the recall
Jan, 21, 2009	FDA, CDC, and state agency confirm source of the outbreak is peanut butter and peanut paste
Jan. 27, 2009	FDA concludes it report on investigation of PCA Blakely plant
Feb. 5, 2009	USDA bans all government contracts with PCA products.
Feb. 13, 2009	PCA files for Chapter 7

("Timeline," 2009)

Here is a short news item from WJBF Channel 6 in Augusta, Georgia, that sums up the crisis:

> The FBI has sealed off the Georgia peanut processing plant linked to a nationwide salmonella outbreak. Agents were at the plant Monday as part of the criminal investigation into alleged wrongdoing. The Food and Drug Administration says the company knowingly shipped out tainted product from this facility that it knew had tested positive for salmonella. ("FBI," 2009)

The FDA investigation found that in 2008, the Peanut Corporation of America's own testing found salmonella in products on seven different occasions. The company then did retesting until a negative test was found. Once a negative test appeared, the products were shipped even though some of the materials in the shipments had tested positive for salmonella. By law, the Peanut Corporation of America had to report only one test, not the results of all the tests. Hence, the Peanut Corporation of America reported only the negative tests to the government.

What made the situation worse for the Peanut Corporation of America was its own words being used against it. E-mails from Stewart Parnell, president of the Peanut Corporation of America, were released during a hearing by the House Energy and Commerce Committee. The messages are clear evidence that Parnell was trying to circumvent laboratory testing that showed salmonella in their products. This included evidence that the company shipped products that had originally tested positive after a negative test was received. When called before Congress, Stewart Parnell used the Fifth Amendment to avoid saying anything to the House Energy and Commerce Committee (Milibank, 2009). Some of the e-mails are included in Exhibit 6.6.

Exhibit 6.6   E-mails From the Peanut Corporation of America

An exchange between Sammy Lightsey and Stewart Parnell

Subject: RE: Granules

We need to discuss this . . . the time lapses, beside the cost is costing us huge $$$$$$ and causing obviously a huge lapses in time from time we pick up peanuts until the time we can invoice. . .

We need to find out somehow what our competition (JIMBOS) is doing and at the very least mimic their policy. . .

We need tp protect our self and the problem is that the tests absolutely give us no protection, just an indication at best. . .

Let's talk.

Stewart

From: Sammy Lightsey

Sent Monday, Septemper 29, 2008 12:40 PM

To: stew.parnell   'David Voth'

Subject: Granules

We received Final Lab result from delbel this morning and we have a Positive for Selmonella. Lot 8266 of Granules produced last thursday. We produced 441 cases of this lot and we produced meal out of the same lot. Samples are going out today for retesting and we will have result on Thursday. Some of this product has been shipped. 280 cases of Medium Chop of Fieldbrook and 40 cases of Meal to kerry ingredients. The customers need to be called and the product placed on HOLD untile this can be cleared. All remaining product is on HOLD in the plant. We have not had any High micro numbers of any kind in Granules and we completely disassembled the line this weekend for cleaning.

(House Energy and Commerce Committee, 2009)

The crisis quickly became framed as an organizational misdeed because management knowingly placed stakeholders at risk. Here are some examples of how the organizational misdeed frame appeared in the media and was reinforced by government officials:

"They tried to hide it so they could sell it," said Georgia Agriculture Commissioner Tommy Irvin. "Now they've caused a mammoth problem that could destroy their company—and it could destroy the peanut industry." ("Calls," 2009)

The company's actions "can only be described as reprehensible and criminal," said Rep. Rosa DeLauro, D-Conn., who oversees FDA funding. "Not only did this company knowingly sell tainted products, it shopped for a laboratory that would provide the acceptable results they were seeking. This behavior represents the worst of our current food safety regulatory system." ("Calls," 2009)

"This company had no conscience in its production practices, sales and distribution," said Senate Agriculture Committee Chairman Tom Harkin (D-Iowa). "That they would knowingly ship products tainted with salmonella to our nation's children almost defies belief." ("Schools," 2009)

The frame is clear; the Peanut Corporation of America knowingly sold products contaminated with salmonella. However, the Peanut Corporation of America did not offer any substantial statements beyond the recall. It remained quiet throughout the salmonella crisis. The initial crisis statements by the Peanut Corporation of America appear in Exhibit 6.2. Its final comments are a statement on its old website that reads:

IMPORTANT NOTICE TO SALMONELLA CLAIMANTS ASSERTING CLAIMS AGAINST PEANUT CORPORATION OF AMERICA (PCA), PLAINVIEW PEANUT CO., LLC (PLAINVIEW) OR TIDEWATER BLANCHING CO., LLC (TIDEWATER)

In order to have your claim considered for payment from a fund established for compensation of injuries or death resulting from an outbreak of Salmonella, you must complete and return the Proof of Claim form and attach the required documentation.

Even if you have previously filed a proof of claim, you must complete and return this proof of claim form and attach the required documentation.

Click here to download Information Page

Click here to download Proof of Claim Form and Exhibit A

This proof of claim form, together with a completed Exhibit A, must be received on or before October 31, 2009—otherwise your claim may be barred.

Proofs of claims must be mailed to [. . .]

Faxes and emails will not be accepted. Proofs of claim should not be sent to the Bankruptcy Court for the Western District of Virginia. Any proof of claim sent to the Bankruptcy Court for the Western District of Virginia will not be accepted or considered for payment. (http://www.peanutcorp.com/)

The bulk of the crisis management effort was performed by the CDC and FDA. The CDC and FDA continually updated the list of recalled products as they increased and provided guidance about salmonella. A sample news release for salmonella is provided in Exhibit 6.3. Of particular note was the use of social media to help people gain access to information about the recall and salmonella. Here is a statement from the CDC:

During the *Salmonella* Typhimurium event of early 2009 and the associated recalls of numerous peanut butter and peanut-containing products, the U.S. Department of Health and Human Services (HHS), Food and Drug Administration (FDA), and Centers for Disease Control and Prevention (CDC) worked together to develop an integrated social media campaign. The goal of the campaign was to provide consumers and partners with social media tools to access up-to-date information about the recalls.

The U.S. Department of Health and Human Services (HHS), Food and Drug Administration (FDA), and Centers for Disease Control and Prevention (CDC) are working together to provide consumers and partners with social media tools to access information about the ongoing peanut butter and peanut-containing product recalls. This page will be updated as new communication approaches are employed. (http://www.fda.gov/Safety/Recalls/Major ProductRecalls/Peanut/ucm164103.htm)

The range of social media was impressive and included blogs, eCards, micro-blogs (Twitter), mobile phone applications, text messaging, videos, podcasts, widgets, social networking sites, and virtual worlds. The government was casting a wide, overlapping set of social media channels to help people stay informed about the recalls and salmonella outbreak. This is an effective online strategy because people seeking information online might use any of these channels. Using multiple channels increases the likelihood of people finding the information they seek.

One of the unique features of the 2009 peanut butter paste salmonella crisis is the collateral damage to companies not involved in the crisis. The recall did garner intense coverage in traditional and online media. That benefits public safety and awareness of tainted products. However, untainted products became caught in the vortex of the crisis. Major manufacturers of peanut butter never used the Peanut Corporation of America's products and were not affected by the recall. Still, a Harvard study found that 25% of the people they surveyed thought major brands, such as Jif and Peter Pan, were part of the recall and were being avoided (Bledon, Weldon, Benson, & Herrmann, 2009). Best estimates indicated that peanut butter sales among the major brands dropped 25% during this time period. Most major peanut butter manufacturers added statements to their home pages telling people they were not part of the recall. The need for crisis management extended to companies not involved in the recall. An illustration of this point is the news release created by the American Peanut Council provided in Exhibit 6.7. The American Peanut Council is a trade association for the peanut industry, and it was taking steps to protect the entire industry.

Exhibit 6.7   News Release from the American Peanut Council

For Immediate Release

American Peanut Council Responds to PCA's Extended Recall

Precautionary recall announced today in public's best interest

1/28/2009, Alexandria, VA—The American Peanut Council (APC) continues to work closely with the U.S. Food and Drug Administration (FDA) and other regulators to fully understand the extended product recall announced by the Peanut Corporation of America (PCA). Late today, PCA expanded its recall to include additional products produced in its Blakely, Georgia facility since January 2007.

At this time, there is no reported evidence that salmonella has been found in any of the newly recalled products; however, this precautionary step is necessary to ensure public health.

"Although we support PCA's precautionary move to recall additional products, since the health and safety of the consumer is our highest priority, one thing is certain— willful neglect of public health and safety cannot be tolerated under any circumstance," said Patrick Archer, president of the American Peanut Council.

This extended recall follows FDA findings announced yesterday, reporting that PCA knowingly released a product with potential salmonella contamination into the food supply.

"This is a clear and unconscionable act by one manufacturer," said Archer. "This act is not by any means representative of the excellent food safety practices and procedures of the U.S. peanut industry."

The www.fda.gov is maintaining a searchable database of products affected by the recall. The APC will continue to maintain a list of unaffected products at www .peanutsusa.com.

The American Peanut Council is a voluntary private trade association that represents all segments of the American peanut industry.

###

AMERICAN PEANUT COUNCIL

1500 King Street, Suite 301

Alexandria, VA 22314

www.peanutsusa.com

("American Peanut Council," 2009)

Discussion Questions

1. What are the dangers of guilt by association?

2. Why did it take so long to warn consumers about the danger?

3. How could you justify the Peanut Corporation of America's limited crisis communication efforts? Do any theories or principles support their choices?

4. Was the Peanut Corporation of American in legal compliance throughout the case?

5. What does this case say about not acting on information discovered in scanning?

6. Why did the American Peanut Council feel the need to get involved?

7. How would you evaluate the government's crisis communication efforts and why?

Websites

CDC timeline for outbreak: http://www.cdc.gov/salmonella/typhimurium/salmonella Outbreak_timeline.pdf

CNN news stories about the Peanut Corporation of America: http://topics.cnn.com/topics/ peanut_corporation_of_america

FDA information about the recall: http://www.fda.gov/Safety/Recalls/MajorProductRecalls/ Peanut/default.htm

Wall Street Journal story with PCA e-mails: http://online.wsj.com/article/SB12343 6949588473457.html

References

About the peanut industry. (n.d.). Retrieved from http://www.peanutsusa.com/USA/index .cfm?fuseaction=home.page&pid=12

American Peanut Council responds to PCA's extended recall. (2009). Retrieved from http:// admin.peanutsusa.com/documents/Document_Library/APC%20statement %201-28-09%20-%20FINAL.pdf

Bettencourt, L. A. (2010). A complex mystery: Finding the sources of foodborne disease outbreaks. Retrieved from http://www.foodsafety.gov/blog/complexmystery.html

Bledon, R. J., Weldon, K. J., Benson, J. M., & Herrmann, M. J. (2009). Following peanut product recall, six in ten Americans taking steps to reduce their risk of getting sick. Retrieved from http://www.hsph.harvard.edu/news/press-releases/2009-releases/peanut -product-recall-survey-americans-reduce-risk-sick.html

Calls for criminal probe in peanut recall begin. (2009). Retrieved from http://www.msnbc .msn.com/id/28896327/wid/11915773/

FBI seals off Blakely, GA peanut plant. (2009). Retrieved from http://www2.wjbf.com/ news/2009/feb/10/fbi_seals_off_blakely_ga_peanut_plant-ar-214783/

Frequently asked questions and answers about the recent salmonella outbreak. (2009). Retrieved from http://www.fda.gov/Safety/Recalls/MajorProductRecalls/Peanut/ResourcesforConsumersandIndustry/ucm150144.htm

House Energy and Commerce Committee. (2009). October 6, 2008 email from Stewart Parnell to Sammy Lightsey. Retrieved from http://democrats.energycommerce.house.gov/Press_111/20090211/parnellemailtolightseyvoth.10.6.2008.pdf

McCarty, D. (2009). Peanut Corp. to liquidate following salmonella deaths. Retrieved from http://www.bloomberg.com/apps/news?pid=newsarchive&sid=a19aOLMU4CQ8&refer=home

Milibank, D. (2009). Mr (tainted) peanut pleads the fifth. Retrieved from http://www.washingtonpost.com/wp-dyn/content/article/2009/02/11/AR2009021104224.html?hpid=topnews

Mohr, A. (2012). The 5 largest food recalls in history. Retrieved from http://finance.yahoo.com/news/5-largest-food-recalls-history-172934187.html

O'Brien, B. (2009). Peanut butter sales prove not so sticky. Retrieved from http://blogs.barrons.com/stockstowatchtoday/2009/02/13/peanut-butter-sales-prove-not-so-sticky/

PCA peanut butter and peanut paste recall. (2009). Retrieved from http://www.schoolkidshealthcareblog.com/2009/pca-peanut-butter-and-peanut-paste-recall.html

Peanut butter and other peanut containing products recall list. (2009). Retrieved from http://www.accessdata.fda.gov/scripts/peanutbutterrecall/index.cfm

Salmonella model press release (all serotypes). (2009). Retrieved from http://www.fda.gov/Safety/Recalls/IndustryGuidance/ucm129275.htm

Schools, disaster victims may have gotten tainted peanut butter. (2009). Retrieved from http://articles.latimes.com/2009/feb/06/nation/na-salmonella-fema6

Timeline of events in peanut-salmonella outbreak. (2009). Retrieved from http://www2.wjbf.com/business/2009/feb/09/timeline_of_events_in_peanut-salmonella_outbreak-ar-215057/

CHAPTER 7

Tetra Pak, Nestlé, and ITX

In 1943, a group of people in Sweden began researching ways to package milk that was both hygienic and used minimal materials. A new technology was developed for coating paper with plastic. In 1946, Dr. Rueben Rausing demonstrated the first tetrahedral package developed by Erik Wallenberg. The company Tetra Pak was founded in 1951 in Lund, Sweden. While originally used for milk, Tetra Pak packaging became used for a variety of liquid food. In the 1970s, Tetra Pak began its international expansion to become the global company it is today. Tetra Pak describes itself as "the world's leading food processing and packaging solutions company. Working closely with our customers and suppliers, we provide safe, innovative and environmentally sound products that each day meet the needs of hundreds of millions of people" ("Our," n.d., About Tetra Pak section). It is currently headquartered in Switzerland.

Tetra Pak's expertise lies in creating safe and responsible packing for liquid food. Because of its expertise, Tetra Pak supplies the packing for a variety of food companies. One company Tetra Pak has worked with is Nestlé. Nestlé began in 1866 when Henri Nestlé started the development of an alternative to breast milk for women who were unable to breast-feed their babies. The original product was known as Farine Lactee ("History," n.d.). Nestlé is now the parent company for hundreds of brands, including Cheerios, Shredded Wheat, Nescafé, Buxton, Poland Springs, Carnation, Nesquik, Juicy Juice, Dancow, Ski, Nanho, Edy's, Hemglass, Skinny Cow, Movenpick, PowerBar, Boost, Baby Ruth, and Wonka Bars.

In 2005, Tetra Pak and Nestlé faced a recall centered in Italy around the discovery of isopropylthioxanthane (ITX) in infant milk. ITX is a fixative in the ink used to print the labels on the liquid milk cartons. The milk cartons in question were produced at a Tetra Pak facility in the Netherlands, filled with milk in the Asturias region in North Spain, and distributed in Italy, Spain, Portugal, Greece, and France. Initial testing of the Tetra Pak-Nestlé infant milk was conducted in July of 2005. The tests found ITX in infant milk from the Marche region of Italy. In early September, the Italian Health Ministry was notified of the contamination but no public statement was made. The Italian Health Ministry used the Rapid Alert System for Food and Feed (RASFF) to alert the EU Commission about the ITX seeping into the infant milk. Later in September, Nestlé recalled milk from the Asturias region of Spain. On October 27, 2005, the products in questions were removed from store shelves in the Italian province of Ascoli Piceno.

On November 9th, 2 million liters of milk were seized by Italian authorities because they were unfit for human use. However, the seizure was not publicized. The products were Latte Mio, Nidina, and Mio Cereali. On November 15th, Nestlé began to recall the same products, but the recall was not publicized. On November 22nd, the recall became public as media covered the seizure of additional milk by the Forestry guard in Italy. The Forestry guard has jurisdiction over food safety in Italy ("Ink," 2005). In the initial media reports, Italian Agriculture Minister Gianni Alemanno proclaimed, "It is incredible that such defenceless beings as babies should face such serious risks in a product as widely used as milk" (Strassheim, 2005, para. 5). The news spread rapidly with such headlines as "Baby milk scare widens in Europe" ("Baby," 2005).

Nestlé management explained the recall in this statement: "This decision was taken as an extreme precautionary measure to reassure consumers. Nestlé believes that the level of ITX measured in the tested produce does not represent a health risk" ("Baby," 2005, p. 7). On November 23rd, Nestlé placed advertisements in Italian newspapers, claiming the recall was voluntary and an "extreme precaution-ary measure to reassure consumers" (Strassheim, 2005, para. 10). That same day, Peter Brabeck-Letmathe, the Nestlé CEO, claimed the Italian government was cre-ating an unnecessary uproar. "It's nothing. It's a storm in a teacup. There is no risk to safety," he told reporters in Zurich. "This has more to do with politics than any-thing else" (Mortished, 2005, p. 69).

Jörgen Haglind, senior vice president of Communications at Tetra Pak, stated:

> The presence of ITX is linked to UV inks used in offset printing; a technology used widely by numerous food packaging companies. Tetra Pak has a long his-tory of holding its packages and packaging equipment to the highest standard of food quality and safety in the industry. Consistent with this, we have decided to change to alternative printing methods that don't use photoinitiators in those products where there is a potential for migration. ("Tetra," 2005, para. 3–4)

Anger begins to emerge about the crisis because of the time lag between when the ITX contamination was found and the removal of the product from the mar-ket. The first reports emerge in September, but it is November before any public action is taken. Also, there are disagreements between the corporations involved and the governmental authorities about the crisis. The corporations believed the contamination was not a health risk, while government authorities differed with that view. Moreover, Nestlé claims it had an agreement with Italian authorities to act slowly on the recall, while the Italian authorities denied there was any such agreement.

Tetra Pak and Nestlé believed there was no risk from the ITX migration. That belief was based on a statement from the European Food Safety Authority (EFSA). That statement is presented in Exhibit 7.1. Both Tetra Pak and Nestlé were using the initial statement to support their claims that there was no danger from ITX migration. As the second statement and letters from the EFSA indicate, the EFSA was not claiming that ITX was safe, only that the agency had not yet fully assessed the risk of ITX. A week later, the preliminary data from the EFSA suggested there was no risk from ITX, but the intense media coverage of the crisis had subsided by that point.

Exhibit 7.1   EFSA Initial Statement on ITX

Press Release

24 November 2005

ITX (Isopropylthioxanthone), a substance utilised in printing inks for certain packaging materials has been recently found in foods including infant formula. On the basis of the very limited data available today, the presence of ITX in food could be considered undesirable but it is not likely to present a health risk at the levels reported. The European Commission has requested that EFSA carry out a risk assessment on ITX. EFSA will provide preliminary advice in the next two weeks and expects to deliver its final opinion no later than March 2006.

For media enquiries, please contact [...]

("EFSA Undertakes," 2005)

Exhibit 7.2   EFSA Clarifying Statement, December 1, 2005

EFSA reaffirms present position on ITX

Contrary to statements being made by third parties, the European Food Safety Authority (EFSA) has not carried out risk assessment of ITX to date. ESFA has not been able to determine the safety of ITX but rather has made a preliminary statement based on very limited data.

Today EFSA sent letters to Nestle and Tetra Pak to express its concern about misinterpretations of EFSA's press statement.

("EFSA Reaffirms," 2005)

Exhibit 7.3   EFSA Press Release, December 9, 2005

EFSA provides advice on the safety of ITX: ITX considered of low health concern

Press Release

9 December 2005

The Scientific Panel on food additives, flavourings, processing aids and materials in contact with food (AFC) of the European Food Safety Authority (EFSA) has adopted an opinion on the possible health risks related to 2-Isopropylthioxanthone (ITX). ITX is a substance used in inks applied to packaging materials, including foods packed in cartons. ITX has recently been found in a number of foods such as ready-to-feed infant formula. In the light of the Panel's conclusions, EFSA advises that the presence of ITX in foods, whilst undesirable, does not give cause for health concern at the levels reported. This confirms previous advice published by EFSA on 24 November 2005.

Following reports of the presence of ITX in foods packed in cartons, the European Commission requested that EFSA provide scientific advice with respect to possible health risks associated with this substance by April 2006. In view of the level of public concern, EFSA's AFC Panel has adopted its final opinion on 7 December.

The Panel's work focused on the assessment of possible exposure to this substance as well as on its genotoxic potential. In carrying out the exposure assessment, the Panel referred primarily to data available on the levels of ITX found by industry in foodstuffs packed in cartons printed with ITX containing inks. The food products analysed in these studies comprise four types of milk-based products, including infant formula, milk and soy beverages as well as fruit juices, fruit nectars and other drinks. It appeared that the composition of the food itself influenced the levels found. According to the reports, the ITX levels in fat-containing foods were higher than in water-based products. Highest levels of ITX were found in milk-based products, followed by "cloudy" products such as orange juice and tomato juice (due to the presence of pulp). ITX was not detectable in 'clear' fruit juices such as apple juice nor was it detectable in water. The pack size appears also to be a factor as levels found in smaller cartons were relatively higher than those in bigger cartons.

The Panel gave special attention to the exposure of infants and young children. Infants who are not exclusively breastfed may be fed with ready-to-feed formulae packed in cartons. A large number of beverages consumed by young children are likely to be packed in cartons, particularly milk-based products and fruit juice in small volume packages. The potential dietary exposure of infants and young children could therefore be higher than that of adults.

Following review of available genotoxicity studies, the Panel concluded that the findings from animal studies did not indicate a genotoxic potential for ITX. EFSA therefore advises that ITX does not give cause for health concern at the levels reported. There are no data available at present on aspects other than genotoxicity. If contamination of foods with ITX was to continue, the Panel would wish to make recommendations about further studies that may be needed.

Following a request of the European Commission, EFSA has also provided scientific advice in the same opinion on another substance also used in inks, 2-ethylhexyl-4-dimethylaminobenzoate (EHDAB). This substance was also found in liquid products such as milk packed in printed carton packaging, but at lower levels than ITX. The Panel concluded that the occurrence of EHDAB in food from its use in inks applied to food packaging materials is of no safety concern.

("EFSA Provides," 2005)

The debate between Nestlé and the Italian government was very heated. The Italian Health Minister Francesco Storace accused Nestlé CEO Brabeck-Lernathe of lying. Storace maintained his office had no agreement with Nestlé to let the ITX contaminated milk be sold while the packing was being changed. The media even characterized Brabeck-Lernathe as being combative in his response to the ITX situations. Italy is Nestlé's fifth biggest market, and the recall was costing over 2 million euros (Mortished, 2005). Brabeck-Lernathe did send a letter of apology to Storace that included the following statement: "However, I acknowledge—and unreservedly apologize for—the memory lapse which caused me to say that the contacts between your Agencia Regionale per la Protezione Ambientale and Nestlé took place in July/August rather than in September" ("Nestlé," 2005, p. B-12). Storace rejected the apology and filed a lawsuit against Brabeck-Lernathe because the apology did not address the issue of the Italian Health Ministry, allowing Nestlé to continue selling the milk once the contamination was known (Mortished, 2005; "Nestlé," 2005).

Though no clear evidence emerged that ITX was a health concern, both Tetra Pak and Nestlé took actions designed to eliminate its use in packaging. ITX is associated with ultraviolet (UV) ink in printing. Tetra Pak switched inks as soon as it learned about the migration into the product ("Chemical," 2005). Tetra Pak stated, "We have decided to change to alternative printing methods that don't use photo initiators in those products where there is a potential for migration" ("Tetra," 2005, para. 4). Safety is all-important to the company. Tetra Pak even phased out the use of ITX-related ink for juice packaging saying, "We take this issue very seriously" (ElAmin, 2005, para. 12). Tetra Pak also noted that the actions were taken even though the World Health Organization does not consider ITX one of the toxic substances that should not come into contact with food. Nestlé noted it changed the printing process (through its suppliers) on its products in October of 2005 (Strassheim, 2005).

By the end, The ITX crisis had become a global concern. Newspapers in the United Kingdom and Ireland reported that ITX could be in their products. Nestlé issued statements in China and Singapore, defending the safety of their milk in those countries. Here is the Nestlé statement from Singapore: "We would like to advise all parties that our infant milk products are safe for consumption and we comply with the strict inspection and safety standards required by the Singapore Agri-Food and Veterinary Authority" (Young, 2005, p. 15). The incidents of ITX in milk were reported in the United States, Canada, and South Africa as well.

Reading Guide

1. If this situation is a crisis, what type of crisis is it?

2. What is the problem and the source(s) of the problem in this case?

3. What government agencies are involved in the case?

4. What corporations are involved in the case?

5. What is the problem and its source in this case?

6. What other stakeholders should be interested in this case?

7. What is ITX?

Discussion Questions

1. What are the dangers of Nestlé getting into a dispute with the government?

2. Who should be responsible for managing the crisis?

3. Why are interpretations of risk so critical in this case?

4. What is the importance of the interpretation of the EFSA statement?

5. When a company makes changes after a crisis, does that imply there was a problem? Defend your conclusion.

6. How and why did this case become global?

7. What is the importance of timing in this case? Why is timing such a critical factor?

8. How can the rhetorical arena be useful in analyzing this case?

Websites

Tetra Pak: http://www.tetrapak.com/Pages/default.aspx
Nestlé: http://www.nestle.com/Pages/Nestle.aspx
Story about Tetra Pak changing its printing: http://www.foodproductiondaily.com/Packaging/Tetra-Pak-to-phase-out-chemical-from-citrus-juice-packaging

References

Baby milk scare over chemical in packaging. (2005, Nov. 26). *Liverpool Daily Echo,* p. 7.

Chemical in cartons to be phased out. (2005, Nov. 24). *Daily Post,* p. 16.

EFSA provides advice on the safety of ITX: ITX considered of low health concern. (2005). Retrieved from http://www.efsa.europa.eu/en/press/news/afc051209.htm

EFSA reaffirms present position on ITX. (2005). Retrieved from http://www.efsa.europa.eu/en/press/news/afc051201.htm

EFSA undertakes risk assessment on ITX. (2005). Retrieved from http://www.efsa.europa.eu/en/press/news/afc051124.htm

ElAmin, A. (2005). Tetra Pak to phase out chemicals from citrus juice packaging. Retrieved from http://www.foodproductiondaily.com/Packaging/Tetra-Pak-to-phase-out-chemical-from-citrus-juice-packaging

History. (n.d.). Retrieved from http://www.nestle.com/AboutUs/History/Pages/History.aspx

Ink could be found in baby's milk. (2005, Nov. 26). *Daily Post,* p. 11.

Mortished, C. (2005, Nov. 25). Nestle chief faces lawsuit over baby milk sales claim. *The Times,* p. 69.

Nestlé recalls baby milk after traces of ink found. (2005, Nov. 23). *The Globe and Mail,* p. B-12.

Our history. (n.d.). Retrieved from http://www.tetrapak.com/about_tetra_pak/the_company/history/pages/ourhistory.aspx

Strassheim, I. (2005, Nov. 23). Italian police seize 30M litres of contaminated baby milk. *Irish Independent.* Retrieved from http://www.independent.ie/world-news/europe/italian-police-seize-30m-litres-of-contaminated-baby-milk-25958199.html

Tetra Pak says no ITX in infant formula packages. (2005, November). Retrieved from http://i-grafix.com/index.php/news/packaging/tetra-pak-says-no-itx-in-infant-formula-packages.html

Young, E. (2005, November 25). Nestle baby milk sold here safe, says AVA. *The Strait Times,* p. 15.

CHAPTER 8

Nestlé and Greenpeace Disagree Over Palm Oil Sourcing

You might have heard of palm oil or even know how it touches your life every day. Palm oil is found in chocolate, margarine, and as a dietary supplement. The baking industry relies heavily upon the use of palm oil, and it is used extensively for home and commercial frying. The oleochemicals from palm oil are used in cosmetics, soaps, detergents, pharmaceuticals, rubber, biofuels, and plastics. In fact, 50% of all consumer goods use some element of palm oil. At this moment, you are probably not far from a product containing palm oil and have probably utilized palm oil at some point during your day. Palm oil is extracted from the fruit of the oil palm, primarily the African oil palm.

Palm oil usage can be traced back to at least the ancient Egyptians. Palm oil, *Elaeis guineensis* to use scientific terminology, is a wild plant in Equatorial Africa and Western Africa. Like many cash crops, palm oil is now grown in many other tropical areas with Malaysia being one of the largest palm oil producers in the world ("Palm," 2007). A cash crop is grown for sale, to earn money, as opposed to use as feed or food. The incentive to increase production of a cash crop is increased revenues. As long as demand is strong, prices remain high even when the supply of the cash crop is increased. The demand for palm oil has been on the rise given its wide array of uses. In the past 5 years, palm oil demand and its use have tripled. The global demand for palm oil makes it a very attractive crop. Critics claim the palm oil is too attractive as a crop ("Palm," 2011).

So how can a cash crop be too attractive? The vast majority of palm oil is now grown in Indonesia, Malaysia, and Papua New Guinea (PNG). The problem is that increased cultivation of palm oil is coming at the cost of the rainforests. Palm oil cultivation is one of the primary reasons for global rainforest deforestation. The rainforests are being cleared so that palm oil trees can be grown. The intense demand for palm oil keeps the prices steady so there is a financial incentive to increase palm oil production. Unfortunately, many growers choose unsustainable methods, such as rainforest destruction, in pursuit of the palm oil revenues ("Palm," 2011).

Rainforest destruction is bad for the entire planet. Rainforest deforestation adds to global warming. But more directly, rainforests are critical habitats for a wide range of animal life and indigenous peoples. Destroying their habitats will lead to the death of these animals and the displacement of indigenous peoples. Animals cannot live when they have no habitat to inhabit. Indigenous people frequently struggle to survive when displaced from their traditional home areas. Among the animals threatened by palm oil cultivation are orangutans, Asian elephants, Sumatran tigers, and Sumatran rhinos. The Dayak and Melanesian tribes have been displaced from their ancestral lands and face uncertain futures in their new locations ("Cruel," 2005). It is against this backdrop of palm oil and rainforest concerns that the Nestlé-Greenpeace palm oil crisis case transpires.

Nestlé defines itself as a nutrition, health, and wellness company. It was founded in 1866 by Henri Nestlé in Vevey, Switzerland. His original product was an infant formula that could be used by mothers who could not produce breast milk. Soon, the brand expanded to include condensed milk. In the early 1900s, Nestlé added chocolate to its mix of products. Today, the stable of Nestlé brands includes such famous names as Butterfinger, Carnation, Coffee-Mate, Dog Chow, Gerber, Kit Kat, Perrier, PowerBar, Smarties, and Wonka ("History," n.d.). This is a broad mix of products. However, most children will associate Nestlé with chocolate. Nestlé is a global brand with sales and operations around the world.

Greenpeace International is a non-governmental organization (NGO). An NGO is independent from the government. Technically, corporations can be included in NGOs. The term *private voluntary organizations* (PVOs) has been created to designate noncorporate organizations. Greenpeace began in 1970 when the Don't Make Waves Committee decided to sail their boat to Amchitka Island in the Aleutians to protest a planned nuclear test there by the U.S. government ("Founders," 2009). Greenpeace now has operations in 40 countries and spans the globe with over 2.8 million supporters. Greenpeace exists to support Earth:

> Greenpeace is an independent global campaigning organisation that acts to change attitudes and behaviour, to protect and conserve the environment and to promote peace by:
>
> **Catalysing an energy revolution** to address the number one threat facing our planet: climate change.
>
> **Defending our oceans** by challenging wasteful and destructive fishing, and creating a global network of marine reserves.
>
> **Protecting the world's ancient forests** and the animals, plants and people that depend on them.

Working for disarmament and peace by tackling the causes of conflict and calling for the elimination of all nuclear weapons.

Creating a toxic free future with safer alternatives to hazardous chemicals in today's products and manufacturing.

Campaigning for sustainable agriculture by rejecting genetically engineered organisms, protecting biodiversity and encouraging socially responsible farming. ("About," n.d., para. 2–8)

Greenpeace is an activist group. Activists can be defined as those who stand up for a cause (Raymond, 2003) and seek to create changes they feel will help to improve society (Thomas, 2003). Problematic corporate behaviors are frequent activist targets for change. Moreover, activists rely heavily upon public relations (Coombs & Holladay, 2010). Greenpeace is no exception to this activist-public relations connection. Two of Greenpeace's core values are expressed in these statements: (1) "We take personal responsibility for our actions, and we are committed to nonviolence. . . . taking action based on conscience—personal action based on personal responsibility. . . . everyone on a Greenpeace action is trained in nonviolent direct action" and (2) "In exposing threats to the environment and finding solutions we have no permanent allies or adversaries" ("Our Core," 2006, para. 2, 4). Raising public debate and exposing people to information are public relations-intensive activities (Heath & Coombs, 2006).

The Events

In March of 2010, Greenpeace began its "Ask Nestlé to give rainforests a break" campaign. The problem behavior was Nestlé sourcing palm oil from the Sinar Mas Group. The Sinar Mas Group is a major Indonesian conglomerate and the largest palm oil producer in the country. Greenpeace claims its investigations prove the Sinar Mas Group is destroying rainforests in efforts to boost the size of its palm oil plantation. As a result of the rainforest destruction, the habitat of orangutans is being destroyed. The Sinar Mas Group denies it is involved in rainforest deforestation (Selamat, 2010). In today's business environment, a corporation is held accountable for what happens in its supply chain. Therefore, if a supplier is acting irresponsibly, the corporation is irresponsible as well. Supply chain responsibility became a visible business concern in the 1990s when activists protested the use of sweat shops by Nike and other apparel manufacturers (Bhattacharya, Smith, & Palazzo, 2010).

Greenpeace wanted to pressure Nestlé into reforming its palm oil sourcing by ending ties with Sinar Mas immediately and committing to sustainable palm oil. The Roundtable for Sustainable Palm Oil, formed in 2004, is the dominant certifier of sustainably produced palm oil. A relatively small percentage of palm oil is certified as sustainable. In 2009, only 1.5 tons of the 45 million tons produced were certified (Selamat, 2010). Earlier in 2010, Unilever had dropped Sinar Mas Group as a palm oil supplier due to lingering doubts about the group's methods.

Greenpeace began its campaign by releasing online a nine-page digital document titled "Caught Red-Handed: How Nestlé's Use of Palm Oil Is Having a Devastating Impact on Rainforest, the Climate and Orang-utans" ("Caught," 2010). The date of the release was March 16 or 17, depending upon the country where the recipients lived. The report used a modified Nestlé's Kit Kat logo with the word *Kit Kat* replaced by "Killer." The document used a number of visuals to reinforce the evidence, showing Nestlé was using a supplier that sourced palm oil irresponsibly. The orangutans emerged as one of the symbols Greenpeace would use to dramatize the palm oil sourcing problems.

Nestlé's initial response on March 17 was a defense of its actions. Here is the first part of the response:

There have been recent questions raised about Nestlé and palm oil.

We share the deep concern about the serious environmental threat to rainforests and peat fields in South East Asia caused by the planting of palm oil plantations. The company recently announced its commitment to using only "Certified Sustainable Palm Oil" by 2015, when sufficient quantities should be available.

Because of our commitment, we are taking all feasible steps to impact our suppliers to assure [them] that we don't buy palm oil which contributes to deforestation.

As a part of this commitment, we have accelerated the investigation of our palm oil supply chain to identify any palm oil source which does not meet our high standards for sustainability. Given our uncompromising food safety standards, we have done this in a deliberate manner as we use palm oil for food products rather than for soap or other personal care products. ("greenEnder," 2010, para. 4–7)

Greenpeace and other critics considered Nestlé's initial response to be ineffective. The 2015 date was 5 years away, and Nestlé seemed to be creating a loophole by noting "when sufficient quantities are available." It is legitimate to note there is a limited supply of certified palm oil, but there are many other suppliers who are recognized as responsible but have yet to be certified. The statement did say Nestlé would stop sourcing from the Sinar Mas Group. However, one of its replacement suppliers is known to source from the Sinar Mas Group. Critics felt Nestlé was simply moving the problem further down the supply chain and that tangible actions needed to be taken now. Here is Greenpeace's reaction to Nestlé's initial response:

Nestlé's concessions don't go nearly far enough. The company seems to agree with Greenpeace that much more has to be done to stop the destruction of

Paradise Forests and peatlands for palm oil, but it hasn't delivered the kind of action we hoped to see. Despite today's announcement, Nestle will still be using palm oil from destructive suppliers like Sinar Mas through indirect supplies. The Greenpeace campaign will continue until Nestle has cut the Sinar Mas group from its supply chain completely and become a public advocate for peatland protection and a deforestation moratorium. ("Greenpeace," 2010, para. 1)

March 17 was also the release of Greenpeace's video on YouTube called *Have a Break?* The video was a parody of a Nestlé's Kit Kat commercial. The key phrase in the advertisement is "give me a break." A man in an office begins to eat a Kit Kat candy bar. Blood begins to run down his face, and we see the candy bar pieces are orangutan digits. The scene then jumps to orangutans in a lone tree with the sound of chainsaws cutting the trees around them. The call is then made for Nestlé to stop destroying orangutan habitat through its irresponsible sourcing of palm oil. Here is the message that went along with the video:

NEED A BREAK? SO DOES THE RAINFOREST.

Nestlé, maker of Kit Kat, uses palm oil from companies that are trashing Indonesian rainforests, threatening the livelihoods of local people and pushing orang-utans towards extinction.

 We all deserve to have a break—but having one shouldn't involve taking a bite out of Indonesia's precious rainforests. We're asking Nestlé to give rainforests and orang-utans a break and stop buying palm oil from destroyed forests. (http://www.greepeace.org/international/campaigns/climate-change/kitkat/)

The orangutans became a condensation symbol for the campaign. A condensation symbol is powerful because the symbol evokes emotion. People have sympathy for the orangutans so they evoke a powerful emotion as a visual in the Greenpeace campaign. Nestlé responded by demanding that the Greenpeace video be removed from YouTube. The Nestlé response created a backlash as people claimed their actions were a form of censorship. Nestlé's actions had the opposite effect of what was intended. Instead of the video disappearing from view, it became more popular as people tried to find it. People wanted to see the video because of the efforts to ban it. As one viewer commented, "Thanks Nestlé—I would've never seen this video if you hadn't kicked it off YouTube" (Ridings, 2010).

 To intensify the pressure on Nestlé, Greenpeace moved the campaign to an additional front, Nestlé's Facebook page. Like many companies, Nestlé has a fan page on Facebook. It is a chance for limited interaction with stakeholders, mostly customers. It is heavily populated with people who like Nestlé. As early as March 17, negative comments began to appear as people learned about the effort to remove the YouTube video. On March 17, Nestlé addressed the issue with a shortened version of the initial response:

Nestlé and palm oil: we're concerned. We announced our commitment to using only Certified Sustainable Palm Oil by 2015. We have accelerated investigation of palm oil supplies to identify any unsustainable palm oil. Given our uncompromising food safety standards, we have done this in a deliberate manner as we use palm oil for food and not soap or other personal care products. More: http://tinyurl.com/nestlepalmoil. (Ridings, 2010, para. 12)

Then, the negative comments began to be posted at the Nestlé Facebook page, including aggressive questions from Greenpeace about the lack of true reform. Some people began using the Killer version of the Kit Kat logo as their profile pictures. It is commonplace on Facebook for people to use an image related to the issues they feel passionate about as their profile picture. On March 19, the following message appeared from Nestlé, with a link to their website: "We welcome all comments but please don't post using an altered version of our logo as your profile pic. And please read our statement to answer many questions" ("6 Painful," 2011, para. 4). This comment triggered a firestorm against Nestlé. People disliked the tone and viewed the effort as censorship. One person wrote: "You NEED to change the tone in your Facebook responses. You're committing social media suicide" (Ridings, 2010, para. 19).

That last message was prophetic. After a number of criticisms, Nestlé threw fuel on the fire by stating on Facebook, "Oh please . . . it's like we're censoring everything to allow only positive comments" ("6 Painful," 2011, para. 5). Nestlé soon lost control of its Facebook page as the messages were predominantly from critics, including self-identified members of Greenpeace. The Nestlé page became a podium for those who disliked the company. The discontent spread throughout the Internet and spawned stories in the traditional or legacy media as well. One term used to describe the situation was "brandjacked." One analysis found that the Facebook situation caused an increase in online mentions of Nestlé. Unfortunately, the majority of those messages were negative. Digging deeper into the online comments was not reassuring for Nestlé. Discussion of Nestlé was up 22% over the previous week, but the discussion of the Greenpeace incident was up 932%. A total of 37% of all online conversations about Nestlé were about the Greenpeace action (Etlinger, 2010). Nestlé was being used as an example of how not to handle a crisis emerging in social media (e.g., "Crises," 2010; Ridings, 2010).

The situation on Facebook was moving quickly, and Nestlé was compounding the negativity of the situation with its own errors. Here is one additional exchange between a person posting to the Facebook page and the Nestlé response:

Comment: "not sure you're going to win friends in the social media space with this sort of dogmatic approach. I understand that you're on your back-foot due to various issues not excluding palm oil but social media is about embracing your market, engaging and having a conversation rather than preaching!"

Nestlé: "Thanks for the lesson in manners. Consider yourself embraced. But it's our page, we set the rules, it was ever thus." ("6 Painful," 2011, Paul Griffin, para. 3 & Nestle, para. 4)

Eventually the following message appeared from Nestlé: "This (deleting logos) was one in a series of mistakes for which I would like to apologise. And for being rude. We've stopped deleting posts, and I have stopped being rude" (Leonard, 2010, para. 20). Essentially, Nestlé stopped providing official posts as activists dominated the page for another few days (Ridings, 2010). The communication mistakes Nestlé made echoed throughout the social media via tweets and blogs about the situation. Widespread, negative social media commentary is a threat to a corporation's reputation. Managers care what is being said about their companies when that message is spreading rapidly among its stakeholders. The negative statements about Nestlé helped to promote Greenpeace's cause.

The Greenpeace campaign ended on May 17, 2010, when Nestlé announced sweeping changes to its palm oil sourcing. Nestlé detailed its new responsible sourcing guidelines and a partnership with The Forest Trust (TFT) to help work to stop deforestation. The TFT will work with Nestlé to create a sustainable supply chain. Nestlé was changing and recognized how its use of palm oil was having a negative impact on society through deforestation. On its website, Greenpeace thanked Nestlé for its changes, officially ended the Ask Nestlé to give rainforests a break campaign, and noted it will monitor Nestlé closely to make sure the company's actions match its words. The Thank You also noted the importance of social media and thanked all those who helped them in the effort. The complete announcements by Nestlé, TFT, and Greenpeace are presented in Exhibit 8.1.

Exhibit 8.1   Nestlé Open Forum on Deforestation, Malaysia

José Lopez, Executive Vice President Nestlé S.A., today announced in Malaysia Nestlé's partnership with TFT (The Forest Trust), reaffirming Nestlé's commitment to ending the deforestation of rainforests.

TFT, a global non-proϕιτ οργανization, will help Nestlé to build responsible supply chains by identifying and addressing embedded social and environmental issues. Nestlé is the first global consumer goods company to become a TFT member.

The partnership starts with palm oil, and Nestlé is studying its supply chains to determine a similarly ambitious target for the pulp and paper it uses. Together with TFT, Nestlé has defined the Responsible Sourcing Guidelines, a set of critical requirements to guide the Nestlé procurement process and to ensure compliance with the Nestlé Supplier Code. The partnership will focus on assessing suppliers' performance with respect to these guidelines and on providing technical support to those who currently do not meet the requirements, but who are committed to achieving them.

Nestlé's actions will focus on the systematic identification and exclusion of companies owning or managing high risk plantations or farms linked to deforestation.

Nestlé has already set the goal that by 2015, 100% of the palm oil it uses will come from sustainable sources. The Company has made strong progress toward that goal; 18% of its palm oil purchases in 2010 come from sustainable sources, and this is expected to reach 50% by the end of 2011.

By setting critical requirements for its procurement process and checking compliance with its Supplier Code, Nestlé wants to ensure that its products have no deforestation footprint.

Responsible Sourcing Guidelines

Together with TFT, Nestlé developed the following requirements for palm oil: The palm oil Nestlé purchases will:

- Be derived from plantations and farms operating in compliance with local laws and regulations
- Protect high conservation value forest areas
- Support the free prior and informed consent of indigenous and local communities to activities on their customary lands where plantations are developed
- Protect peatlands
- Protect forest areas of "high carbon" value

To further implement the Responsible Sourcing Guidelines, Nestlé and TFT will:

- Communicate these guidelines strongly and clearly to the global commodity industry, particularly the palm oil and pulp and paper sectors
- Continue to focus its procurement to already certified suppliers
- Conduct and ensure field audits of its existing suppliers to determine their performance against the guidelines
- Exclude all suppliers found to be in breach of the guidelines
- Implement technical assistance programs to support those willing to proceed to sustainability
- Identify new suppliers who comply or could with technical assistance comply with the guidelines
- Provide regular and transparent feedback on its findings and its performance against these guidelines.

These Responsible Sourcing guidelines are enforced with immediate effect. TFT's work with Nestlé has already begun and Nestlé will continue to communicate on its progress.

("Nestlé Open Forum," 2010)

Exhibit 8.2   Nestlé Becomes TFT's Newest Member

17 May 2010

TFT to Follow Palm Oil Back to Source for Nestlé;

Swiss Giant Commits to Excluding Suppliers that Destroy Forests

Greenpeace Welcomes Agreement as "Very Positive"

The Forest Trust (TFT) announced today that Swiss consumer goods company Nestlé has agreed to a plan that will rid its products of palm oil purchased from suppliers whose activities are destroying vulnerable tropical forests in the developing world.

Under the terms of their agreement, the Geneva-based nonprofit will work with Nestlé to transform its purchasing power into a force for forest conservation, according to TFT's executive director Scott Poynton. Auditors from the Geneva-based NGO will be in Southeast Asia before the end of May to start work on making Nestlé's supply chains in the region responsible.

"For the first time ever, a global company is saying that it doesn't want its products to have a deforestation footprint, and it is taking action to live up to its words," Poynton said. "This is the whole push behind TFT's model-to get one end of the supply chain to take responsibility for what happens at the other end. This is a game-changer."

In a statement today, Nestlé said its actions "will focus on the systematic identification and exclusion of companies owning or managing high risk plantations or farms linked to deforestation."

"Nestlé has entered into a partnership with The Forest Trust (TFT), a global non-profit organization that will help Nestlé to build responsible supply chains by identifying and addressing embedded social and environmental issues," the statement said. "The partnership (with TFT) starts with palm oil, and Nestlé is studying its supply chains to determine a similarly ambitious target for the pulp and paper it uses."

Greenpeace, which was instrumental in outlining the measures that would be seen as meaningful, called the agreement "a very positive step."

"Nestlé's new policy sends a very clear message to companies that are destroying forests and peatlands for new plantations," said Andy Tait, Senior Campaign Advisor for Greenpeace. "If you don't stop deforestation and protect peatlands, your days of supplying to global brands such as Nestlé are over. This is a very positive step forward by Nestle, but delivery is critical, and we will be monitoring progress carefully."

The company has committed as well to ensure that suppliers act to safeguard the rights of forest communities in developing palm oil plantations, Poynton said. "As part of the agreement, TFT will audit Nestlé's suppliers and will help identify and exclude those that are not doing the right thing," said Poynton, an Australian forester. "And if there are suppliers that want to change the way they operate, our team on the ground will help them to improve their practices in order to comply with Nestlé's purchasing requirements."

Potential impact of corporate giant's decision

With sales of CHF 107.6 billion in 2009, Nestlé is one of the world's top 50 companies. It employs 278,000 people and has 449 factories in 83 countries. Nestlé products are sold in almost every country in the world.

"The impact of Nestlé's announcement is huge because the company is so important globally," Poynton said. "Nestlé does not use a huge volume of palm oil or pulp and paper compared to other companies. The focus for the first time is on products, and if Nestlé's decision inspires other companies to engage in the same process, we can stop wringing our hands about carbon baselines and forest carbon markets. Demand for sustainable products can work its magic without them."

Nestlé has a policy that by 2015 the company will obtain 100 percent of the palm oil it uses from sustainable sources. This year, 18 percent of its palm oil purchases will come from sustainable sources, rising to 50 percent by the end of 2011, according to the company statement.

Nestlé says in its statement that the company has worked with TFT to come up with "a set of critical requirements" that will guide the Nestlé procurement process and ensure compliance with the Nestlé Supplier Code. "The partnership will focus on assessing suppliers' performance with respect to these guidelines and on providing technical support to those who currently do not meet the requirements, but who are committed to achieving sustainability."

The statement notes as well that Nestlé worked with TFT to come up with the following requirements for palm oil purchases. Such purchases will:

- Be derived from plantations and farms operating in compliance with local laws and regulations;
- Protect high conservation value forest areas;
- Support the free prior and informed consent of indigenous and local communities to activities on their customary lands where plantations are developed;
- Protect peatlands; and
- Protect forest areas of "high carbon" value.

And to further implement the "Responsible Sourcing Guidelines," the two partners will:

- Communicate these guidelines strongly and clearly to the global commodity industry, particularly the palm oil and pulp and paper sectors;
- Continue to focus its procurement to already certified suppliers;
- Conduct and ensure field audits of its existing suppliers to determine their performance against the guidelines;
- Exclude all suppliers found to be in breach of the guidelines;
- Implement technical assistance programs to support those willing to proceed to sustainability;
- Identify new suppliers who comply, or could comply with technical assistance, with the guidelines; and
- Provide regular and transparent feedback on its findings and its performance against these guidelines.

"We're getting going immediately, no delays, we're going for it," Poynton said. "Our guys are heading to Singapore in less than two weeks to meet Nestlé's procurement staff and we're away. It's game on."

("Nestlé Becomes," 2010)

Exhibit 8.3   Sweet Success for Kit Kat Campaign: You Asked, Nestlé Has Answered

Feature story—May 17, 2010

A big "Thank You!" to the hundreds of thousands of you who supported our two-month Kit Kat campaign by e-mailing Nestlé, calling them, or spreading the campaign message via your Facebook, Twitter and other social media profiles. This morning, Nestlé finally announced a break for the orang-utan—as well as Indonesian rainforests and peatlands—by committing to stop using products that come from rainforest destruction.

The new policy commits Nestlé to identify and exclude companies from its supply chain that own or manage "high risk plantations or farms linked to deforestation." This would apply to notorious Sinar Mas, a palm oil and paper supplier that Greenpeace has repeatedly caught destroying the rainforest—if it fails to meet Nestlé's new criteria—and also have implications for Cargill, one of Nestlé's palm oil suppliers which purchases from Sinar Mas.

Nestlé's announcement sends a strong message to the palm oil and paper industry that rainforest destruction is not an acceptable practice in today's global marketplace—and it wouldn't have happened without you. From the very beginning, the strength of our Kit Kat campaign has been the truly amazing support from the public—online and offline—both concerned consumers and social media-savvy activists alike.

The support from the online community has been clear since day one when our "Have a break?" video's removal from YouTube sparked online calls of censorship, several spin-off uploads to YouTube, and drove hundreds of thousands of views on the video within hours of it being re-uploaded to Vimeo—the total number of views on all versions of the video is now over 1.5 million!

Facebook was another key online arena for the Kit Kat campaign, where a steady stream of pressure was applied to Nestlé via comments you left on its Facebook Fan page. While many of you also "wore your support on your sleeve" Facebook-style by changing your profile pictures to images of orang-utans, rainforest, and our campaign Kit Kat "killer" logo.

The power of social media combined dramatically with our direct actions to deliver the message directly to Nestlé at events like its Annual General Meeting on April 15th. Outside the meeting venue, shareholders were greeted by protesting orang-utans as they arrived, while inside our activists hid in the ceiling in order to drop down over shareholders heads just as the meeting began to deploy banners asking Nestlé to give orang-utans a break. Online our supporters were sending tweets to shareholders throughout the meeting via a fake Wi-Fi network we had set up, which sent shareholders directly to greenpeace.org/kitkat when they connected.

Online and offline the message to Nestlé has been strong and relentless over the past two months—give rainforests and orang-utans a break. All of it—from protesting orang-utans on the streets to Facebook status updates—has brought us to today's commitment. Congratulations and thank you to everyone who helped us get here—now go on and announce it to the world. Please boast about your involvement in the success of our Kit Kat campaign on Facebook and Twitter—or any of your other social network profiles—you deserve it!

Our goal remains the complete protection of Indonesia's rainforests and carbon-rich peatlands. We will be watching Nestlé closely to make sure it sticks to its word and puts them into action fast. We will also continue to investigate and expose unscrupulous palm oil and paper companies that destroy rainforests and to pressure the Indonesian government to act. In the meantime, today's new Nestlé "no deforestation footprint" policy is something to celebrate. We hope it will inspire action by other international companies—like Carrefour and Wal-mart—to hear our message that there is no room for forest destruction in the products we buy.

Let's celebrate our sweet success!

You deserve a huge round of applause for helping us get that well-deserved break for the orang-utan and for Indonesian rainforests! Do some online boasting.

("Sweet Success," 2010)

Reading Guide

1. If this situation is a crisis, what type of crisis is it?

2. What is the problem and the source(s) of the problem in this case?

3. What stakeholders should be interested in this case?

4. Who is Sinar Mas and what role does it play in the case?

5. What actions did Nestlé take that made people angry?

Discussion Questions

1. What is a condensation symbol, and why does it matter that orangutans were used in this case?

2. Are the efforts to restrict Sinar Mas as a supplier ethically justified?

3. What role did social media play in intensifying the situation?

4. What clear flaws were there in Nestlé's social media communication?

5. Why did Nestlé choose TFT as a partner and not Greenpeace when it decided to change its palm oil sourcing?

6. Why is timing such an important factor in this case?

7. How might threat assessment from contingency theory or ideas from paracrisis be useful in analyzing this case?

Websites

Responsible palm oil sourcing: http://www.rspo.org/?q=page/789

Sinar Mas: http://www.sinarmas.com/en/

SourceWatch critique of Sinar Mas: http://www.sourcewatch.org/index.php?title=Sinar_Mas

References

About. (n.d.). Retrieved from http://www.greenpeace.org/international/en/about/

Bhattacharya, C. B., Smith, N. C., & Palazzo, G. (2010). Marketing's consequences: Stakeholder marketing and supply chain CSR issues. *Business Ethics Quarterly, 20*(4), 617–641.

Caught red-handed: How Nestlé's use of palm oil is having a devastating impact on rainforests, the climate and orang-utans. (2010). http://www.greenpeace.org/international/en/publications/reports/caught-red-handed-how-nestle/

Coombs W. T., & Holladay, S. J. (2010). *Public relations strategy and application: Managing influence.* Malden, MA: Blackwell.

Crises planning: Prepare your company for social media attacks. (2010). Retrieved from http://www.web-strategist.com/blog/2010/03/22/prepare-your-company-now-for-social-attacks/

Cruel oil. (2005). Retrieved from http://www.cspinet.org/palmoilreport/PalmOilReport.pdf

Etlinger, S. (2010). Brand monitoring: What we can learn from the Nestle-Facebook crisis. Retrieved from http://horngroup.blogs.com/horn_group_weblog/2010/03/brand-monitoring-what-we-can-learn-from-the-nestlefacebook-crisis.html

Founders of Greenpeace. (2009). Retrieved from http://www.greenpeace.org/international/en/about/history/founders/

greenEnder. (2010). Retrieved from http://www.mizozo.com/world/03/2010/23/greenpeace-nestl-s-powerbar-kitkat-crunch-crisp-an....html

Greenpeace response to Nestlé's statement on sourcing Indonesian palm oil. (2010, March 17). Retrieved from http://www.greenpeace.org/usa/en/media-center/news-releases/greenpeace-response-to-nestle/

Heath, R. L., & Coombs, W. T. (2006). *Today's public relations: An introduction.* Thousand Oaks, CA: Sage.

History. (n.d.). Retrieved from http://www.nestle.com/AboutUs/History/Pages/History.aspx

Leonard, A. (2010). Nestle's brave Facebook flop. Retrieved from http://www.salon.com/news/social_media/index.html?story=/tech/htww/2010/03/19/nestle_s_brave_facebook_flop

Nestlé becomes TFT's newest member. (2010, May). Retrieved from http://www.tft-forests.org/news/item/?n=10303

Nestlé open forum on deforestation, Malaysia. (2010). Retrieved from http://www.nestle.com/Media/MediaEventsCalendar/ArchivedEvents/Pages/AllEvents.aspx?Name=2010-Nestle-open-forum-on-deforestation-Malaysia&Title=Nestl%C3%A9%20pen%20forum%20n%20deforestation,%20Malaysia&IsArchieved=true&EventYear=2010&PageName=2010.aspx

Our core values. (2006). Retrieved from http://www.greenpeace.org/international/en/about/our-core-values/

Palm oil, gift to nature, gift to life. (2007). Retrieved from http://americanpalmoil.com/publications/Brief%20Palm%200il%20Story.pdf

Palm oil: A global threat to rainforests. (2011). Retrieved from http://ran.org/content/problem-palm-oil

Raymond, D. (2003). Activism: Behind the banners. In S. John & S. Thomson (Eds.), *New activism and the corporate response* (pp. 207–225). New York, NY: Palgrave MacMillan.

Ridings, M. (2010). Take a look at what Nestle thinks a brand manager does. Retrieved from http://www.techguerilla.com/nestle-facebook-greenpeace-timeline-in-proces

Selamat, F. (2010). Nestle drops Indonesia's Sinar Mas as palm oil supplier. Retrieved from http://www.foxbusiness.com/story/markets/industries/retail/correct—nestle-drops-indonesias-sinar-mas-palm-oil-supplier/?utm_source=feedburner&utm_medium=feed&utm_campaign=Feed%3A+foxbusiness%2Flatest+%28Text+-+Latest+News%29&utm_content=Yahoo+Search+Results

6 painful social media screw-ups. (2011). Retrieved from http://money.cnn.com/galleries/2011/technology/1104/gallery.social_media_controversies/2.html

Sweet success for Kit Kat campaign: You asked, Nestlé has answered. (2010). Retrieved from http://www.greenpeace.org/international/en/news/features/Sweet-success-for-Kit-Kat-campaign/

Thomas, C. (2003). Cyberactivism and the corporations: New strategies for new media. In S. John & S. Thomson (Eds.), *New activism and the corporate response* (pp. 115–135). New York, NY: Palgrave MacMillan.

CHAPTER 9

Carrefour, China, and the Olympic Torch Relay

Carrefour, founded in 1958, is an international chain of hypermarkets based in Levalloius-Perret, France. Hypermarkets are a combination of supermarket and department store. The hypermarkets carry both groceries and other consumer goods, such as clothing and electronics. Carrefour opened the first hypermarket in Europe in June of 1963. Walmart is the largest chain of hypermarkets. Carrefour is the second largest retailer in the world by revenue. *Carrefour* is French for "crossroads" ("History," 2011). While little known in the United States, Carrefour is a major, global brand with a strong presence in Europe, Argentina, Brazil, China, Taiwan, Colombia, Dominican Republic, and Saudi Arabia. In 2008, Carrefour's efforts to expand its share of the Chinese market were well under way. It was an exciting time in China with the Summer Olympics being hosted by Beijing in 2008. But exciting times can bring both opportunity and threat.

Beijing was announced as host of the Summer Olympics in July of 2001. China was very excited given that they were the favorite to host the 2000 Summer Olympics, but in 1993, Sydney received the bid. There were lingering concerns among many on the Olympic selection committee about China's record of human rights and suppression of dissent (Riding, 1993). Hosting the Summer Olympics is a major public diplomacy victory for a country. The Olympics signal a country has arrived as a major actor on the world stage and generates favorable international media coverage for the host nation (Manheim, 1994). Hosting the Summer Olympics was a significant point of pride for the Chinese people and a chance for China to enhance its international reputation.

However, there were those who opposed China hosting any Olympic Games. Many human rights organizations were angered that China could host the Summer Olympics given its poor human rights record, including the occupation of Tibet. Human Rights Watch led the chorus of those opposed to Beijing hosting the

Summer Olympics. Protestors attacked all the top-level Summer Olympics sponsors, including Atos Origin, Coca-Cola, General Electric, Manulife, Johnson & Johnson, Kodak, Lenovo, McDonald's, Omega (Swatch Group), Panasonic, Samsung, and Visa. The protests were originally designed to pressure the Olympic Committee into changing its mind about allowing China to host the Summer Games, then shifted to increasing international visibility of China's human rights record ("Rights," 2008).

A tradition in the modern Olympic Games is to have the Olympic torch tour a number of countries. The idea is to share the Olympic spirit and to build anticipation for the games. The torch relay is a very symbolic event that begins with the torch being lit on Mount Olympus in Greece and culminates in the torch finally lighting the Olympic flame at the host city. It is a relay because a series of runners take turns carrying the torch. The 2008 Olympic Torch Relay would last 129 days and was labeled the *Journey of Harmony*. Unfortunately, the protestors knew they could not protest the games in China, so they created disharmony along many points, during the Journey of Harmony. Disharmony occurred in the United States, Australia, Japan, the United Kingdom, South Korea, and France. It was in France that the protests were the most intense. During the French leg, security had to be increased, the route was shortened, and at times, the torch was kept in the support van rather than being carried by a runner. The protestors were trying to extinguish the torch and actually accomplished that goal once in France. By attacking the torch, the protestors hoped to create awareness about Tibet and other Chinese human rights issues. It should be noted that the support van carries the true flame, so the Olympic flame was never really extinguished. This precaution is employed because the individual torches have been known to fail or to be extinguished by accident.

At the center of the torch protests was 27-year-old Jin Jing. Jin Jing is a Paralympic fencer who uses a wheelchair. When protesters tried to take the torch from her on April 7th, she fought them off until security could drag the protestors away from her. Jin became a hero in China for her valiant efforts. She was dubbed "the angel in the wheelchair" and praise for her could be found on Chinese television, in Chinese newspapers, and in online music video tributes (Graham-Harrison, 2008). Here is Jin's account of the events:

> When the second torchbearer was accepting the flame from the first, I was waiting at my position as the third torchbearer. At the time the security around me was relatively light, there were only a few police officers and three, maybe two, escort runners around me. Several Tibetan separatists and members of "Reporters without Borders" came over to protest.
>
> They began lunging towards me, trying to grab the torch from my hands. I tried to hide the torch with my body and managed to keep it from them. I was focused on the three or four separatists attacking me. I'm not sure how many were behind me. I felt people trying to take the torch from me. That's when some of the escort runners, as well as the tourist guide assigned to me in Paris, came over to help me, drawing the attackers away. People ask me how I dealt

with the danger. I don't think I thought too much about it. I trusted the escorts around me. They were the ones, along with my guide, that faced the danger. ("Interview," 2008)

The protestors were successful in drawing attention to calls for Tibet's independence and human rights issues in China because the international media flocked to cover the torch attacks. As one analyst of the torch protest noted, "The pro-Tibet protestors have managed to turn the Olympic torch processions in London and Paris into huge publicity stunts. They have gathered global media coverage for their cause" ("Olympic," 2008, para. 2).

The Chinese people were angered by the torch attacks (Graham-Harrison, 2008). Hosting the Olympics was a point of national pride, and the attack on the torch was viewed as an attack on China. The torch attacks stirred nationalistic feelings in China. Some Chinese citizens were angry and wanted to vent that anger. But France is thousands of miles away. How could the angry citizens strike back against the villainous French? The answer was to vent their anger on symbols of France that existed in China. Symbols of France include products and companies associated with France. After the torch attack, websites began appearing, calling for boycotts of French companies, such as Louis Vuitton and Carrefour. The boycott messages began to spread online and via mobile phones. Carrefour soon found itself at the center of the boycott because of its high visibility as a French company. In April of 2008, the web portal Netease.com conducted a poll about the boycott. Though unscientific, the poll had 43,000 respondents, and 95% supported the boycott of Carrefour ("Carrefour Charming Solution," 2008). The situation would get worse before it would get better for Carrefour.

It is important to consider the context leading up to the torch attacks in France. In the previous month, there had been protests in Tibet that drew negative international media from the efforts to end those protests. Moreover, French President Nicholas Sarkozy had suggested he might not attend the Summer Olympics due to concerns about human rights issues in China. The Chinese government has been actively using the news media to counter claims being made by Tibetan independence proponents (Matlack, 2008). There were heightened tensions about the Beijing Olympics prior to the torch attack in France.

The angry online comments and protest calls quickly morphed into two greater problems. First, the online messages became rumors that Carrefour and some of its investors supported Tibetan independence. Supporting an unpopular cause only increased the online anger flowing from China and focused additional negative attention on Carrefour. Second, the anger moved from the online world to the real world as Chinese citizens began demonstrating at Carrefour stores. Rumors occur when untrue information circulates about a person, product, or organization. Neither Carrefour nor any of its large investors supported pro-Tibetan independence groups, so the online information linking Carrefour and some of its large investors to Tibetan independence groups was a rumor. As the rumor spread, Carrefour began to deny the allegations that the company was linked to pro-Tibetan groups.

The rumor was actually two rumors. One rumor held that Carrefour itself was supporting pro-Tibetan independence groups ("Protest-Hit," 2008). The other rumor said a major Carrefour investor was funding pro-Tibetan independence groups. Here is an example of the latter rumor:

> "No one should shop at Carrefour, because the biggest shareholder of Carrefour donated huge money to the Dalai Lama, a lot of French people support the independence of Tibet, and even the French president has announced boycott of the Beijing Olympics," says the message (Liu, 2008, para. 2).

Online, people were urged to boycott Carrefour: "If you are a patriotic Chinese, forward this text message to your friends and family and do not shop at Carrefour" (Matlack, 2008, para. 3). The anger drove many Chinese citizens to move the protests from the online to the real world. As one protestor phrased it, "We want to let all foreigners know that China is very angry today. We have to let Chinese people in China know that we are united" (McDonald, 2008, para. 4). In Mid-April, protestors appeared at Carrefour stores in Beijing, Shanghai, Changsha, Fuzhou, Chongqing, and Shenyang (McDonald, 2008; "More," 2008). The number of protestors ranged from a few hundred to over a thousand. Carrefour also canceled its planned marketing efforts for the May 1 holiday. Carrefour seemed shocked by the protests and did not respond to the torch attack backlash for almost a week.

Carrefour China's vice president Gean Luc Lhuillier presented the initial Carrefour response at a press conference. He stated: "We and all our employees feel regretful about what happened in Paris and support the Beijing Olympics 100 percent" ("Carrefour China Reiterates," 2008, para. 2). Carrefour Chairman Jose Luis Duran echoed those sentiments:

> Obviously, recent sabotage incidents in Paris during the Olympic torch relay hurt feelings of the Chinese people, made them angry and triggered their protests. I hope that the preparations for the Olympics will be implemented with a harmonious atmosphere. The success of the Beijing Olympics will benefit all the people. ("Carrefour Supports," 2008, para. 6–7)

Later, Chairman Duran denied any Carrefour store provided financing to pro-Tibetan independence groups, saying, "These allegations are groundless. Carrefour and its branches have given no direct or indirect support to any political or religious group. Whether in China or anywhere else, Carrefour has never done these and will never do these" ("Carrefour Supports," 2008, para. 9–10). Vice president Lhuillier directly denied the Internet rumors linking Carrefour to pro-Tibet independence groups as well. Lhuillier stated, "Carrefour is innocent, but we understand the feeling of the Chinese people. . . . Carrefour never ever did and will not do anything concerned with politics and religion" ("Carrefour China Reiterates," 2008, para. 4).

The Chinese government found itself in a difficult position. The Chinese government had been defending its policies; thus, a nationalistic spirit was being cultivated in China. However, the anti-Carrefour boycotts were becoming a distraction from the Olympics. The international media were following the boycotts. Instead of positive news stories about the Olympics, there were stories about the protests that would mention the problems in Tibet. At first, there was little action taken by the Chinese government. As the protests lingered and larger protests were planned for the May 1st holiday, the government began to actively discourage the anti-Carrefour boycotts. First, the Chinese government requested that citizens switch to more positive displays of patriotism. Government editorials and statements asked people to display patriotism "rationally" (Lawrence, 2008). An example of a rational display of patriotism was to see that the games were a success and that "the best way to love your country is to do your job well" ("China Protests French," 2008, para. 20). Later, the Chinese government began deleting calls for boycotts from websites, and police turned people away from some proposed protest sites (Anderlinin, 2008; McDonald, 2008). The message was clear that the Chinese government no longer wanted any overt protests related to the torch attack.

One could argue that anger from torch protests would have dissipated on its own. However, crisis communication was used to hasten that dissipation. Carrefour had more at stake than some bad publicity and lost revenues from poor May 1, 2008, holiday sales. China remains a critical market for Carrefour. Carrefour had been operating in China since 1995, starting with a joint venture. In 2000, Carrefour had become the largest retailer in China by carefully cultivating its China market strategy. For instance, Carrefour considers China as a number of smaller markets rather than one large market. Moreover, Carrefour cultivates a sense of being local by stocking many items manufactured in China. In fact, some Chinese citizens did not join the anti-Carrefour boycott because the company bought locally and employed locally ("Chinese," 2008). Carrefour remained committed to growth in the China market, opening its 218th hypermarket in January of 2013 ("Carrefour China Opened," 2013). There have been past problems for Carrefour in China. In 2007, three customers in Chongqing were crushed to death when a cooking oil sale, during escalation of cooking oil prices, created a stampede ("Three," 2007). Two Carrefour executives were convicted of safety lapses and sentenced to jail (Buckley, 2010).

Carrefour's journey in China shows the dangers of globalization. Having a global footprint creates unexpected risks. Carrefour was drawn into a problematic situation through no fault of its own. The only reason Carrefour was a boycott and protest target was because the company was French. Not all risks are easy to identify in today's world.

A final contextual consideration in this case is postcolonial studies. Postcolonial studies represent a very broad concept, crossing a number of academic disciplines. A central aspect of postcolonial studies is trying to understand the social, political, and cultural effects on countries that have been ruled and exploited by colonial powers. In particular, the past colonization can impact current relationships between countries ("Introduction," n.d.). Postcolonialism has relevance for China and protests by Chinese citizens against corporations that represent past colonial powers.

The move to exploit the large market in China is not a modern phenomenon. In the 1800s, colonial powers in Europe, including France, established spheres of influence in China. Essentially, these spheres of influence were territories in China that were controlled by European powers. France had control over three southern provinces in China. Japan is another colonial power that controlled regions, starting in the 1930s ("Open," n.d.). In 2005 and 2012, there were large and often violent protests in China, targeting Japanese businesses (Pan, 2005). The protests in September of 2012 forced many Japanese businesses in China to close for a time and included such brand names as Panasonic, Honda, Toyota, and Sony ("China," 2012). Part of the current anger can be tied to previous exploitive behaviors by former colonizing agents.

Reading Guide

1. If this situation is a crisis, what type of crisis is it?

2. What is the problem and the source(s) of the problem in this case?

3. What stakeholders should be interested in this case?

4. Why does the Olympics play a major role in the case?

5. Who were the main actors engaging in communication in the case?

6. What role did technology play in the case?

Discussion Questions

1. Were the attacks on the Olympic torch ethical? Why or why not?

2. Could Carrefour have anticipated the attacks on them after the torch attack? Why or why not?

3. How ethical were the Chinese government's efforts to stop the online protest activities?

4. What did the Chinese government stand to lose in the case?

5. How credible was Carrefour's response to the situation?

6. What does this case tell us about the unpredictability of crises?

7. What does this case tell us about guilt by association?

8. How might postcolonial studies help crisis managers formulate a crisis response?

9. What crisis theory or principles might fit well with ideas from postcolonial studies?

Websites

Carrefour: http://www.carrefour.com/

YouTube video of Paris Olympic Torch Protest: http://www.youtube.com/watch?v=LxT_icmQiq4

British news story about protests over Tibet: http://www.telegraph.co.uk/sport/olympics/2525087/Beijing-Olympics-Protests-around-the-world-as-Games-open-in-style.html

References

Anderlinin, J. (2008). China moves to rein in Carrefour protestors. Retrieved from http://www.ft.com/intl/cms/s/0/c03f9250–173b-11dd-ae27–0000779fd2ac.html#axzz1eAzeWHag

Buckley, C. (2010). China Carrefour managers jailed for deadly stampede. Retrieved from http://www.reuters.com/article/idUSL555655120081106

Carrefour: Charming solution. (2008). Retrieved from http://www.carrefour.com/search/site/Charming%2520Solution

Carrefour China opened 3 new stores. (2013). Retrieved from http://www.carrefour.com/current-news/carrefour-china-opened-3-new-stores

Carrefour China reiterates support for Beijing Olympics. (2008, April 29). Retrieved from http://www.china.org.cn/olympics/news/2008–04/29/content_15031311.htm

Carrefour supports Beijing Olympics. (2008). Retrieved from http://www.chinadaily.com.cn/olympics/2008-04/23/content_6638543

China protests French retailer Carrefour. (2008). Retrieved from http://www.msnbc.msn.com/id/24218173/

China protests: Japanese firms suspend some operations. (2012). Retrieved from http://www.bbc.co.uk/news/business-19620114

Chinese netizens calling on boycott of Carrefour in wake of troubled Olympic torch relay. (2008). Retrieved from http://josieliu.blogspot.com/2008/04/chinese-netizens-calling-on-boycott-of.html

Graham-Harrison, E. (2008). Disabled torch bearer becomes Chinese hero. Retrieved from http://abcnews.go.com/International/story?id=4634434&page=1

History. (2011). Retrieved from http://www.carrefour.com/content/presentation-group

Interview with torch bearer Jin Jing. (2008, April 7). Retrieved from http://torchrelay.beijing2008.cn/en/torchbearers/headlines/n214299940.shtml

Introduction to postcolonial studies. (n.d.). Retrieved from http://www.bbc.co.uk/news/business-19620114

Lawrence, D. (2008). Carrefour boycott had China reining in supporters. Retrieved from http://www.bloomberg.com/apps/news?pid=newsarchive&sid=aw1fsXdRYEvU&refer=asia

Liu, J. (2008). Guest blogger: Chinese netizens call for boycott of Carrefour. Retrieved from http://chinadigitaltimes.net/2008/04/chinese-netizens-calling-on-boycott-of-carrefour-in-the-wake-of-troubled-olympic-torch-rely-josie-liu/

McDonald, J. (2008). Protests target Carrefour stores in China. Retrieved from http://www.usatoday.com/news/world/2008–05–01–3419792923_x.htm

Manheim, J. B. (1994). Strategic public diplomacy & American foreign policy: The evolution of influence. New York, NY: Oxford University Press.

Matlack, C. (2008). France's Carrefour feels China's ire. Retrieved from http://www.businessweek.com/globalbiz/content/apr2008/gb20080422_316128.htm

More protests erupt at China Carrefour stores. (2008). Retrieved from http://goldsea.com/805/01carrefour.html

Olympic torch tour as public relations disaster. (2008). Retrieved from http://www.zonaeuropa.com/20080410_1.htm

Open door policy. (n.d.). Retrieved from http://www.britannica.com/EBchecked/topic/429642/Open-Door-policy

Pan, P. P. (2005). Japan-China talks fail to ease tensions. Retrieved from http://www.bbc.co.uk/news/business-19620114

Protest-hit, Carrefour cancels China sales (2008). Retrieved from http://www.reuters.com/article/2008/04/25/us-china-carrefour-idUSPEK37001320080425

Riding, A. (1993, September 24). Olympics: 2000 Olympics to Sydney in surprise setback for China. Retrieved from http://www.nytimes.com/1993/09/24/sports/olympics-2000-olympics-go-to-sydney-in-surprise-setback-for-china.html

Rights group decries Olympic sponsors. (2008). Retrieved from http://www.upi.com/Top_News/2008/08/19/Rights-group-decries-Olympic-sponsors/UPI-99351219195808/

Three die in China sale stampede. (2007). Retrieved from http://news.bbc.co.uk/2/hi/asia-pacific/7088718.stm

CHAPTER 10

Sparboe Farms and McDonald's Part Company Over Animal Cruelty

When the British were building their global empire, they exported part of their culture to their colonies. One of those exports was the "full breakfast." In most English-speaking locales, the full breakfast features eggs and bacon. Of course, the full breakfast is localized to include aspects of the local culture (Lemm, n.d.). In the United States, McDonald's fused the full breakfast with America's love for fast food to create the Egg McMuffin. The Egg McMuffin is a portable full breakfast. The basic Egg McMuffin is an egg, bacon, cheese, and a muffin. Of course, you can also get one with sausage, only sausage, and a few other variations if you prefer. The Egg McMuffin is a popular breakfast item in the United States and many other countries. In the United States, you could even say the Egg McMuffin is iconic—a well-known sign.

In November of 2011, McDonald's announced it was dropping the egg supplier that provided most of the eggs for the Egg McMuffins west of the Mississippi River. Such a change is major news because of the iconic nature of the Egg McMuffin and the size of the contract. The reason for the contract change was not food safety. It was animal welfare. The supplier, Sparboe Farms, was the subject of a news story that was about to air on two ABC news shows, *20/20* and *World News with Diane Sawyer*. The reports were documenting abuse of chickens at a Sparboe Farm facility. The report was built around undercover video provided by the animal rights activist group Mercy For Animals (Galli, Hill, & Momtaz, 2011; Reddy, 2011). Parts of the McDonald's announcement are located In Exhibit 10.1.

Exhibit 10.1 McDonald's Announces Dropping Sparboe as a Supplier

McDonald's Statement on Dropping Sparboe Farms as an Egg Supplier

"McDonald's expects all of our suppliers to meet our stringent requirements for delivering high quality food prepared in a humane and responsible manner. Based upon recent information, we have informed our direct supplier, Cargill, that we are no longer accepting eggs from its supplier, Sparboe. This decision is based on McDonald's and Cargill's concern regarding the management of Sparboe's facilities."

("McDonald's," 2011, para. 1)

"Regarding the undercover videos, the behavior on tape is disturbing and completely unacceptable. McDonald's wants to assure our customers that we demand humane treatment of animals by our suppliers. We take this responsibility—along with our customers' trust—very seriously. It's important to note that the most alarming actions on video did not occur at Sparboe's Vincent, Iowa facility that supplies McDonald's. Nonetheless, our extremely high standards for our suppliers prohibit this conduct."

("McDonald's," 2011, para. 4)

"McDonald's cares about how our food is sourced and we have a long history of action and commitment to improve the welfare of animals in our supply chain. We are a founding member of the Coalition for Sustainable Egg Supply (CSES) and are participating in an unprecedented three-year study that compares traditional, cage-free, and enriched laying hen housing systems on a commercial scale. For our customers, that means we're working with scientists and suppliers to determine the most optimal hen housing method considering impacts on hen health & welfare, food safety, environment, and other important factors."

("McDonald's," 2011, para. 5)

The story seemed to break very suddenly. However, common in investigative journalism, the target knew about the story well in advance. Both Sparboe and McDonald's were aware the story was being developed and the general content of the story to be aired on November 18, 2011. Moreover, McDonald's had been under pressure from Mercy For Animals to drop Sparboe Farms as a supplier due to the animal cruelty at the supplier.

Mercy For Animals had created a website titled "McDonald's Cruelty" that documented the terrible ways that chickens were being abused at Sparboe Farms. The centerpiece of the website was the undercover video that members of Mercy For Animals filmed while they worked at Sparboe Farm facilities in Iowa, Minnesota, and Colorado. Here is a description of what the undercover video found:

- Hens crammed into filthy wire cages with less space for each bird than a standard-sized sheet of paper to live her entire miserable life, unable to fully stretch her wings or engage in most other natural behaviors

- Workers burning off the beaks of young chicks without any painkillers and callously throwing them into cages, some missing the cage doors and hitting the floor
- Workers grabbing hens by their throats and ramming them into battery cages
- Rotted hens, decomposed beyond recognition as birds, left in cages with hens still laying eggs for human consumption
- A worker tormenting a bird by swinging her around in the air while her legs were caught in a grabbing device—violence described as "torture" by another worker
- A worker shoving a bird into the pocket of another employee without any regard for the animal's fear and suffering
- Chicks trapped and mangled in cage wire—others suffering from open wounds and torn beaks
- Live chicks thrown into plastic bags to be suffocated ("New," 2011, para. 3–10).

In addition to the inhumane treatment, Mercy For Animals is opposed to the battery cage method of raising chickens. Battery cages are crammed with chickens and are considered to be an inhumane and unhealthy way for chickens to live by many groups. Farms are often composed of hundreds to thousands of cages filled with chickens. Organizations such as Whole Foods and Subway had already prohibited eggs from producers using the battery cage method.

McDonald's was the target because of its purchasing power. As Mercy For Animals explains on the website,

> As the largest egg purchaser in the United States, McDonald's has enormous power in effecting improved standards of care for egg-laying hens. Accordingly, MFA is also asking that McDonald's actively support a recent agreement between the United Egg Producers and The Humane Society of the United States that seeks to establish federal regulations that would provide hens enough space to turn around, as well as environmental enrichments, such as perches and nesting boxes. The agreement is a modest but important first step in establishing minimal standards for care of birds on a federal level. Sadly, Sparboe Egg Farms is aggressively opposing the implementation of even these meager reforms to reduce animal suffering. ("New," 2011, para. 16)

McDonald's did not like being drawn into the negative publicity surrounding animal cruelty (Galli et al., 2011; Reddy, 2011). Crises can vary in their degree of symbolic impact—how much emotion the topic generates among stakeholders. The symbolic impact of animal cruelty is high; thus, it is not surprising that McDonald's severed its connection to Sparboe Farms before the animal cruelty video appeared on television. McDonald's was distancing itself from Sparboe Farms before most of its stakeholders were aware of the animal cruelty problems.

In addition to animal cruelty, the news stories about the contract cancellation noted the Food and Drug Administration (FDA) had sent Sparboe Farms a Warning Letter about multiple health violations at a number of its egg farms.

The Warning Letter can be found at the end of the case. Here is the FDA's explanation of a Warning Letter:

When FDA finds that a manufacturer has significantly violated FDA regulations, FDA notifies the manufacturer. This notification is often in the form of a Warning Letter.

The Warning Letter identifies the violation, such as poor manufacturing practices, problems with claims for what a product can do, or incorrect directions for use. The letter also makes clear that the company must correct the problem and provides directions and a timeframe for the company to inform FDA of its plans for correction. FDA then checks to ensure that the company's corrections are adequate. ("What," n.d., para. 1–2)

An FDA Warning Letter is a serious concern. Sparboe Farms was not just facing a horrifying undercover video expose but pressure from the FDA to improve its operations. The complete FDA Warning Letter text can be found in Exhibit 10.2.

Exhibit 10.2   FDA Warning Letter

Sparboe Farms / Prairie Complex 11/16/11

Department of Health and Human Services Public Health Service, Food and Drug Administration, Minneapolis District Office, Central Region

November 16, 2011

WARNING LETTER, Via UPS Overnight

Refer to MIN 12–09

Beth Sparboe Schnell, Owner

Dear Ms. Schnell:

The United States Food and Drug Administration (FDA) inspected your shell egg production facilities located at:

1140 Timber Drive, Goodell, IA 50439 on April 25–29, 2011 (Inspection 1); 65018 U.S. Highway 12, Litchfield, MN 55355 on April 25-May 5, 2011 (Inspection 2); 6339 Weld County Road 47, Hudson, CO 80642 on May 9–12, 2011 (Inspection 3); 2088 120th Street, Humboldt, IA 50548 on June 20–21, 2011 (Inspection 4); and 1979 Iowa Avenue, Britt, IA 50423 on July 20–22, 2011 (Inspection 5).

We found that the above-listed facilities have serious violations of the Prevention of Salmonella Enteritidis (SE) in Shell Eggs During Production, Storage, and Transportation regulation (the shell egg regulation), Title 21, Code of Federal Regulations, Part 118 (21 CFR 118). The failure to adequately implement the requirements in 21 CFR 118 causes your shell eggs to be in violation of section 361(a) of the Public Health Service Act (the "PHS Act"), Title 42, U.S.C. section 264(a). In addition, these violations render your shell eggs adulterated within the meaning of section 402(a)(4) of the Federal

Food, Drug, and Cosmetic Act (the "FFD&C Act"), 21 U.S.C. section 342(a)(4), in that they have been prepared, packed, or held under insanitary conditions whereby they may have become contaminated with filth, or whereby they may have been rendered injurious to health. You can find the FFD&C Act, the PHS Act, and the shell egg regulation through links on FDA's home page at www.fda.gov.

The significant violations, with references to each specific farm, are as follows:

1. You failed to have and implement a written SE prevention plan that is specific to each farm where you produce eggs, as required by 21 CFR 118.4. Specifically, your written SE prevention plans obtained during Inspection 1 in Goodell, IA, Inspection 2 in Litchfield, MN, Inspection 3 in Hudson, CO, Inspection 4 in Humboldt, IA, and Inspection 5 in Britt, IA, are not specific to each farm.

2. You induced molt in a flock but then failed to perform environmental testing for SE in the poultry house at four to six weeks after the end of the molting process as required by 21 CFR 118.5(b). Specifically, during Inspection 2 in Litchfield, MN, investigators noted that you failed to environmentally test the poultry house (house #(b)(4) four to six weeks after the end of the molting process. Your written response dated May 25, 2011, states that your SE prevention plan calls for environmental testing four to six weeks after the end of the molting process; however, you did not provide any records to demonstrate that environmental testing did, in fact, take place in this circumstance. To the extent that you are asserting that environmental testing was performed four to six weeks after the end of the molting process in the poultry house (house #(b)(4), you are required under 21 CFR 118.10(a)(3)(vi) to maintain records documenting the results of the SE testing that is required by 21 CFR 118.5.

3. You failed to use appropriate methods to achieve satisfactory rodent control when monitoring indicated unacceptable rodent activity within a poultry house, as required by 21 CFR 118.4(c)(1).

• During Inspection 1 at Goodell, IA, it was noted that when your monitoring indicated unacceptable rodent activity, appropriate measures were not used to achieve satisfactory rodent control. Specifically, your Biosecurity Program and Procedures Manual Version #4, dated September 2009, states the rodent index should be lower than (b)(4). A review of the records for the previous ten months (June 2010-April 2011) found the rodent index exceeded (b)(4) on most of the dates when it was calculated; however, your records indicate that neither your firm nor your contracted pest control company took remedial action to achieve satisfactory rodent control. Your written response dated May 18, 2011, stated that a rodent index of (b)(4) was "a goal, not the starting point for our evaluation," and that adjustments on the rodent control index have been done based on historical trends for the Goodell facility with a new rodent index of (b)(4). However, your response did not indicate that you had concluded that a rodent index of (b)(4) represents an acceptable level of rodent activity, nor did it indicate any basis for such a conclusion. Changing threshold levels to reflect historical levels of rodents is not an acceptable correction. You are required to use appropriate methods to achieve satisfactory rodent control when your monitoring indicates unacceptable rodent activity.

- During Inspection 2 at Litchfield, MN, it was noted that your Biosecurity Program and Procedures Manual Version #4, dated September 2009, states the rodent index should be lower than (b)(4). Between July 9, 2010, and April 22, 2011, the rodent index continuously ranged from (b)(4)((b)(4) rodents caught) to (b)(4) ((b)(4) rodents caught), which exceeded your rodent index of (b)(4) and thus required corrective action according to the pest control section of your firm's SE prevention plan. However, no corrective actions were taken to achieve satisfactory rodent control. Your written response dated May 25, 2011, stated that you will change the rodent index threshold level at which you will take corrective action. However, your response did not indicate what your revised rodent index threshold level would be, nor did it indicate that the revised rodent index would reflect an acceptable level of rodent activity. Changing threshold levels in light of historical levels of rodents is not an acceptable correction. You are required to use appropriate methods to achieve satisfactory rodent control when your monitoring indicates unacceptable rodent activity.

- During Inspection 4 at Humboldt, IA, it was noted that your SE plan stated that action would be taken if a rodent index of (b)(4) was reached. Your rodent monitoring logs indicated that the rodent index exceeded (b)(4) on June 14, 2011 (houses #(b)(4)), May 31, 2011 (houses #(b)(4)), May 24, 2011 (house #(b)(4), May 17, 2011 (house (b)(4) and May 10, 2011 (house #(b)(4). However, no corrective actions were documented. Your written response dated July 12, 2011, stated that in the future, corrective actions will be implemented at a rodent index of (b)(4). We note that, at the time of the inspection, your SE plan stated that you follow FDA's Industry Guidance for rodent indexing. This statement is in conflict with your threshold of a rodent index of (b)(4) which is not consistent with FDA's Draft Guidance for Industry: Prevention of Salmonella Enteritidis in Shell Eggs During Production, Storage, and Transportation, which we believe to be the Industry Guidance that is referenced in your SE plan. Please note that whatever monitoring method you use, you are required to use appropriate methods to achieve satisfactory rodent control when your monitoring indicates unacceptable rodent activity.

- During Inspection 5 at Britt, IA, it was noted that when monitoring indicated unacceptable rodent activity, appropriate methods were not used to achieve satisfactory rodent control. Specifically, on November 2, 2010, you recorded a rodent index of (b)(4) for house #(b)(4). Although your SE plan as of November 2, 2010, did not require action at any rodent index level, your Britt Complex Manager acknowledged during the inspection that a rodent index of (b)(4) indicated a problem that needed to be addressed. However, your records indicate that no action was taken to address this unacceptable rodent activity.

4. You failed to remove vegetation and debris outside a poultry house that may provide harborage for pests, as required by 21 CFR 118.4(c)(3). Specifically, during Inspection 5 at Britt, IA, FDA investigators observed a pile of lumber between houses #(b)(4) as well as thick grass standing approximately 4.5 feet tall between houses #(b)(4) FDA investigators observed a rodent run out from under the pile of lumber.

5. You failed to have and implement a written SE prevention plan that includes an appropriate monitoring method for flies and you failed to use appropriate methods to

achieve satisfactory fly control when monitoring indicated unacceptable fly activity within a poultry house as required by 21 CFR 118.4(c)(2).

- During Inspection 1 in Goodell, IA, it was noted that, though you use fly cards for monitoring, an unacceptable level of fly activity had not been determined and was not addressed in the Salmonella Prevention Program or your firm's procedures as required under 21 CFR 118.4(c)(2). In your written response dated May 18, 2011, you stated that you updated the Goodell SE Prevention Program to specify fly monitoring activity and set a threshold with corrective actions when those are reached. However, your written response did not indicate what the threshold is for unacceptable fly activity, nor did it indicate what the corrective actions are.

- During Inspection 2 in Litchfield, MN, it was noted that your SE prevention plan references your Biosecurity Program and Procedure Manual #4, which requires fly control procedures in writing; however, there are no written procedures for monitoring of flies and you do not determine if fly activity is acceptable or unacceptable, as required under 21 CFR 118.4(c)(2). Your written response dated May 25, 2011, stated that you will include a written Fly Control Program with threshold levels and take corrective actions when necessary. However, your response did not indicate what the threshold levels will be or what the corrective actions will be.

- During Inspection 5 in Britt, IA, it was noted that the presence of flies is not monitored by appropriate monitoring methods as required under 21 CFR 118.4(c)(2). Specifically, your fly index action level of (b)(4) is based on historical levels of flies, as opposed to being based on a determination of what level of fly activity is unacceptable.

6. You failed to procure pullets that are SE monitored or to raise pullets under SE monitored conditions, as required by 21 CFR 118.4(a). Specifically, you failed to comply with the requirement in 21 CFR 118.4(a)(2) that the pullet environment be tested for SE when pullets are 14 to 16 weeks of age, and that you have and implement a written SE plan that calls for such testing. You also failed to maintain records documenting that pullets were raised under SE monitored conditions, as required by 21 CFR 118.10(a)(2).

- During Inspection 2 in Litchfield, MN, it was noted that house #(b)(4) was populated on or around February 12, 2011, with pullets that were never environmentally monitored. Your written response dated May 25, 2011, states that you will revise your SE prevention plan to state that "pullets" (which we understand to mean the pullet environment) will be tested for SE when pullets are between 14 and 16 weeks of age. We will verify this correction at our next inspection.

- During Inspection 4 in Humboldt, IA, it was noted that house #(b)(4) was populated on or about September 26, 2010, with pullets that were never environmentally monitored. We acknowledge that, during the course of Inspection 4, you corrected your SE plan to call for pullet environment testing at 14–16 weeks.

- Your SE prevention plan for all five farms stated that environmental sampling of pullets is done at 12 weeks of age. Your written response dated May 25, 2011, stated that corrective actions were being implemented for all pullet flocks to be environmentally monitored between 14 to 16 weeks of age; however, FDA observed that the SE prevention plans of the farms that were subsequently inspected had not been revised to reflect this correction. We acknowledge that during Inspection 4 in Humboldt, IA, you corrected that farm's SE prevention plan in the presence of FDA investigators to call for pullet environment testing at 14–16 weeks.

• During Inspection 2 in Litchfield, MN, your records indicated that two of your poultry houses had been populated with pullets that were environmentally monitored when they were approximately 19 weeks of age. Your written response dated May 25, 2011, stated that you do not test any of your pullets at 19 weeks of age, and that pullets at this age are already at the layer facility. Your response seems to indicate that a recordkeeping error had been made. Under 21 CFR 118.10(a)(2), you must maintain records documenting that pullets were raised under SE monitored conditions, including environmental testing records for pullets.

7. You failed to maintain practices that will protect against cross-contamination when persons move between poultry houses as required by 21 CFR 118.4(b)(3). Specifically, during Inspection 1 in Goodell, IA, management stated that employees move between SE-positive houses and SE-negative houses without taking precautions that would prevent cross-contamination, and FDA investigators found that your SE prevention practices failed to address cross-contamination from personnel movement between poultry houses. Your written response dated May 18, 2011, stated that personnel working at Goodell will institute immediately a new series of steps to ensure all precautions have been taken to prevent cross-contamination between SE-positive and SE-negative houses including powder foot baths and hand sanitizers when exiting SE positive houses. You further stated that this correction had been included in the updated Goodell SE Prevention Program. We will verify this correction at our next inspection.

8. You failed to prevent stray poultry, wild birds, cats, and other animals from entering poultry houses as required by 21 CFR 118.4(b)(4).

• During Inspection 1 in Goodell, IA, a wild bird was observed in house #(b)(4). Bent, broken, or separated bird netting was observed in five of the poultry houses, and broken louvers were observed on ventilation fans in one house. Your written response dated May 18, 2011, stated that all bird netting to prevent the introduction of wild birds and all louvers on ventilation fans would be immediately repaired. We will verify these corrections at our next inspection.

• During Inspection 3 in Hudson, CO, a hole was observed in the bird netting located along the northwest corner eave of layer house #(b)(4) South. The hole measured approximately 48 inches in length and 24 inches in width. We acknowledge that the hole was repaired during the course of the inspection.

9. You failed to sample the environment using a sampling plan appropriate to the poultry house layout as required by 21 CFR 118.7(a). Specifically, at all five of your facilities you did not sample your manure pits, though they appeared to be accessible and were, in fact, accessed by FDA during Inspection 1 (Goodell, IA) and Inspection 2 (Litchfield, MN, where FDA's environmental sampling found the presence of SE, as discussed below). Instead of sampling your manure pits, you sampled (b)(4). Additionally,

at Goodell, IA, you only sampled from the (b)(4). Your written response dated May 18, 2011, stated that Goodell's updated SE Prevention Program "has addressed the sampling method and follows FDA August 2010 guidelines and provided an optimal method in case manure sampling cannot be accomplished." We will verify this correction at our next inspection.

10. You failed to maintain records documenting rodent and other pest control measures as required by 21 CFR 118.10(a)(3)(ii). Specifically, during Inspection 3 in Hudson, CO, FDA investigators found that, as of May 9, 2011, you had not maintained any fly monitoring documentation. We acknowledge that your Production Manager stated that documentation began during the course of the inspection, and one monitoring log was provided. We will verify your continued compliance at our next inspection.

11. You failed to include the date and time of the activities reflected in your records, as required by 21 CFR 118.10(b)(2). Specifically, during Inspection 5 in Britt, IA, FDA investigators observed that your House Fly Activity Log, your Fly Control Logs, and your Rodent Index Monitoring Records did not document the times of the activities that the records reflect. We acknowledge that during the course of the inspection, you revised your House Fly Activity Log and your Fly Control Logs to include a space to record the time of the activity. We will verify your corrective actions at our next inspection.

12. You failed to provide the location of your farm on all of your required records, as required by 21 CFR 118.10(b)(1). Specifically, during Inspection 3 in Hudson, CO, records related to rodent monitoring and refrigeration monitoring did not contain the location of your farm.

13. You failed to include in your required records the signature or initials of the person performing the operation or creating the record, as required by 21 CFR 118.10(b)(3). Specifically, during Inspection 4 in Humboldt, IA, rodent monitoring logs did not have the signature or initials of the person performing the operation. Your written response dated July 12, 2011, stated that the Humboldt SE Prevention Program has made the appropriate correction for the Rodent Control Representative to initial or sign the monitoring records. We will verify this correction at our next inspection.

This letter is not intended to be an all-inclusive list of your firm's violations. You are responsible for ensuring that your shell egg production facility operates in compliance with all applicable statutes and regulations, including the FFD&C Act, the PHS Act, and the shell egg regulation. You also have a responsibility to use procedures to prevent further violations of the applicable statutes and regulations.

You should take prompt action to correct the violations cited in this letter. Failure to promptly correct these violations may result in FDA taking regulatory action without further notice, such as seizure, injunction, or the initiation of administrative enforcement procedures under 21 CFR 118.12(a).

In addition to the above violations, we also have the following comments:

• Under 21 CFR 118.8(a), you must conduct testing to detect SE in environmental samples using the method entitled "Environmental Sampling and Detection of Salmonella in Poultry Houses," April 2008, or an equivalent method in accuracy, precision, and sensitivity in detecting SE. At the time of these inspections, your SE prevention plan for all five of your farms required environmental sampling in your high-rise style layer houses of (b)(4) with (b)(4). This method has not been recognized by FDA as being equivalent to the method entitled "Environmental Sampling and Detection of Salmonella in Poultry Houses," April 2008. We acknowledge that your latest written response dated July 12, 2011 (Humboldt, IA), states that the revised (July 1, 2011) version of your SE prevention plan calls for "appropriate FDA-approved sampling materials for environmental sampling procedures." If you are continuing to use a method that differs from the method specified in 21 CFR 118.8(a) and that has not been recognized by FDA as being equivalent to that method, we encourage you to submit documentation to FDA that will allow the agency to make a determination regarding equivalency.

- Additionally, FDA environmental sampling conducted at Litchfield, MN, (Inspection 2) indicated the presence of Salmonella enteriditis in poultry houses #(b)(4) We acknowledge that, upon being notified of these findings, you initiated egg testing in keeping with 21 CFR 118.6, the results of which have all been negative.

Within 15 working days of receipt of this letter, you should notify this office in writing of the specific steps that you have taken to correct the above violations and prevent their recurrence. Include an explanation of each step being taken to correct the violations and prevent their recurrence, as well as copies of related documentation. If you cannot complete corrective action within 15 working days, state the reason for the delay and the time within which you will complete the corrections.

Please send your reply to the Food and Drug Administration, Attention [. . .], at the address in the above letterhead. If you have questions regarding any issues in this letter, please contact Ms. Wisecup at [. . .].

Sincerely,

/S/

Elizabeth A. Waltrip

Acting Director

Minneapolis District

("Sparboe Farms/Prairie," 2011)

Investigative reports are unique crises in that the organization knows exactly when the crisis will hit. Sparboe Farms had time to prepare for the ABC news stories. Sparboe Farms crafted a part of its website designed to address the animal cruelty and the FDA Warning Letter. The centerpiece of Sparboe Farm's response was a statement by its president, Beth Sparboe Schnell. There was a video of her statement on the website along with a letter from her. Here are excerpts from the letter:

> I was deeply saddened to see the story because this isn't who Sparboe Farms is. Acts depicted in the footage are totally unacceptable and completely at odds

with our values as egg farmers. In fact, they are in direct violation of our animal care code of conduct, which all of our employees read, sign and follow each day. ("Letter," 2011, para. 2)

Upon learning of the video, Sparboe Farms launched a comprehensive internal investigation. We have completed many interviews and reviewed audits, records and training documents. We have identified four employees who were complicit in this disturbing activity and they have been terminated. Management changes have taken place, and our investigation is ongoing. We will hold any others involved accountable for their actions. We are documenting all corrective actions taken. ("Letter," 2011, para. 3)

For 57 years, the Sparboe family and hundreds of dedicated employees have worked hard every day to properly care for our chickens so they will produce well for thousands of loyal customers whom, in turn, will provide American families with safe, nutritious, affordable eggs. Our company has long been an industry leader in food safety and supports scientific research for improvements to hen well-being. That is why the video footage and media coverage is so shocking. ("Letter," 2011, para. 6–7)

The website also provided detailed information about Sparboe Farm's certification by the U.S. Department of Agriculture, health and safety efforts, animal care guidelines, and FDA egg safety rules. There was also a timeline of the events surrounding the investigation. A version of that timeline is found in Exhibit 10.3.

Exhibit 10.3   Sparboe Farms Timeline

Timeline for Sparboe Exposé and Response

November 1st: ABC news notifies Sparboe Farms about allegations of animal abuse and requests comment. Sparboe launches an internal audit and requests details from ABC News.

November 3rd: Sparboe requests information from ABC News again while its audit continues.

November 4th: ABC News gives Sparboe still pictures from video clips. Sparboe requests more video from ABC News and begins examining the pictures to determine who was in violation of its own codes of conduct.

November 5th: Another request is made for video from ABC News.

November 6th: Sparboe internal investigation team meets and plans its actions.

November 7th: ABC supplies some video clips to Sparboe. The internal team goes to the sites they have identified so far from the material supplied by ABC.

November 8th: Third party audit is initiated at the suspected operations. The employees in the videos are identified and fired. A request is made for additional video from ABC News.

November 9th: The internal team continues employee interviews and terminates those employees found to be involved in the abuse. Sparboe Farms gives a statement to ABC News.

November 10th: The audit results show Sparboe Farms is in full compliance with animal welfare policies.

An ABC news crew is allowed into the Sparboe facility to film for the segment. ABC News acknowledges that Mercy For Animals is their source for the undercover video.

November 11th: Sparboe tells all of its employees about the continuing investigation and potential for media coverage.

November 13th: Retraining efforts begin for all barn workers.

November 14th: Sparboe Farms reiterates to employees that there is a confidential hotline for calling in concerns anonymously. The hotline includes reporting violations of animal welfare policies. ABC News tells Sparboe to direct requests for additional video to Mercy For Animals.

November 15th: Sparboe sends a written request to Mercy For Animals for all recordings (see "Sparboe Farms Update," 2012, Timeline of Responses section, para. 1–15).

November 16th: "FDA's Minneapolis District Office issues warning letter recapping violations found during inspections conducted between April 25 and July 22 at five Sparboe Farms. Sparboe responded to each 483 within 15 days as required, documenting immediate implementation of corrective actions." (*"Sparboe Farms Update," 2012, Most Recent Activity section*, para. 20)

November 17th: "In a conference call with the FDA, Sparboe learned that some of the corrective actions taken related to 483s were insufficient. Immediate steps were initiated to rectify." (*"Sparboe Farms Update," 2012, Most Recent Activity section*, para. 19)

November 18th: "In addition to the four employees already fired, management changes have taken place, and our investigation is ongoing." *("Sparboe Farms Update,"* 2012, Most Recent Activity section, *para. 18)*

("Sparboe Farms Update," 2012)

On November 19, 2011, Sparboe Farms took its response action a step further. Sparboe Farms announced it would create a task force that would find ways to increase the company's animal care and food safety. Here is the opening statement from the announcement:

Sparboe Farms announced today that it is creating a Sustainability Task Force that is charged with reviewing all current company practices in the areas of food safety, animal care and sustainability. The task force will also develop additional best practices in those areas for all of the company's production and processing facilities.

Beth Sparboe Schnell, president and owner of Sparboe Farms, said she decided to take the additional step of creating a Sustainability Task Force "so that we can make our company better." ("Sparboe Farms Creates," 2011, para. 1–2)

The announcement also restated that Sparboe Farms had conducted an internal investigation and terminated the four employees found to be in violation of the company's animal care code of conduct. Sparboe also reminded people that the FDA Warning Letter had been addressed and that the situation was animal cruelty and at no time was there a threat to public health.

This case is a further illustration of how companies are connected to and held accountable for the actions of their suppliers. Organizations can be quick to sever ties with a supplier if there are questions about that supplier's behavior or policies. McDonald's is in a unique position because it is the market leader in the fast-food industry. Any time stakeholders take issue with what are deemed irresponsible behaviors, the market leader is the first to feel the stakeholder wrath. Consider how Nike was targeted for sweatshop concerns in the apparel industry in the 1990s. McDonald's may be more sensitive to stakeholder concerns because of its leadership position. Moreover, McDonald's has made public commitments to a sustainable supply chain in its sustainability messages. Consider this passage from McDonald's own discussion of suppliers:

> **Ethics**—We envision purchasing from suppliers that follow practices that ensure the health and safety of their employees and the welfare and humane treatment of animals in our supply chain. ("Our," 2012, para. 2)

McDonald's was risking a backlash from stakeholders if it did not act on the exposé of Sparboe Farms and animal cruelty.

Reading Guide

1. If this situation is a crisis, what type of crisis is it?

2. What is the problem and the source(s) of the problem in this case?

3. What stakeholders should be interested in this case?

4. What organizations are involved in the case?

5. What is an FDA warning letter?

Discussion Questions

1. Why is Sparboe Farms receiving an FDA warning letter important to this case?

2. What conclusions do you reach about Sparboe Farms' practices after reading the government statements?

3. What assets are Sparboe Farms trying to leverage in their response?

4. How would you justify McDonald's "quick" decision to cut ties with Sparboe Farms?

5. Was it fair to target McDonald's in this campaign? Justify your answer.

6. What makes the animal cruelty label so powerful for stakeholders?

7. How might the rhetorical arena be useful in this crisis? What theories or principles could be coupled with the rhetorical arena to gain insights into this crisis communication effort?

8. What, if anything, could Sparboe Farms have done to protect itself more effectively in this crisis?

Websites

"McDonald's Cruelty": http://mcdonaldscruelty.com/

Sparboe Farms: http://sparboe.com/

FDA Warning Letter: http://www.fda.gov/ICECI/EnforcementActions/WarningLetters/default.htm

References

Galli, C., Hill, A., & Momtaz, R. (2011). McDonald's dumps McMuffin egg factory over health concerns. Retrieved from http://gma.yahoo.com/mcdonalds-dumps-mcmuffin-egg-factory-over-health-concerns-205521245.html

Lemm, E. (n.d.). What is a full breakfast? Retrieved from http://britishfood.about.com/od/faq/f/breakfast.htm

Letter from President Beth Sparboe Schnell. (2011). Retrieved from http://www.sparboeupdate.com/letter-from-beth-schnell/

McDonald's statement of Sparboe allegations. (2011). Retrieved from http://www.aboutmcdonalds.com/mcd/media_center/recent_news/media_press_releases/mcdonalds_statement_on_sparboe_allegations.html

New Mercy For Animals undercover investigation. (2011). Retrieved from http://www.mcdonaldscruelty.com/

Our sustainability supply chain vision. (2012). Retrieved from http://www.aboutmcdonalds.com/mcd/sustainability/our_focus_areas/sustainable_supply_chain.html

Reddy, L. (2011). Activists call for end to "cruel" battery cages for chickens. Retrieved from http://abcnews.go.com/Blotter/activists-call-end-cruel-battery-cages-chickens/story?id=14989778

Sparboe Farms creates sustainability task force to review food safety and animal care practices. (2011, November 19). Retrieved from http://www.prnewswire.com/news-releases/sparboe-farms-creates-sustainability-task-force-to-review-food-safety-and-animal-care-practices-134179803.html

Sparboe Farms/prairie complex 11/16/11 (2011). Retrieved from http://www.fda.gov/ICECI/EnforcementActions/WarningLetters/ucm280413.htm

Sparboe Farms update on undercover video. (2012, April). Retrieved from http://thebeefbeat.com/

What is an FDA warning letter? (n.d.). Retrieved from http://www.ehow.com/facts_7408023_fda-warning-letter_.html

CHAPTER 11

BP Texas City Explosion

On March 23, 2005, tragedy struck Texas City, Texas, when Beyond Petroleum's (BP's) Texas City refinery had an explosion in the isomerization (ISOM) unit that killed 15 workers and injured 180 others. The explosion occurred when vapors overflowing from the blowdown drums in the ISOM ignited. The Texas City refinery is the third largest in the United States. It has 29 oil-refining units and processes about 460,000 barrels of crude oil each day. That is about 3% of the daily gasoline demands of the United States ("Welcome," n.d.). All 15 workers who died were contract workers at the facility and were near temporary trailers being used to support maintenance and turnaround work at the refinery. Houses three quarters of a mile from the blast were damaged, and over 43,000 residents had to shelter-in-place for a few hours. BP's Texas City facility had a poor safety track record. There had been multiple accidents and four deaths as recently as 2004. In the past 10 years, the ISOM unit itself had had eight other vapor releases (Mac Sheoin, 2010).

Here is the initial statement by BP:

Don Parus, BP's Texas City, Texas, refinery manager has confirmed that there have been fatalities from an explosion that occurred this afternoon at about 1:20 p.m. at the company's isomerization unit at the facility.

"The accident has caused injuries to multiple BP workers, and it is with deep sadness that I must report that there have been fatalities," Mr. Parus said.

Parus said BP was not able to confirm the exact number of injuries or of fatalities at this time, but said the company was cooperating closely with the Texas City medical examiner on site.

"Our primary focus is on the safety and condition of our employees and other workers. We are directing all of our emergency efforts in response to the situation. The fire is out, and we are working with local authorities to bring the situation fully under control and to provide emergency medical care for the injured."

"We have not had time to investigate causes, and we will not speculate," Parus said. "But at this time, terrorism is not a primary focus of our concern."

Emergency response crews have set up three triage locations on the BP property.

The company also has set up environmental monitoring around the refinery. Efforts are continuing to account for all personnel.

Parus said that there has been some impact on the local community properties but it is being assessed.

"Our primary objectives right now are to treat the injured and to account for all personnel."

"I wish to stress that our deepest sympathy and concern go out to the families of the injured and the deceased. We are already working with local authorities to reach out to these families." ("BP Texas City Refinery Manager Confirms," 2005)

BP updated the crisis response twice on March 24:

I'm Don Parus, BP's Texas City, Texas, refinery manager. I apologize for the delay but we have been working on the scene and working to bring you updated information.

Words cannot begin to express how I and the people of BP feel right now. This is an extremely sad day for Texas City and BP.

To the best of our knowledge, at this time we believe there have been 14 fatalities. We are currently working with the medical examiner's office to confirm this information. As soon as we have any new information, we will provide you with an update.

We know that more than 70 people have received medical treatment, and some have been released.

There are still some people who are not accounted for. We have a process to account for everyone working in the plant at the time of the incident and we are proceeding with that process. This is a major focus at this time.

So is supporting those who were injured and the families of those killed in this incident.

We have called in extended staff to provide every possible assistance to the families.

We are taking the following actions:

- We are providing employee assistance program (EAP) counseling and pastoral help to responders, employees, workers, and families.
- We are continuing to work to account for all personnel.
- We are continuing to secure affected areas, and helping ensure that proper humanitarian assistance is available at the site and area hospitals.
- We also are calling more people to help.
- The company also is working with officials to mobilize the incident investigation team.

The fire at the company's isomerization unit occurred at about 1:20 this afternoon and was extinguished at 3:22 pm. The cause of the explosion and fire is not known. ("BP Texas City Refinery Manager Provides Update," 2005)

Second update on March 24, 2005:

> Ross Pillari, President of BP America, arrived in Texas City this morning and made the following statement.
>
> "I am here today to express BP's deep regret over yesterday's accident. Our thoughts and prayers are with the families of those who died and with those from the workforce and the community who were injured.
>
> Throughout the day and the weeks to come we will continue to cooperate with all local, state and federal authorities. We will also commit our full corporate resources to investigating the cause of the accident.
>
> I am here to support our staff, the community and our contractors as they continue to work to assist families and the community." ("BP Texas City Refinery Explosion," 2005)

After the initial shock of the explosion, attention shifted to identifying the cause of the tragedy. The question was why were the vapors coming from the blowdown drums, and how did they ignite? BP launched its own investigation while the U.S. government's investigation was conducted by the U.S. Chemical Safety and Hazard Investigation Board (CSB), the government agency tasked with investigating chemical accidents. There was also another governmental investigation launched by the U.S. Occupational Safety and Health Administration (OSHA). In May of 2005, BP released its initial report of the event. The vapor release was caused by overfilling at the ISOM unit when operators were restarting the unit. The ignition source was a pickup truck that was idling near the vapor cloud. These were the basic facts of what happened. The larger question was why did the vapor cloud form?

BP's initial report identified worker error as the cause. Hourly workers had failed to follow the proper procedures for the start-up of the ISOM unit (Belli, 2005). Workers had turned off an overflow warning light in order to reduce the time it took to restart the unit. Because the warning light was off, BP personnel did not know they were overfilling a tank, causing the vapor to pour out of the blowdown drum. Later investigations would agree that BP personnel did take shortcuts that were unsafe. However, the initial BP report was immediately criticized for being incomplete.

One critic of the report was the Center for Chemical Process Safety (CCPS). The CCPS is a nonprofit organization "that identifies and addresses process safety needs within the chemical, pharmaceutical, and petroleum industries. CCPS brings together manufacturers, government agencies, consultants, academia and insurers to lead the way in improving industrial process safety" ("About CCPS," n.d.). The CCPS's agenda is about chemical safety, it had no preexisting conflict with BP. The CCPS argued that the failure to follow procedures is not a root cause but merely a symptom of an underlying root cause. An investigation must look beyond the human error for the root cause and not end with it (Belli, 2005). One widely used definition of root cause is a factor that if corrected will prevent a recurrence of the problem ("What's," 2008).

Another critic was the United Steelworkers (USW) who represent many of the employees at the Texas City refinery. The USW does have an adversarial relationship with BP that could bias their view of the BP's initial report. The USW argued that management was blaming hourly workers for problems created by management. Those problems include a lax safety culture and cost cutting measures that had eroded safety at the Texas City facility. Leo Gerard, president of USW, stated: "As a union, we will do everything in our power to ensure that our members who were disciplined by BP are treated fairly and are not blamed for mistakes made by their supervisors or by higher-level BP management" (Belli, 2005, para. 12).

Though biased, the USW's comments reflect wider concerns raised in traditional news and social media reports about lax safety at BP's Texas City refinery that were driven by the need for profit (Elkind, Whitford, & Burke, 2011). Here is a sample of skeptical news media comments from Loren Steffy, a columnist with the *Houston Chronicle*:

> Unit operators and their managers didn't follow proper procedures, the report found. They didn't properly supervise the startup of the isomerization unit where the blast occurred, and they didn't evacuate people when they became aware of vapor releases and rising pressure in the unit.
>
> The report doesn't answer several key questions: Who hired those employees? Who trained them? Who supervised them?
>
> The report also found that the location of the contractor trailers, where many of the victims died, added to fatalities and injuries. So did the failure to evacuate nonessential personnel before the isom unit startup. A flare system, which BP had twice before decided not to install, would have reduced the severity of the incident, the report found.
>
> Are we to believe that low-level employees were in charge of the placement of contractor trailers? Did low-level employees decide to forgo the investment in a flare system? Did low-level employees set staffing levels for the control room and the isom unit? (Steffy, 2005)

Note how Steffy is questioning BP's report that blames low-level workers for larger safety decisions and policies. The concern is raised that there are larger safety issues at play and that the problem goes much higher in the management structure than the initial report identifies.

The U.S. Chemical Safety and Hazard Investigation Board (CSB) investigation was conducted throughout 2005 and 2006 with the cooperation of BP. Even BP did not seem satisfied with its own initial report. On August 17, 2005, BP announced it was creating an independent panel to review "the safety management systems and corporate safety culture of BP Products North American Inc., the subsidiary responsible for its U.S. refining operations" ("BP to Appoint," 2005, para. 1). The announcement was influenced by a recommendation by CSB to BP. The panel would be composed of an external chairperson, safety experts, and BP personnel. John Browne, the CEO of BP at the time of the explosion, stated, "The Texas City explosion was the worst tragedy in the recent history of BP, and we will do everything possible to ensure nothing like this happens again" ("BP to Appoint," 2005, para. 3). Eventually, respected former Secretary of State James Baker would chair the independent investigation commissioned by BP.

Simultaneous with the investigations, BP was taking steps to improve safety at Texas City. On September 22, 2005, BP initiated specific recommendations prescribed by OSHA, including hiring a process safety expert to review and update safety programs, hiring an expert to review the safety communication and commitment at the refinery, and improving health and safety training for refinery workers ("BP Agrees," 2005). Other actions taken by BP included hiring Colin MacLean to lead the turnaround at Texas City, hiring AlixPartners to aid in the turnaround, and undertaking 500 discrete safety-enhancing initiatives within one year of the explosion (Finley & Roberts, 2006). Exhibit 11.1 lists the specific actions BP reported taking as of December 9, 2006.

Exhibit 11.1   Detailed Actions BP Initiated After Texas City Explosion

Actions Taken to Ensure Safe and Reliable Equipment Operations

- $1 billion investment to modernize Texas City
- Create Focus on the Future program to coordinate new initiatives
- Execute engineering analysis of process units
- Introduce program to ensure proper initiation of work and oversight process to stop work if there are significant deviations
- Overhaul the entire steam system at Texas City
- Review relief valve revalidation and flare system for the process unit
- Started to replace blow down stacks
- Began regular alarm and site notification reviews
- Began process to manage and to evaluate safety critical systems
- Centralized review of all projects and maintenance work in progress

Actions Taken to Refine and Implement HSSE Policies

- Hire independent expert to execute facility citing study for safe worker housing
- Move all occupied trailers from areas that are potentially hazardous
- Relocate 400 employees to newly leased office space in Texas City
- Redesign parking to reduce vehicles on site and start transit system and vehicle parking policy
- Hire experts to identify opportunities for improvements in safety management
- Require supervisors be present for all critical operations including start ups and shut downs
- Implement leadership audits to monitor proper use of safety procedures, shut downs, and start ups
- Hire consultant to help with process safety management system
- Institute improvements to responsiveness, emergency response process, and enhance readiness
- Execute a series of crisis response drills
- Upgrade the site-wide security process
- Application of the new risk assessment standards
- Application of a pre-start up safety review process

Actions Taken to Develop People, Skills, and Behavior

- Hire new refinery manager
- Simplify the organizational structure to clarify accountability
- Clarify the roles and responsibilities [of] associates with start up, evacuation, maintenance, and operation
- Institute specific control and communication policies to make sure employees are following procedures
- Institute site-wide communication effort to increase safety vigilance and encourage feedback on safety-related issues
- Begin program to enhance operator training and frontline leader education
- Hire consulting firm to help design improved work environment and conduct leadership training
- Hire consultants for control of work and maintenance
- Refinery leadership will increase its visible presence to help drive the operational, safety, and maintenance changes

("Fatal Accident Report," 2005)

BP's final incident investigation report was released on December 9, 2005. The findings reflect a broader view of the safety issues preceding the March 2005 explosion than was found in the initial report. Here is a section of the BP news release that notes the causes of the tragedy:

The final report confirms the critical factors which led to the explosion and greatly increased its consequences. Those critical factors were identified in an interim report published May 17. The final report also identifies the following underlying causes:

- Over the years, the working environment had eroded to one characterized by resistance to change, and lacking of trust, motivation, and a sense of purpose. Coupled with unclear expectations around supervisory and management behaviors this meant that rules were not consistently followed, rigor was lacking and individuals felt disempowered from suggesting or initiating improvements.
- Process safety, operations performance and systematic risk reduction priorities had not been set and consistently reinforced by management.
- Many changes in a complex organization had led to the lack of clear accountabilities and poor communication, which together resulted in confusion in the workforce over roles and responsibilities.
- A poor level of hazard awareness and understanding of process safety on the site resulted in people accepting levels of risk that are considerably higher than comparable installations. One consequence was that temporary office trailers were placed within 150 feet of a blowdown stack which vented heavier than air hydrocarbons to the atmosphere without questioning the established industry practice.

- Given the poor vertical communication and performance management process, there was neither adequate early warning system of problems, nor any independent means of understanding the deteriorating standards in the plant. ("BP Issues," 2005, para. 9–14)

Note how the final incident investigation acknowledges a wider problem with the safety culture at Texas City.

On January 16, 2007, the Baker Report was released. The Baker Report was the culmination of the independent committee BP created to investigate the explosion headed by James Baker. The Baker Report was a strong critique of BP management's failure to maintain an effective safety culture. Here is a segment of the report pertaining to safety culture:

Process safety leadership.

The Panel believes that leadership from the top of the company, starting with the Board and going down, is essential. In the Panel's opinion, it is imperative that BP's leadership set the process safety "tone at the top" of the organization and establish appropriate expectations regarding process safety performance. Based on its review, the Panel believes that BP has not provided effective process safety leadership and has not adequately established process safety as a core value across all its five U.S. refineries. While BP has an aspirational goal of "no accidents, no harm to people," BP has not provided effective leadership in making certain its management and U.S. refining workforce understand what is expected of them regarding process safety performance. BP has emphasized personal safety in recent years and has achieved significant improvement in personal safety performance, but BP did not emphasize process safety. BP mistakenly interpreted improving personal injury rates as an indication of acceptable process safety performance at its U.S. refineries. BP's reliance on this data, combined with an inadequate process safety understanding, created a false sense of confidence that BP was properly addressing process safety risks. The Panel further found that process safety leadership appeared to have suffered as a result of high turnover of refinery plant managers. ("Report of," 2007, p. xii)

As media sources were quick to note, the Baker Report was critical of BP's top management for neglecting safety through cost-savings measures and process safety. The implications were that the tragedy could have been avoided if management had shown more interest in maintaining an effective safety culture (Mufson, 2007; "Report Accuses," 2007).

On March 22, 2007, the CSB released its final report on the Texas City tragedy. This report cited and echoed the Baker Report by noting the failure of BP's top management to take safety seriously and to invest in safety at the Texas City refinery. Carolyn Merritt, a President Bush appointee, was chairperson of the U.S. Chemical Safety and Hazard Investigation Board at the time of the report. In an interview with *60 Minutes* about the report and tragedy at Texas City, she said: "These things do not have to happen. They are preventable. They are predictable, and people do not have to die because they're earning a living" (Schorn, 2009, para. 18). When asked if Texas City could have been avoided, her answer was, "Absolutely" (Schorn, 2009, para. 19). Two years after the explosion, Texas City was still making negative headlines for BP. The reports were reaffirming earlier allegations that BP's top management had facilitated the crisis by neglecting safety.

In addition to the investigations, lawsuits extended the Texas City crisis for BP. In 2010, BP was found guilty of not making their promised safety changes in a timely enough fashion and was fined $50.6 million (Fowler & Hatcher, 2010). In 2006, BP settled the highest profile lawsuit from a family member. A number of smaller lawsuits remained open for BP ("BP Settles," 2007). On November 9, 2006, the settlement with Eva Rowe, a young woman who lost both parents at Texas City, was the last settlement. However, her settlement allowed her attorney to release internal documents BP provided for the trial. Her attorney is Brent Coon. Here is a summary of the key terms in Eva Rowe's settlement:

- BP releases over 7 million documents
- $30 million donated to Texas A&M University Mary Kay O'Connor Process Safety Center, University of Texas Medical Branch at Galveston, Truman G. Blocker Adult Burn Unit, and the College of the Mainland, in Texas City, in the memory of the 15 victims.
- The University of Texas Medical Branch at Galveston, Truman G. Blocker Adult Burn Unit, receives 12.5 million dollars in memory of all 15 people who died in the Texas City explosion
- The Texas A&M University Mary Kay O'Connor Process Safety Center, receives 12.5 million dollars
- The College of the Mainland, in Texas City, receives 5 million dollars to provide safety and process technology training for refinery and chemical plant workers
- The St Jude's Hospital receives 1 million dollars
- Hornbeck High School in Hornbeck, LA receives 1 million dollars
- A $1 million donation was to be made to Eva Rowe's parents' favorite charity, the Cancer Center at St. Jude's Children's Research Hospital in Memphis, Tenn., in their memory (Hatcher, 2010; see also "The Terms of Settlement in the Case of Eva Rowe," n.d., at http://texascityexplosion.com/site/terms_of_settlement)

Brent Coon has kept the Texas City tragedy alive by creating the Remember the 15 website. The "15" is in reference to the people killed at Texas City. Coon held public ceremonies on the second and fifth anniversaries of the Texas City tragedy. Below is the mission statement for Remember the 15:

We are here to remember and honor the 15 people who tragically lost their life and the many others whose lives were forever changed as a result of the March 23rd, 2005 BP Texas City plant explosion.

We are here to remember commitments made by many of us five years ago. For BCA, it was promises to our clients to be aggressive and thorough in discovering the root causes of this tragedy. Promises to the general public to disclose all the results of our independent investigations. Promises of spreading awareness in order to improve safety conditions for all industrial plants so that tragedies such as this may be prevented in the future. For the USW and safety organizations, it was a promise to work with the industry to use this information to make petrochemical facilities a safer place to work. For enforcement agencies, it was to tighten regulatory mandates and improve oversight. For the judiciary, it was to ensure that all parties to the litigation receive justice. And for all of us, it was to leave this tragedy with lessons learned and make sure they are never forgotten.

On the fifth year anniversary of the Texas City plant explosion, we came together to commemorate those who lost their life and take a look back at what progress has been made. These promises and the calls for action that followed, for all the lives that were touched, will never be broken.

—Brent Coon, Founder—Brent Coon & Associates. ("Mission," n.d.)

The two anniversaries, especially the fifth anniversary, drew some news media attention (e.g., Hatcher, 2010). Here is how the Remember the 15 website describes the fifth anniversary event:

About the Event

As lead counsel in the lawsuit against BP, Brent Coon & Associates hosted a very special presentation examining the progress and promises made since the explosion at the British Petroleum Texas City Plant on March 23, 2005 that left 15 people dead. The event marked the five year anniversary of the explosion and included key recipients of the $44 million in charitable donations, union leaders directing the safety negotiations, regulatory agency officials, worker's safety activists and victim's family members.

This event marked the culmination of BCA's collective research effort aimed at determining what safety measures have been enacted, where BP's safety conditions and procedures currently stand, whose lives have been improved, what advances have been made as a result of the charitable contributions, and how the victims have adjusted with the loss of their loved ones.

The ceremony was well attended by members of the media and those affected by the explosion, ensuing litigation and the far reaching effects of the settlement. The ceremony was also broadcast online to hundreds of interested parties across the nation. ("About the Event," 2010)

This is a description of the second anniversary event:

About the 2nd Anniversary Event

On March 23, 2005, an explosion rocked the BP Texas City oil refinery, spewing flames and smoke into the air. 15 workers—moms and dads, sons and daughters—lost their lives. Hundreds more were injured, and countless families shattered.

In the aftermath of the explosion, heroes emerged. Family members, friends and survivors banded together to seek justice. They launched a campaign to challenge one of the world's oil giants, taking on a company hell bent on profits at any cost.

Through countless legal battles, public appeals and aggressive grassroots action, the victims of the BP Texas City explosion exposed a pattern of reckless cost-cutting, insufficient government oversight and a blatant disregard for human life.

Along the way, there have been some victories—helping bring to light the depths of corporate irresponsibility at BP—but perhaps more importantly—revealing a broader industry-wide culture that puts profits over people. That's why more must be done to prevent another Texas City from happening—and you can help.

On Friday, March 23rd, 2007, families came together to mark the second anniversary of that terrible, and largely preventable, accident. We gathered on the steps of the State Capitol in Austin, Texas to announce a new legislative initiative—the Remember the 15 Bill—designed to change the way oil and chemical companies do business in Texas.

The earliest drafts of the Remember the 15 Bill were inspired and championed by Eva Rowe. Eva lost her mom and dad in the blast, turning a young, shy small-town woman into an activist and advocate for change. The bill, if enacted, would strengthen worker safety protections, toughen environmental regulations, and bolster government oversight.

This is a fight about saving families, protecting the environment and holding big corporations responsible for their actions. It is also a battle for justice that continues to this day—and we hope you will join with us. ("About the 2nd Anniversary," 2007)

The anniversaries provided a news hook for stories that help to keep a crisis "alive" for stakeholders.

The BP documents received limited public release. Coon moved them from public to private access following the Deep Horizon disaster in the Gulf. However, one memo did generate negative attention for BP on the Internet. The memo was a safety assessment conducted by BP. The safety assessment decision involved what types of trailers to use for temporary employees. Keep in mind that the workers who died were in or near just such trailers. Here is part of the message from one blog that carried the memo:

"Right there we found a presentation on the decision to buy the trailers that showed BP using 'The Three Little Pigs' to describe the costs associated with the four [refinery housing] options." Says Coon: "I thought you've got to be f——— kidding me. They even had drawings of three pigs on the report."

The two-page document, prepared by BP's risk managers in October 2002 as part of a larger risk preparedness presentation, and titled "Cost benefit analysis of three little pigs," is harrowing:

"Frequency—the big bad wolf blows with a frequency of once per lifetime."

"Consequence—if the wolf blows down the house then the piggy is gobbled."

"Maximum justifiable spend (MJS)—a piggy considers it's worth $1000 to save its bacon."

"Which type of house," the report asks, "should the piggy build?"

It then answers its own question: a hand-written note, "optimal," is marked next to an option that offers solid protection, but *not* the "blast resistant" trailer, typically all-welded steel structures, that cost 10 times as much.

At Texas City, all of the fatalities and many of the serious injuries occurred in or around the nine contractor trailers near the isom unit, which contained large quantities of flammable hydrocarbons and had a history of releases, fires, and other safety incidents. A number of trailers as far away as two football fields were heavily damaged. (Outzen, 2010, para. 13–20)

The blogs used the memo as further evidence that BP management was callous and cavalier about worker safety at Texas City. In 2010, BP's Deep Horizon disaster pushed Texas City to the background of discussions about BP.

Reading Guide

1. If this situation is a crisis, what type of crisis is it?

2. What is the problem and the source(s) of the problem in this case?

3. What stakeholders should be interested in this case?

4. How were BP's various reports on the crisis investigation received by stakeholders?

5. What government agency investigates chemical accidents?

6. Who headed BP's independent investigation?

7. What actions were taken to keep alive the memory of the explosion?

Discussion Questions

1. Do you think BP's long list of correctives will help to restore its reputation? Why or why not?

2. What was the problem with the initial findings that blamed low-level employees for the explosion?

3. What evidence is there to support the claim that the explosion was avoidable and why is that so important in the case?

4. How would you rate the credibility of the various reports about the explosion? Which would be the most credible and why?

5. What effect would the anniversaries have on BP's reputation, and why would it have those effects?

6. How important is it for an organization's comments to align with their safety culture and record?

7. What impact does BP's past safety record have on the effectiveness of its crisis communication?

8. How might the association with a lawyer erode the impact of the memorial website and efforts?

Websites

Remember the 15: http://rememberthe15.com/
Brent Coon's website about the explosion: http://www.texascityexplosion.com/
Baker Report: http://www.texascityexplosion.com/
U.S. Chemical Safety Board: http://www.csb.gov/

References

About CCPS. (n.d). Retrieved from http://www.aiche.org/CCPS/About/index.aspx

About the event. (2010). Retrieved from http://rememberthe15.com/about_five_year

About the 2nd anniversary. (2007). Retrieved from http://www.rememberthe15.com/about_second

Belli, A. (2005, May 20). BP's finding that staff at fault in blast is disputed. Retrieved from http://www.chron.com/news/article/BP-s-finding-that-staff-at-fault-in-blast-is-1930706.php

BP agrees to safety improvements at Texas City following settlement with OSHA. (2005). Retrieved from http://www.bp.com/genericarticle.do?categoryId=2012968&contentId=7009570

BP issues report on fatal explosion: Announces $1 billion investment in Texas City. (2005). Retrieved from http://www.bp.com/genericarticle.do?categoryId=2012968&contentId=7012963

BP settles more claims from Texas refinery fire. (2007, February 23). Retrieved from http://www.nytimes.com/2007/02/23/business/worldbusiness/23iht-bp.4705364.html

BP Texas City refinery explosion. (2005). Retrieved from http://www.bp.com/genericarticle.do?categoryId=2012968&contentId=7005041

BP Texas City refinery manager confirms fatalities from explosion. (2005). Retrieved from http://www.bp.com/genericarticle.do?categoryId=2012968&contentId=7004999

BP Texas City refinery manager provides update on explosion. (2005). Retrieved from http://www.bp.com/genericarticle.do?categoryId=2012968&contentId=7005000

BP to appoint independent panel to review U.S. refinery safety. (2005, August 17). Retrieved from http://www.bp.com/genericarticle.do?categoryId=2012968&contentId=7008210

Elkind, P., Whitford, D., & Burke, D. (2011, February). BP: "An accident waiting to happen." *Fortune, 163*(1), 105–132.

Fatal accident report investigation report: Isomeriation unit explosion final report. (2005). Retrieved from http://www.bp.com/liveassets/bp_internet/us/bp_us_english/STAGING/local_assets/downloads/t/final_report.pdf

Finley. F. & Roberts, K. (2006). BP tackles Texas City failing. Retrieved from http://www.chemicalprocessing.com/articles/2006/055/

Fowler, T., & Hatcher, M. (2010). BP accepts $50.6 million fine, but 05 blast still dogs company. Retrieved from http://www.chron.com/business/article/BP-accepts-50-6Mfine-but-05-blast-still-dogs-1699938.php

Hatcher, M. (2010, March 23). Five years later: BP settlement money helps with safety training. Retrieved from http://apps.chron.com/disp/story.mpl/business/6927302.html

Mac Sheoin, T. (2010). Chemical catastrophe: From Bhopal to Texas City. Retrieved from http://monthlyreview.org/2010/09/01/chemical-catastrophe-from-bhopal-to-bp-texas-city

Mission. (n.d). http://rememberthe15.com/mission

Mufson, S. (2007). BP failed on safety, report said. Retrieved from http://www.washingtonpost.com/wp-dyn/content/article/2007/01/16/AR2007011600208.html

Outzen, R. (2010). BP shocking memo. Retrieved from http://www.thedailybeast.com/articles/2010/05/25/shocking-bp-memo-and-the-oil-spill-in-the-gulf.html?cid=hp:mainprom01

Report accuses BP over safety. (2007). Retrieved from http://www.guardian.co.uk/business/2007/jan/16/bp

Report of the BP U.S. refineries independent safety review panel. (2007, p. xii). Retrieved from http://www.bp.com/liveassets/bp_internet/globalbp/globalbp_uk_english/SP/STAGING/local_assets/assets/pdfs/Baker_panel_report.pdf

Schorn, D. (2009). The explosion at Texas City. Retrieved from http://www.cbsnews.com/2100-18560_162-2126509.html

Steffy, L. (2005). Reminders of death linger 5 years after BP blast. Retrieved from http://www.texascityexplosion.com/site/headlines?post_id=831

Welcome to BP Texas City refinery. (n.d.). Retrieved from http://www.bp.com/sectiongenericarticle.do?categoryId=9030612&contentId=7055884

What's a root cause. (2008). Retrieved from http://www.idcon.com/reliability-tips-81.html

CHAPTER 12

Sigg and BPA

I n the early 2000s, plastic water bottles became a target for people with environmental concerns. From 2000 to 2010, the annual bottled water usage of an individual in the United States rose from 16.7 to 28.3 gallons per year (Koch & Marohn, 2011). The initial problem was the waste generated by one-time-use plastic bottles and their dependence on petrochemicals as a main ingredient. Advocates against bottled water argued that it was essentially the same as tap water and in many cases tap water is actually a healthier alternative than bottled water while also being much cheaper ("True," 2010). One of the lead organizations for the bottled water issue was Ban The Bottle. This group advocates drinking water but utilizing reusable water bottles instead of one-time-use plastic bottles. The group recommends hydration stations on college campus. Hydration stations are designed to allow people to quickly fill their water bottles and represent a faster and easier alternative to using drinking fountains (Koch & Marohn, 2011).

As early as 2005, the concerns about plastic water bottles shifted to the controversial issue of bisphenol A or BPA. Scientists and governments from around the world were concerned that this common ingredient in many plastics could have harmful health effects on people, especially infants. The scrutiny intensified in 2007 and 2008 as new studies emerged that suggested a danger from BPA. Canada and some other countries banned the use of BPA from many products in 2009. BPA can leach from a plastic bottle or liners into the food the plastic is designed to contain. Leaching was most likely to occur when the plastic was heated or frozen. BPA is controversial because those in the plastic industry, led by the American Chemistry Council (ACC), argue that its dangers have yet to be proven ("American," 2010). A sample statement from the ACC about BPA is provided in Exhibit 12.1. Still, many environmental and health conscious stakeholders consider BPA to be negative and have sought ways to avoid it in their lives.

Exhibit 12.1   Sample American Chemistry Council Statement on BPA

ARLINGTON, VA (Jan. 15, 2010)—The American Chemistry Council (ACC) issued the following statement today in reaction to the Health and Human Services (HHS) and Food and Drug Administration (FDA) announcement on bisphenol A (BPA):

The HHS statement today confirms that exposure to BPA in food contact products has not been proven harmful to children or adults. However, the agency suggests that more research needs to be done and provided guidance on how parents can choose to limit infant exposures.

Regulatory agencies around the world, which have recently reviewed the research, have reached conclusions that support the safety of BPA. Extensive scientific studies have shown that BPA is quickly metabolized and excreted and does not accumulate in the body. BPA is one of the most thoroughly tested chemicals in commerce today.

ACC and our members are committed to the safety of our products, and we will continue to support laws and regulations that protect consumer safety. While ACC recognizes that HHS and FDA are attempting to address public confusion about BPA, we are disappointed that some of the recommendations are likely to worry consumers and are not well-founded.

Plastics made with BPA contribute safety and convenience to our daily lives because of their durability, clarity and shatter-resistance. Can liners and food-storage containers made with BPA are essential components to helping protect the safety of packaged foods and preserving products from spoilage and contamination. ACC remains committed to consumer safety, and will continue to review new scientific studies concerning the safety of BPA.

(American Chemistry Council, 2010)

Exhibit 12.2   Nalgene Statement on BPA

Information on BPA

As a responsible manufacturer of polycarbonate consumer products, **NalgeNunc International** has monitored scientific research concerning the safety of our products including Bisphenol-A for many years.

Based on the findings of the Food and Drug Administration, The Environmental Protection Agency, The American Plastics Council and other reliable sources from around the world, we continue to firmly believe in the safety of our products.

NalgeNunc International also believes in providing its customers with the most factual information currently available on this subject. You can view the most up to date information here.

("Our," n.d.)

The desire to avoid BPA included both multiuse plastic bottles as well as one-time-use plastic bottles. Nalgene is a major producer of multiuse plastic bottles. In 2007, it was reported that some of their bottles contained BPA (MacDonald, 2007). Nalgene maintains there never was a danger from the BPA in some of their bottles but eliminated the chemical due to consumer concerns. The Nalgene statement is presented in Exhibit 12.2. Consumers began to avoid Nalgene bottles and look for alternatives. The search for an alternative to Nalgene and other multiuse plastic bottles was a boon to Sigg, a Swiss-based company that happened to make stainless steel water bottles. The trend is captured in the following news story:

> Once ubiquitous on university campuses, where they emerged as the accessory of choice among young, outdoorsy types, Nalgene bottles are being displaced by metal bottles, says Valhalla sales associate—and University of British Columbia student—Aja O'Gorman. "It's like the whole 'buy green' movement: it's cool to have a conscience." Plus, she says, they look a lot nicer. Sigg, the Swiss maker of the most coveted—and priciest—products in the category, was even recognized by New York City's Museum of Modern Art for its chic shapes and design. (MacDonald, 2007, p. 89)

Similar news stories could be found across the United States and Canada, documenting how eco and health conscious consumers were dumping plastic (e.g., Nalgene) for stainless steel (e.g., Sigg).

In 2008, Sigg saw sales of its stainless steel water bottles increase five times from those in 2007 (Austen, 2008). Sigg promoted itself as a safe alternative to plastic, and the news media endorsed Sigg and a handful of other stainless steel bottles as a means of avoiding BPA (e.g., Turner, 2008). For instance, the *New York Magazine* hailed Sigg as a nontoxic alternative ("Nontoxic," 2008), while other stories noted some retailers were pulling Nalgene and other multiuse plastic bottles off their shelves over health concerns with BPA (King, 2008). Sigg was benefiting from multiuse plastic bottles being linked to BPA. Sigg bottles were even listed as a common must-have for back to school in 2008 (Hulette, 2008). Again, scientists still debate the exact threat from BPA, but the perception of risk is what is most important to stakeholders. The perception among health conscious stakeholders was that BPA presented a danger to their lives that they should eliminate (Moran, 2009). Experts argued that media coverage of BPA was driving sales on non-BPA products, such as Sigg ("Are," 2009). Sigg was attracting stakeholders who wanted to avoid BPA because they considered BPA to be a health threat. The anti-BPA stakeholders are driven by a desire to eliminate that chemical from their lives. Sigg was being presented as an attractive option for the anti-BPA stakeholders.

In August of 2009, the non-BPA benefit for Sigg came to a crashing halt. It was in August that people learned some Sigg bottles manufactured before August of 2008 did contain BPA. The pre-August 2008 Sigg bottles had epoxy liners, and those liners contain BPA even though Sigg had promoted itself as BPA safe since 2007.

The dispute over being safe became a focal point in the story. Those active in the health and environment-friendly social media were very upset. Here are a few samples:

By Light Green Stairs: Sigg Bottles Had BPA before August 2008

August 21st, 2009

Last year, I wrote glowing reviews about SIGG bottles here and at Tree Hugging Family. I also recommended them to my friends and family. I bought one for my husband who has taken it to work with him each day for more than a year now.

Today, I feel very betrayed. In my Tree Hugging Family post, I defended SIGG's decision to not disclose the ingredients of their liner since it was a proprietary secret. I also linked to a letter that was posted on mysigg.com, written by the President on March 12, 2007 in which he said:

"I can assure you that SIGG bottles are absolutely not made with a plastic liner and are in fact lined with a proprietary non-toxic, water-based resin which has been refined over decades of study and is extremely safe & stable."

and he continued to state:

"As you may know, the BPA issues surrounding Lexan plastic bottles (poly-carbonate #7) involve the migration of chemicals from the plastic into the contents of the bottles. On the other hand, SIGG bottles have been thoroughly tested in Europe to ensure 0% leaching of any substance—**no trace of BPA**, BPB or any phthalates."

These are direct quotes from Steve Wasik, President SIGG USA. (I added the bold font, not words.) Now, a letter dated August 2009 by Steve Wasik, CEO, SIGG Switzerland even begins with somewhat of a defense of BPA! He goes on to say that:

"Within the reusable bottle water category, polycarbonate plastic bottles (#7) came under scrutiny in early 2008 because they were found to leach BPA. As a result, many consumers turned to metal bottles (aluminum and stainless steel) because these bottles had no issues with BPA migration. Prior to its transition, **SIGG utilized a water-based epoxy liner which contained a trace amount of BPA**."

Perhaps the consumer is supposed to read between the lines. What he was really saying is zero leaching, but we know BPA is present. How am I sup-posed to believe anything they say now? I didn't want a bottle with trace amounts of BPA.

SIGG will have to go a very long way to win back the support of the green community. As part of making this right, I believe that SIGG should offer all consumers who purchased a SIGG prior to August 2008 (within reason) a free replacement bottle—IF they even want it. Contact SIGG.

SIGG knew that consumers were buying their bottles because they wanted an alternative to BPA. They certainly were crafty to make sure they never exactly said that their bottles didn't contain BPA. They simply said no leaching of BPA in a way that implied BPA wasn't present. Plus, they challenged groups (like Organic Consumers Association) that said their bottle contained BPA, and they even accepted an apology.

Shame on you SIGG. (Rowland, 2009)

From Blisstree: Way to go with the BPA SIGG!

So in case you haven't heard, one of the hottest buzzes around the ecosphere is the SIGG issue. Long story short . . .

1. Most greenies love SIGG it's a valuable water bottle option when compared to disposable plastic bottles. In fact, I have written about them a lot.

2. Back in 2007 SIGG's CEO noted that SIGG bottles were BPA trace free.

3. Fast forward to August 2009 and now SIGG's CEO (yeah the same guy, Steve Wasik) is all, well, the older bottles DO have BPA, but no worries.

4. Let the drama begin.

Now, I already posted about this, my friend posted about this, and as to not rehash the topic over and over here are some useful links:

- Does SIGG Owe Consumers New BPA-Free Water Bottles?—I say yes.
- My pal Peggy a long time SIGG advocate is super peeved. Read her views in **SIGG Bottles Had BPA Before August 2008** and here at Blisstree as well.
- Here's SIGG's letter from August 2009 noting yup we've got a BPA issue.
- Treehugger's take: SIGG Update: Did We Get It Right?

I'll end with this. Shame on SIGG, like green advocates don't already have to defend green products enough. Thanks for making it this much harder. (Chait, 2009)

Sigg was defining non-BPA as no leaching of BPA from its liners, not that the liners were free of BPA. From Sigg's perspective, if the BPA could not leach, there was no threat from the BPA, hence the bottles were free of BPA. Sigg provided a five-point explanation of BPA and its products starting with an explanation of BPA and why it is used in the container industry.

1) What is Bisphenol A (BPA) and how is it generally used? Bisphenol A (BPA) is a chemical building block that is used primarily to make polycarbonate plastics and epoxy resins. Cured epoxy resins are inert materials and have been used as protective liners in metal containers for more than 40 years to maintain the quality of foods and beverages. They have achieved wide acceptance for use as protective coatings because of their combination of toughness, adhesion, formability and chemical resistance. BPA is still used today in the cans of your favorite Cola for example. ("Sigg Has BPA," 2009)

Next, Sigg explained why BPA was used in its own products. This is a key point because Sigg is recognizing there was BPA in some of its bottles:

2) Did SIGG use BPA in its bottles? Yes. Prior to August 2008, SIGG utilized a water-based epoxy liner that contained a trace amount of BPA. These bottles were thoroughly and regularly tested in the U.S. and Switzerland and all tests revealed absolutely no migration or leaching of BPA or any other substance from the former protective liner. ("Sigg Has BPA," 2009)

Sigg then went on to explain how they were no longer using BPA in any of their bottles. Ending the use of BPA was intended to reassure its customers.

3) Are you still using the water-based, epoxy resin liner in any of your bottles? No. We no longer use this liner at all. Today and since August 2008, we make all of our SIGG bottles with a powder-based, co-polyester liner that we call the EcoCare liner. BPA is not one of the ingredients in the formula of this liner. ("Sigg Has BPA," 2009)

Because of the concerns about BPA, Sigg included an explanation of why the BPA in their containers was safe. The use of any amount of BPA was the primary objection from its customers.

4) Are older SIGG bottles that contain BPA safe? Yes. U.S. and worldwide regulatory bodies continue to deem the component safe and independent research has shown that these bottles do not leach. We stand behind the quality and safety of all our SIGG bottles including those with our former liner. ("Sigg Has BPA," 2009)

Finally, Sigg provided details about how customers could determine if they had a Sigg bottle that contained BPA. Customers who were concerned about BPA could now determine whether or not their Sigg bottle contained any BPA.

5) How do I know which liner is in my SIGG bottle? If you purchased your SIGG before August 2008, you very likely have the water-based, epoxy resin liner. Consumers can determine their liner type with a quick visual inspection. The EcoCare liner has a dull, pale yellow appearance while the former liner has a shiny copper bronze appearance. ("Sigg Has BPA," 2009)

From the message, you can see the line of reasoning, no leaching = no BPA. Unfortunately for Sigg, their vocal customers did not accept that logic.

Customers were angry about what they saw as deception, especially stakeholders who were anti-BPA. The customers demanded new bottles that had no BPA because that is what they wanted and thought they'd had in the first place. The plastics industry had made the same argument about no leaching, but a segment of the customers just wanted no BPA, period. Perceptions of risk are a common disconnect between corporations and customers. Corporate scientists define risk as probability and base their decisions on logic. Stakeholders frequently define risk as possibility, and these evaluations are laced with emotion. Robert Heath's work in crisis communication has noted the criticality of corporations understanding what drives the risk perceptions of their stakeholders (e.g., Heath & Palenchar, 2000). Sigg was using a scientific view of BPA.

Many customers bought Sigg bottles because they believed the bottles had no BPA in them at all, according to how the people were defining no BPA. Refer to the earlier blog posts to get a sense of the anger and desire for a replacement.

The power of online communication is a significant part of this story. Customers reacted negatively to Sigg's initial response. They sent e-mails to Sigg, wrote blogs, and sent Tweets on the issue. The customer reactions reflected the perceptual nature of risk. The BPA may not leach from the epoxy, but many customers bought Sigg bottles because they wanted to avoid any contact with BPA for themselves or their children when using the products. If BPA is there, people can perceive it as a threat and as undesirable. The sentiments were echoed in the traditional or legacy news media as well. Instead of a must have, Sigg bottles now were something to avoid (Doshi, 2009).

Sigg needed to change its communicative response because the negative online comments and related traditional or legacy media coverage indicated its current course of action was ineffective. Instead of reducing customer anger over the BPA concern, it was intensifying the anger. The change was signaled by an apology from the CEO. The apology begins with an acknowledgement that the initial message Sigg delivered was wrong:

> Dear SIGG Customer, (STAMFORD CT)—Last month, I wrote a letter to try and provide you with as much factual and historical information as I could in regards to the evolution of the SIGG bottle liner. I also suggested that people could email me if they had any questions and comments. After reading and responding to hundreds of emails and viewing nearly as many blog & Twitter posts, I realize that my first letter may have missed the mark. What I should have said simply and loudly to all of our loyal SIGG fans is: I am sorry that we did not make our communications on the original SIGG liner more clear from the very beginning. (Zmuda, 2009)

The next section details the lessons Wasik said he learned from the incident:

> I have learned much over the past 2 weeks. I learned that many of you purchased SIGG bottles—not just because they were free from leaching and safe—but because you believed that SIGGs contained no BPA. I learned that, although SIGG never marketed the former liner as "BPA Free" we should have done a better job of both clearly communicating about our liner as well as policing others who may have misunderstood the SIGG message. For over 100 years, SIGG has earned a reputation for quality products and service—and we do not take that for granted. From the day we made our announcement last month, we made a commitment consistent with SIGG values that we would offer anyone who is concerned about BPA an opportunity to swap their old SIGGs for new SIGGs with the new EcoCare liner. Today, I am announcing that this voluntary Exchange Program will be in place until October 31, 2009 to ensure that our customers have ample time to send their former liner bottles back to us should they choose to do so. Once again, I truly apologize for the lack of clarity in our previous communications. All of us at SIGG hope that we will have an opportunity to regain your confidence and trust. Sincerely, Steve Wasik, CEO, SIGG Switzerland. (Zmuda, 2009)

The apology was followed by a plan, announced on October 1, 2009, to allow people to replace the older BPA bottles with the newer, BPA-free bottles. The recall announcement was another opportunity for Sigg to discuss how customers convinced them to change their behavior: "Back in April 2008, the popular blog Tree Hugger ran a story, 'Are SIGG Aluminum Bottles BPA Free?' The story ended with: 'Conclusion: We are not sure if the lining of SIGG bottles is made with BPA or not, but we like the results of the testing, which is what really matters.' The testing of course showed that SIGG bottles did not leach any chemicals, which we too thought, 'is what really matters.' Based on the mail we received this past month, some people disagreed" ("Sigg Has BPA," 2009). The first paragraph reviews Sigg's claim that the BPA would not leach and that customers care more about the BPA than the leaching.

The second paragraph emphasized how many customers bought the bottles because they believed the bottles had no BPA:

> At the same time, we learned that some people in North America purchased SIGG bottles—not just because they were Swiss-made, beautifully designed and free from leaching—but because they thought SIGGs contained no BPA. We learned that we could have done a better job of more clearly communicating about our liners. We are very sorry for any confusion. ("Sigg Has BPA," 2009)

Sigg ended by providing details about the recall. Sigg would offer a voluntary exchange program for the bottles with BPA:

> To ensure that our North American customers remain completely satisfied with SIGG, we have offered those concerned with our old liner an opportunity to swap their old SIGGs for new SIGGs with the new EcoCare liner. This voluntary exchange program began in August and will run for nearly 3 months expiring on Oct 31, 2009. ("Sigg Has BPA," 2009)

Note how the crisis was about two months old before the replacement was offered to customers outraged that BPA was in the products they purchased specifically to avoid BPA.

The fallout from the BPA crisis went beyond customers for Sigg. Sigg was a partner with Patagonia, an outdoor company well known for its environmental commitment. Sigg was producing a line of bottles with the Patagonia logo that was sanctioned by the Patagonia CEO, Yvon Chouinard. Patagonia ended their partnership as result of the BPA crisis. Here is part of the statement announcing the end of the partnership:

> "We did our homework on the topic of BPA, going all the way back to 2005 when this subject first emerged in discussions in scientific journals," says Rick Ridgeway, Patagonia's vice president of environmental initiatives. "We even arranged for one of the leading scientists on BPA research to come to our company to educate us on the issue. Once we concluded there was basis for concern, we immediately pulled all drinking bottles that contained BPA from our shelves and then searched for a BPA-free bottle. We very clearly asked SIGG if there was BPA in their bottles and their liners, and they clearly said there was not." (Chua, 2009)

The Patagonia endorsement was important for Sigg. Not only was Patagonia a valuable retail outlet, but there is also its credibility among environmentally conscious consumers, such as those that are anti-BPA. Patagonia is well known among environmentally conscious consumers for its commitment to the environment. Exhibit 12.3 provides Patagonia's mission statement and vision of the company ("Our," n.d.). This history of environmental commitment is what gives Patagonia its credibility on environmental-related issues, such as BPA.

Exhibit 12.3   Patagonia Mission and Vision

Our Reason for Being

Build the best product, cause no unnecessary harm, use business to inspire and implement solutions to the environmental crisis.

Patagonia's Mission Statement

Patagonia grew out of a small company that made tools for climbers. Alpinism remains at the heart of a worldwide business that still makes clothes for climbing—as well as for skiing, snowboarding, surfing, fly fishing, paddling and trail running. These are all silent sports. None requires a motor; none delivers the cheers of a crowd. In each sport, reward comes in the form of hard-won grace and moments of connection between us and nature.

Our values reflect those of a business started by a band of climbers and surfers, and the minimalist style they promoted. The approach we take towards product design demonstrates a bias for simplicity and utility.

For us at Patagonia, a love of wild and beautiful places demands participation in the fight to save them, and to help reverse the steep decline in the overall environmental health of our planet. We donate our time, services and at least 1% of our sales to hundreds of grassroots environmental groups all over the world who work to help reverse the tide.

We know that our business activity—from lighting stores to dyeing shirts—creates pollution as a by-product. So we work steadily to reduce those harms. We use recycled polyester in many of our clothes and only organic, rather than pesticide-intensive, cotton.

Staying true to our core values during thirty-plus years in business has helped us create a company we're proud to run and work for. And our focus on making the best products possible has brought us success in the marketplace.

("Patagonia," n.d.)

Sales declined for Sigg as rivals used the bad press about Sigg to promote their bottles as really free of BPA ("EcoUsable," 2009). The exact concern over BPA that had increased Sigg sales was now decreasing its sales. In 2011, Sigg's U.S. branch filed for bankruptcy. The bankruptcy claim noted the negative effect of the BPA crisis on sales.

Reading Guide

1. If this situation is a crisis, what type of crisis is it?

2. What is the problem and the source(s) of the problem in this case?

3. What stakeholders should be interested in this case?

4. What are the organizations involved with this case?

5. What was the initial response from Sigg? How did they change that response?

6. What is BPA, and why are people concerned about it?

Discussion Questions

1. How does the BPA debate illustrate principles of risk communication?

2. How did BPA help and then hurt Sigg?

3. What effect did BPA have on Nalgene?

4. What role did social media play in the case?

5. What do you think a label means when it says "BPA free"? Why does that matter in this case?

6. How does this case illustrate the importance of perceptions in crisis? How was this crisis perception driven?

7. Why do emotions become more important than scientific evidence when risk is an important element of a crisis?

8. What role did the timing of the crisis response play in the crisis?

Websites

Facts about BPA associated with the chemical industry: http://factsaboutbpa.org/

American Chemical Council information on BPA: http://plastics.americanchemistry .com/BPA

Mayo Clinic information about BPA: http://www.mayoclinic.com/health/bpa/AN01955

References

American Chemistry Council. (2010, January 15). American Chemistry Council reacts to statement from HHS and FDA on bisphenol A. Retrieved fromhttp://www.american chemistry.com/Media/PressReleasesTranscripts/ACC-news-releases/American -Chemistry-Council-Reacts-to-Statement-from-HHS-and-FDA-on-Bisphenol-A.html

Are green cleaning products recession-proof? Many manufacturers think so. (2009, February 1). *Nutrition Business Journal*, p. 12.

Austen, I. (2008, April 25). Plastic-bottle scare is a boon for some. *The New York Times*, p. C-1.

Chait, J. (2009, August). Way to go with BPA Sigg! Retrieved from http://archive.blisstree .com/live/way-to-go-with-the-bpa-sigg/

Chua, J. M. (2009). Patagonia to Sigg: We're finished! Retrieved from http://www.treehugger .com/files/2009/09/sigg-patagonia.php

Doshi, S. (2009, September). 6 reasons to ditch that plastic bottle. *San Jose Mercury News*, p. D-1.

EcoUsable offers the safe alternative to aluminum water bottles. (2009, September 23). Retrieved from http://www.businesswire.com/news/home/20090923005431/en/EcoUsable -Offers-Safe-Alternative-Aluminum-Water-Bottles.

Heath, R. L., & Palenchar, K. J. (2000). Community relations and risk communication: A longitudinal study of the impact of emergency response messages. *Journal of Public Relations Research, 12*, 131–161.

Hulette, E. (2008, August 16). Top 5 must-have items for back-to-school. *The Maryland Gazette*, p. B1.

King, R. S. (2008, May 4). Retailers yanking plastic bottles. *New Haven Register*, p. B2.

Koch, W., & Marohn, K. (2011, September). Hydration stations sweep colleges to promote tap water. *USA Today*. Retrieved from http://www.usatoday.com/news/education/story/ 2011–09–14/water-bottle-college/50403454/1#uslPageReturn

MacDonald, N. (2007, October 15). Plastic bottles get the eco-boot. *Maclean's*, p. 89.

Moran, S. (2009, January 26). Save your money, body and planet: These healthful, helpful tips hit that trifecta. *Star Tribune*, p. 1E.

Nontoxic alternatives. (2008, April 27). Retrieved from http://nymag.com/shopping/ features/46457/

Our reason for being. (n.d.). Retrieved from http://www.patagonia.com/us/patagonia.go? assetid=2047

Patagonia. (n.d.). Retrieved from http://www.patagonia.com/us/patagonia.go?assetid=2047

Rowland, P. (2009, August). Sigg bottles had BPA before August 2008. Retrieved from http:// lightgreenstairs.com/2009/08/

Sigg has BPA: Reputation in peril [Blog]. (2009, October 28). Retrieved from http://prstrategy andapplication.wordpress.com/tag/risk-communication/

True ingredients of bottled water (2010). Retrieved from http://www.banthebottle.net/ articles/

Turner, K. (2008, June 7). Shop around for a safe water bottle. *The Star Phoenix*, p. E3.

Zmuda, N. (2009, September 14). Sigg tries damage control on BPA issue. *Water &Recycling News*, p. 24.

CHAPTER 13

West Pharmaceutical Services' Dust Explosion

O n January 29, 2003, a deadly dust explosion occurred in Kinston, North Carolina. The West Pharmaceutical Services facility in Kinston was destroyed by an explosion that killed six workers and injured 38. The blast was so large it was felt 25 miles away. The ensuing fire burned for 2 days. The dust was a result of the facility's manufacturing of rubber stoppers for syringes. The precise culprit was polyethylene dust (*Final*, 2004). In addition to the deaths and injuries, the West Pharmaceutical facility in Kinston was completely destroyed. West Pharmaceutical had to cope with the human and financial toll the crisis would exact on its company.

Here is how West Pharmaceutical describes itself:

West Pharmaceutical Services is a leader in developing delivery systems that enhance the administration of pharmaceuticals. The products we make and the services we provide improve health care for people around the globe.

Chances are, West has already been a part of your life. You may have used a prescription drug that was safely packaged using West designed and manufactured components. You may have had your blood drawn for testing or donation with disposable devices that included West elastomeric components. Each and every day, millions of West's products are used around the world.

In the pharmaceutical and medical device industries, the West name is well-known. In that global arena, West has earned the reputation as a leader in the design and manufacture of products that ensure the safe delivery of pharmaceutical, health care and personal care products. Since its founding by Herman O. West in Philadelphia in 1923, our company has played a major role in advancing the progress of health care. ("West," 2011)

The Kinston facility employed 225 workers. The focus of the facility was on manufacturing intravenous components, syringe plungers, and rubber compounding (Jonsson, 2003).

Combustible dust is a significant threat in any industry where such dust occurs. For West Pharmaceutics, the problem was rubber dust. People often do not realize that the right dust (combustible) can cause a major explosion. The explosiveness of dust is explained by the "Dust Fire and Explosion Pentagon." This Pentagon contains the five factors necessary for a dust explosion: (a) sufficient amount of combustible dust, (b) oxygen, (c) an ignition source, (d) suspended dust, and (e) dust in a confined space (Rutledge, 2011). Dust is composed of fine particles created when materials are finely divided. When a combustible material and some noncombustible materials are dust, they can burn rapidly. When the right amounts of this dust are suspended in the air, it can create an explosion due to the rapid burning. The explosions can be deadly and even destroy an entire building.

A variety of materials can form combustible dust including aluminum, magnesium, wood, coal, plastics, sugar, paper, soap, rubber, dried blood, and some textiles. Industries at risk of combustible dust include food, grain, wood, pulp and paper, tobacco, plastics, rubber, metal, pesticides, and pharmaceuticals ("Combustible," 2011). It takes only 1/32 of an inch of dust over 5% of a room's surface to create an explosion risk. The ignition source can be as simple as a static electric charge. Hence, controlling for a combustible dust explosion can be a challenge but is not impossible. Organizations must be cognizant of the dust threat and work to reduce ignition sources, the suspension of dust, and the accumulation of dust—the three controllable elements of the Pentagon. Management cannot control oxygen or confined spaces (Rutledge, 2011). The January 2003 explosion at Kinston was a deadly convergence of the five elements of the Dust Fire and Explosion Pentagon.

Exhibit 13.1   Initial Statement by West Pharmaceutical

LIONVILLE, Pa.–(BUSINESS WIRE)–Jan. 29, 2003–West Pharmaceutical Services, Inc. (NYSE: WST) confirms that an explosion of unknown origin has occurred today at its manufacturing plant on Rouse Road in Kinston, North Carolina. The facility employs 255 people and is used to manufacture syringe plungers and intravenous (IV) fitments used for drug delivery systems and compounds rubber materials for distribution to other West manufacturing locations.

According to Don Morel, President and Chief Executive Officer, West Pharmaceutical Services, "We are obviously stunned by the news of this incident at our Kinston facility. Our overriding concern lies with the well-being and safety of our employees, their loved ones and the surrounding community. We are in the process of gathering information and will issue a more comprehensive statement when we have the facts to share."

After speaking with West officials today, the New York Stock Exchange temporarily suspended trading of West stock. No information on the reopening of trading is currently available.

Based at West's international headquarters in Lionville, Pennsylvania, Morel and a company crisis management team are traveling immediately to the Kinston facility to guide West's continuing response to the incident.

("West Pharmaceutical Comments on Plant Explosion," 2003)

A crisis involving the death of employees is traumatic for employees, their friends and families, and the community. As with any accident, there is confusion at first. West Pharmaceutical Services management expressed concern for any victims and noted the need to investigate the cause of the accident.

The next day, January 30, West Pharmaceutical Services provided an update on the situation. Part of crisis communication is releasing new information to stakeholders. The complete update is provided in Exhibit 13.2. Note that the message still began with the concern for the victims.

Exhibit 13.2   First Update by West Pharmaceutical

LIONVILLE, Penn.–(BUSINESS WIRE)–Jan. 30, 2003–Don Morel, President and Chief Executive Officer, West Pharmaceutical Services, Inc. (NYSE: WST) provides the following update on the explosion of unknown origin that occurred yesterday at its pharmaceutical rubber manufacturing plant on Rouse Road in Kinston, North Carolina. The facility employs 255 people and is used by West to manufacture syringe plungers and intravenous (IV) components and compounds rubber materials for use in West facilities throughout the United States. Kinston is one of West's five U.S. rubber compounding facilities, and one of ten worldwide.

"The worldwide West family sends its thoughts and prayers to the victims of this devastating incident, as well as to their families and loved ones," Morel said. "We deeply appreciate the outpouring of offers of support and help from people far and wide, and the continuing efforts of the rescue and recovery teams. Our primary focus right now is helping those in need, restoring safety to the area and working with federal, state and local officials to identify the root cause of this situation."

Injury Toll

"To date, our understanding is that three employees have been confirmed dead with 27 others injured, including eight in critical condition. We are in continuing contact with area hospitals and will provide additional information as we learn more."

Victim and Family Support

"I have personally had the opportunity to meet with members of the affected families and will be visiting with victims at area hospitals during the day. West has grief counselors on-site providing the victims and families with counseling. We are meeting with all Kinston employees today regarding the medical and salary benefits available to them from the company, as well as alternative employment possibilities that may exist at other West facilities. We are also in the process of identifying what might be available in the form of disaster relief."

Cause of Explosion

"We do not know the cause of the explosion at this time. We are working cooperatively with local and federal officials in an effort to determine the cause of this incident and will provide additional information as we get the facts. This is a process that could take days or longer."

Impact on West Business

"Clearly, the Kinston plant itself is not currently operational. However, while I and others at West are focused on this catastrophe, our operations and manufacturing teams worldwide are implementing our disaster recovery plans to utilize alternate manufacturing facilities and to minimize any possible disruption to our customers.

In addition, trading of West stock on the New York Stock Exchange has resumed, effective today, following yesterday's temporary suspension."

("West Pharmaceutical Provides Update on Plant," 2003)

The situation has a more somber tone because now actual numbers are appearing for the deaths and injuries from the crisis. Included is new information about the company, providing grief counseling to victims and their families. The cause is still under investigation as well. A new element is added to the message related to business continuity. Business continuity refers to the actions taken to keep an organization operational after a crisis (Coombs, 2012). The need for continuing operations is critical to customers. Investors and employees are affected as well. Investors want to know the effect on their investment while employees want to know what will happen to jobs and benefits.

The third update on February 4 from West Pharmaceutical focused almost exclusively on business continuity issues. An excerpt from the update can be found in Exhibit 13.3.

Exhibit 13.3 Third Update by West Pharmaceutical (February 4)

The severely damaged building hosts the Automated Compounding System (ACS), where bulk rubber materials are mixed into formulations for molding into medical device components, as well as a molding and finishing area, where finished components are produced. The ACS area was most severely damaged in the explosion and fire and is presumed to be a total loss at this time. Although West's access to the building has been very limited until today, initial visual observations by West personnel suggest that damage to the production facility is far less severe and it appears that a substantial part of the machinery, tooling and finished inventory may be recoverable.

The ACS at the Kinston plant is the largest of West's five U.S. rubber compounding facilities, and one of ten worldwide. To ensure the continued availability of critical healthcare products, rubber compounding requirements previously handled by the Kinston ACS will be shifted to alternate West facilities on an interim basis. West is working with its customers and the Food and Drug Administration to manage the temporary transfer of molding and finishing operations to other facilities in order to minimize interruptions in supply.

"We are encouraged by the progress of the work thus far, in collaboration with our customers, in devising alternate production plans," said Don Morel, West's President and Chief Executive Officer. "We are additionally encouraged by the condition of the equipment and tooling in the molding and finishing areas of the building. In the last two days, our manufacturing and engineering personnel and technical consultants were able to visit the building to begin evaluating the damage first-hand. While it is still too early to estimate all of the damage and effects, our preliminary assessment is that the situation is much more manageable than we first imagined. We now need to complete a more detailed assessment."

"It is obviously critical that any work we do in the damaged site can be safely performed, and we will work with environmental authorities to ensure that this is the case," Morel continued. "We are pursuing our own investigation into what happened and we will continue to cooperate with the ongoing investigations by North Carolina Departments of Labor and Natural Resources, The United States Chemical Safety Board, the Environmental Protection Agency, the Bureau of Alcohol, Tobacco, and Firearms and all local authorities who are investigating last Wednesday's events."

("West Pharmaceutical Provides Update on Kinston Plant," 2003, para. 1–5)

The message describes how West Pharmaceutics Services is working with its customers to maintain the supplies the customers need. There is also a reminder that the case is still being investigated.

The fourth update on February 11 builds upon the business continuity aspect of the crisis; it can be found in Exhibit 13.4.

Exhibit 13.4 Fourth Update by West Pharmaceutical (February 11)

LIONVILLE, Pa., Feb 11, 2003 (BUSINESS WIRE)—West Pharmaceutical Services, Inc. (NYSE: WST) today provides an update on recovery and manufacturing plans in reference to the explosion that occurred on January 29 at its plant in Kinston, North Carolina. The severely damaged building houses the Automated Compounding System (ACS), where bulk raw materials are compounded into rubber formulations for molding into medical device components, as well as a molding and finishing area, where finished components are produced. In addition to supplying stock for the Kinston molding operation, the ACS compounded rubber materials for distribution to other West manufacturing locations.

Recovery efforts at the site are well underway. Substantially all of the finished goods from the molding facility have been removed and are being shipped to customers subject to quality assurance approval. The majority of the molding tools has been recovered and, based on a preliminary assessment, appears to be in useable condition. The tooling has been shipped to other West facilities in Florida, Nebraska, Singapore and the U.K., where it will be put into service, subject to cleaning and further evaluation to determine suitability for production. This process should be completed within the next two to four weeks.

To accommodate the loss of the ACS facility, some rubber compounding production will move to West's St. Petersburg, Florida and Kearney, Nebraska operations, with other capacity shifting to Singapore and European operations to support mold tooling moved to those venues. In addition, previously approved U.S. suppliers will be re-qualified for support as needed.

"The responsiveness of our recovery and logistics teams has produced an initial assessment of our recoverable assets and a better understanding of our near-term customer needs," said Donald E. Morel, Jr, Ph.D., Chief Executive Officer and President of West. "This information will allow us to prioritize our production schedules as appropriate to assure continuity of supply to our customers. At this point, we believe that a substantial portion of the Kinston compounding and molding production can be incorporated into our other manufacturing facilities by late April or early May.

We hope to be able to rebuild in Kinston and we are accelerating our efforts to resume production there," added Dr. Morel.

West is increasing production at its other facilities around the world to offset the loss of production at the Kinston plant. West is also in the process of relocating some of the many skilled employees from Kinston to other West U.S. facilities on a temporary basis. Transfers will begin next week as employees' skills and interests are matched with current and anticipated manufacturing needs.

"I'm proud of the effort and dedication shown by our employees in response to the challenges presented by the Kinston situation," said Dr. Morel, "and we continue to be heartened by the support shown our company and employees worldwide, by our customers, shareholders and the Kinston community."

("West Pharmaceutical Provides Update on Assessment," 2003)

West Pharmaceutical is emphasizing how it is increasing production elsewhere to compensate for lost production from the Kinston facility. A new theme that emerges in this update is the commitment to rebuild the Kinston facility. There are 255 jobs associated with the facility, and it is important to the Kinston community. During this time, the community had committed $600,000 toward rebuilding the facility (Jonsson, 2003).

While the third and fourth updates were focused on business continuity, West Pharmaceutical Services still had a concern for the victims. On February 14, management announced there would be a memorial service to honor those lost and the survivors of the crisis. Here is the announcement:

Feb 14, 2003 (BUSINESS WIRE)—

West Pharmaceutical Services, Inc. (NYSE: WST)

WHAT: "A Service of Healing and Remembrance." A closed memorial service will be held to honor the survivors and commemorate the lives of those that were lost during the Kinston plant tragedy.

WHEN: Monday, February 17, 2003, 5:30 p.m.

WHO: For West employees and families of those injured and lost in the tragedy that occurred on January 29th at the Kinston plant.

Reverends Harold Burton and Jerry Waters will preside over the Memorial Service. Remarks will be delivered by Senator Elizabeth Dole on behalf of George W. Bush, President of the United States; West President and CEO Don Morel; Governor Michael F. Easley (tentative); West Kinston Plant Manager Thomas Clagon and West employees.

WHERE: Lenoir Community College, Waller Building Auditorium, 231 Highway 58 South, Kinston

MEDIA: Broadcast and radio outlets: Satellite information: AMC 2, transponder 1 Ku band, Downlink Frequency 11720 Vertical, Audio Subcarriers 6.2 / 6.8

Troubleshooting phone number: [. . .]

Media needs to show credentials to attend. Please contact [. . .] in order to receive your credentials.

Print and online outlets: The constraints of the size of the auditorium will determine the number of cameras allowed into the memorial. Be sure to have a telescopic lens. Flashes will not be necessary. Media is invited to watch the memorial on televisions in rooms adjacent to the auditorium. Please arrive by 5:00 p.m.

("Memorial Service," 2003)

Inclement weather caused the memorial service to be moved from the 18th to the 20th. Exhibit 13.5 contains the statement West Pharmaceutical Services provided about the event.

Exhibit 13.5   Inclement Weather for Memorial Service Announcement

LIONVILLE, Pa., Feb 20, 2003 (BUSINESS WIRE)—West Pharmaceutical Services, Inc. (NYSE: WST) announces a memorial service to be held today, February 20, to honor survivors and to commemorate the lives lost during the explosion that occurred on January 29 at its plant in Kinston, North Carolina. The memorial service, entitled, "A Service of Healing and Remembrance," is to be held at 5:30 p.m. at the Lenoir Community College in Kinston.

The private memorial has been organized by West for the employees and families of the West Pharmaceutical Services Kinston Plant and those of the two independent contractors working in the facility. The West employees recovering at the North Carolina Jaycee Burn Center at the University of North Carolina Hospitals in Chapel Hill, along with their families, will be able to view the memorial service via a televised satellite feed to the hospital.

Reverends Harold Burton and Jerry Waters will preside over the service. Senator Elizabeth Dole (R-North Carolina) will deliver remarks on behalf of President George W. Bush. Also providing remarks will be Donald E. Morel, Jr., PhD, President and Chief Executive Officer of West, North Carolina Governor Mike Easley and West employees.

"This is a time of great sorrow for our company. It is fitting that we come together to remember those who lost their lives, and to offer our prayers for the injured and all families who will be forever changed as a result of this tragic accident," said Donald E. Morel, Jr. "We will also pay tribute to the firemen, police, National Guard, emergency responders, doctors, nurses, relief agencies, clergy and community volunteers who have all given so much of themselves to support our employees and their families."

As part of West's continuing effort to assist their Kinston employees, the Company has established the Kinston Employee Fund in coordination with the American Red Cross and The United Way in Kinston. The fund has received donations from around the world.

("West Pharmaceutical Announces Plant Memorial Service," 2003)

The Service of Healing and Remembrance was about the victims, including those who were lost and those who survived. Also, there was information about a fund to help employees. Later in February, West Pharmaceutical Services addressed concerns about jobs for current employees of the Kinston facility. The plan was to have many of the employees work at a West Pharmaceutical Services facility in Nebraska to help with the increased production load there. The statement can be found in Exhibit 13.6.

Exhibit 13.6   Production Statement

LIONVILLE, Pa., Feb 21, 2003 (BUSINESS WIRE)—West Pharmaceutical Services, Inc. (NYSE: WST) announces that employees from its Kinston, North Carolina manufacturing facility, where an explosion occurred on January 29, will be temporarily relocated to its facility in Kearney, Nebraska.

In an effort to restore production to pre-casualty levels, West will increase production at other selected West facilities. Approximately 60 employees from West's Kinston facility will temporarily relocate to West's Kearney, Nebraska facility for compression molding of syringe plungers and intravenous (IV) components. Employees will work on a three-week rotation, returning to Kinston every fourth week. West will provide transportation, accommodations and a per diem allowance, as well as a designated displacement premium, to each of these employees.

Kinston employees traveling to temporary positions in Nebraska include those with skills in the compounding, molding and trimming processes required for the production of medical device components, as well as those who can provide important maintenance and management support. These employees will continue to retain the same healthcare benefits, vacation and pension as the Kinston facility employees. In addition, the temporarily transferred employees will receive pay for travel time. Overtime, taxes and holidays will be subject to the local rules governing the Kearney, Nebraska facility.

"Our Kinston workers are among some of West's most highly-skilled and we are pleased that so many have volunteered to participate in this temporary relocation," said Rick Luzzi, Senior Vice President of Human Resources at West. "With their commitment and our network of facilities, we hope to achieve minimal disruption to the supply of our critical medical products to healthcare providers and patients around the world."

("West Pharmaceutical Announces Temporary Relocation," 2003, para. 1-4)

Additional information for employees about their benefits followed quickly with this information about help from the State. The full statement about the benefits can be found in Exhibit 13.7. Though not provided by the company, the benefits would help those employees who were unemployed due to the facility's destruction.

Exhibit 13.7   Benefits Announcement

LIONVILLE, Pa., Feb 28, 2003 (BUSINESS WIRE)—West Pharmaceutical Services, Inc. (NYSE: WST) expresses its support and appreciation to North Carolina Governor Mike Easley (D) for his decision to sign legislation yesterday allowing West workers who were employed at the Kinston plant, destroyed in an explosion on January 29, to receive immediate unemployment benefits from the State.

This legislation, approved by the General Assembly and signed by the Governor, allows for the Employment Security Commission (ESC) to waive the standard one-week waiting period for unemployment benefits, traditionally reserved for verifying eligibility. West employees will now be eligible for State unemployment benefits as of March 1.

"We are grateful to the General Assembly for their timely passage of this important legislation which allows our workers to receive benefits without delay," said Donald E. Morel, Jr., President and CEO of West. "It is clear that West, along with Governor Easley and a host of federal, state and local officials, is committed to the best interests of West employees. With this intention, I will continue to work closely with all elected officials including the Governor and his staff over the coming months to find creative ways to continue to aid West employees and their families and to pursue our intentions to rebuild in North Carolina."

("West Pharmaceutical Thanks General Assembly," 2003, para. 1–3)

In May of 2003, West Pharmaceutical Services returned to the theme of rebuilding. This was a specific announcement that supported the initial commitment to rebuild. It can be found in Exhibit 13.8. The focus is on the future. The new facility will benefit the employees and the community as the lost facility is replaced.

Exhibit 13.8   Rebuilding Announcement

LIONVILLE, Pa.–(BUSINESS WIRE)–May 16, 2003–West Pharmaceutical Services (NYSE: WST) today announced the signing of an agreement to purchase land and a partially completed industrial building in Lenoir County, N.C. The Company plans to use the site to rebuild the Kinston, N.C. molding operations destroyed in an explosion and fire on January 29, 2003. At a special meeting held on Friday, May 9, the Lenoir County Board of Commissioners approved the sale of a county-owned building to West along with an economic incentive package. In addition, North Carolina Governor Michael Easley announced on May 14 that North Carolina will invest $250,000 in the project, which involves a $16 million investment by West and will employ over 200 people.

West's new facility is located in the Lenoir County Business/Industrial Park on U.S. Highway 70, approximately four miles from the fire-damaged building. The previously unoccupied structure was developed and built by the county and consists of approximately 100,000 square feet of flexible industrial space on an estimated 25 acres of land. West intends to make significant improvements to the building beginning this summer. West plans to occupy the facility by the end of the year and will be in full operation in 2004.

"West has been an integral part of the Kinston community for nearly 30 years, employing a dedicated and skilled workforce. It has always been our hope and intent to remain in Kinston, and we are excited to have arrived at a solution that will make this happen," said Donald E. Morel, Jr., Ph.D., Chairman, CEO and President of West Pharmaceutical Services. "We are very grateful to the City of Kinston, Lenoir County and the State of North Carolina for working diligently with us to develop a solution that benefits our employees, our company and our local, county and state organizations. Their consistent support and quick responses will enable us to accelerate our rebuilding program, put our Kinston employees back to work and continue to provide products critical to our healthcare customers."

("West Pharmaceutical Announces Agreement to Rebuild," 2003, para. 1–3)

In July of 2003, West Pharmaceutical Services broke ground on the new facility. The complete groundbreaking statement can be found in Exhibit 13.9. While moving forward, West Pharmaceutical Services included recognition of those who were lost in the crisis. There was hope tempered with remembrance.

Exhibit 13.9   Groundbreaking Statement

West Pharmaceutical Services, Inc. (NYSE: WST) today announced that it will hold a Groundbreaking Ceremony on July 1 at noon to mark the formal start of a project to re-establish a compression molding operation in Kinston, NC. West's plant in Kinston was destroyed as the result of an accident on January 29, 2003. The ceremony will be held at the new site, located in the Lenoir County Business/Industrial Park on U.S. Highway 70, approximately four miles from the fire-damaged building.

Several local, state and federal officials are scheduled to speak, including Bruce Parson, President, Kinston/Lenoir County Chamber of Commerce; Kinston Mayor Johnnie Mosley; Chairman Oscar E. Herring, Lenoir County Board of Commissioners; Congressman Frank W. Ballance, Jr. (D-NC); and Senator John Edwards (D-NC). Also providing remarks will be Donald E. Morel, Jr., Ph.D., Chairman and Chief Executive Officer of West Pharmaceutical Services.

"While we continue to grieve for the loss of our friends and colleagues who lost their lives in the Kinston plant tragedy, we must look ahead and work collectively towards a future of productive growth," said Dr. Morel. "Today's groundbreaking is an important first step on our road to recovery, and we at West are very grateful to the City of Kinston, Lenoir County, the State of North Carolina and our employees for their consistent support and generosity during these difficult times and throughout the rebuilding process."

("West Pharmaceutical Announces Groundbreaking," 2003, para. 1–3)

Remembrance would be a continuing theme for West Pharmaceutical Services as the new facility approached completion in 2004. Prior to the next facility opening, the first anniversary of the tragedy would be observed. West Pharmaceutical Services led the anniversary observance. The company's statement about the anniversary observance can be found in Exhibit 13.10. The memories of the victims of the explosion were being honored by being remembered.

Exhibit 13.10   Anniversary Service

LIONVILLE, Penn.–(BUSINESS WIRE)–Jan. 29, 2004–West Pharmaceutical Services, Inc. (NYSE: WST) held a commemorative service today in honor of those lost and injured during an accidental explosion at its Kinston, N.C. facility one year ago. The service was held at Immanuel Baptist Church in Kinston for employees and the families of the deceased, and was made available company-wide via a live audio hook-up.

The ceremony was conducted by Reverend John Hoye and consisted of music and prayers. In opening remarks, Troy Player, Kinston plant manager, said: "I joined West several months after the accident, and since that time, I have learned there is a distinct strength of character in every West employee."

Donald E. Morel, Jr., Ph.D., the Company's Chairman and Chief Executive Officer of West Pharmaceutical Services, addressed the audience on a solemn note, listing those whose lives were lost and those who suffered serious injuries. He acknowledged the community's vital role in recovery, and cited the groundbreaking for a new manufacturing facility as a sign of renewal. Dr. Morel convened the event with a moment of silence, observed at West facilities worldwide, at the exact moment when the accident occurred.

"Today, as we gather here in sadness to remember the six people we have lost and to support the many who continue to cope, we do so with the knowledge that our community is strong, even in the wake of tragedy," said Dr. Morel.

("West Pharmaceutical Holds Commemorative," 2004, para. 1–4)

The memory would be permanent as West Pharmaceutical Services decided to place commemorative plaques in the lobby of its new facility. A special ceremony was held before the facility was officially opened. Here is a description of the event:

KINSTON, N.C.—(BUSINESS WIRE)—June 9, 2004—West Pharmaceutical Services (NYSE: WST) today dedicated two memorial plaques for permanent display in the lobby and garden of its new Kinston facility. In a private service attended by Kinston employees and the families of those who lost their lives in the January 29, 2003, accident, West established a memorial to honor the six people lost in the explosion.

"It is especially appropriate for West to establish a memorial to our colleagues at the new West facility in Kinston," said Donald E. Morel, Jr., Ph.D., Chairman and Chief Executive Officer of West Pharmaceutical Services, Inc. "As we embark upon a new beginning, the plaques will help keep the memories of six special people in our collective thoughts."

The memorial plaque inscriptions read "We remember our colleagues" and list the six employees who passed away: James C. Byrd, Kevin M. Cruiess, Butch Grant, William A. Gray, Milton A. Murrell and Faye Jones Wilkins. ("West Pharmaceutical Dedicates Memorial," 2004, para. 1–3)

West Pharmaceutical created a permanent memorial to those employees who lost their lives in the tragedy. The new facility was officially reopened for production on August 26, 2004 ("West Pharmaceutical Announces Official Opening," 2004).

During the entire rebuilding process, the incident was still under investigation. West Pharmaceutical had cooperated with the U.S. Chemical Safety Board (CSB), the Federal body charged with investigating these types of industrial accidents. In September of 2004, the CSB released its results. Here are the primary results presented in the report:

1. Revise policies and procedures for new material safety reviews. (2003–07-I-NC-R1) In particular:

- Use the most recent versions of material safety data sheets (MSDSs) and other technical hazard information.

- Fully identify the hazardous characteristics of new materials, including relevant physical and chemical properties, to ensure that those characteristics are incorporated into safety practices, as appropriate.

- Include an engineering element that identifies and addresses the potential safety implications of new materials on manufacturing processes.

2. Develop and implement policies and procedures for safety reviews of engineering projects. (2003–07-I-NC-R2) In particular:

- Address the hazards of individual materials and equipment and their effect on entire processes and facilities.

- Consider hazards during the conceptual design phase, as well as during engineering and construction phases.

- Cover all phases of the project, including engineering and construction performed by outside firms.

- Identify and consider applicable codes and standards in the design.

3. Identify West manufacturing facilities that use combustible dusts. Ensure that they incorporate applicable safety precautions described in NFPA 654, Standard for the Prevention of Fire and Dust Explosions From the Manufacturing, Processing, and Handling of Combustible Particulate Solids. (2003–07-I-NC-R3). In particular:

- Ensure that penetrations of partitions, floors, walls, and ceilings are sealed dust-tight.

- Ensure that spaces inaccessible to housekeeping are sealed to prevent dust accumulation.

4. Improve hazard communication programs so that the hazards of combustible dust are clearly identified and communicated to the workforce. In particular, ensure that the most current MSDSs are in use and that employees receive training on the revised/updated information. (2003–07-I-NC-R4)

5. Communicate the findings and recommendations of this report to the West Pharmaceutical Services, Inc., workforce. (2003–07-I-NC-R5). (*Final*, 2004, pp. 61–62)

West Pharmaceutical Services issued a response to the CSB report. The complete statement can be found in Exhibit 13.11.

West Pharmaceutical took some exceptions with the CSB report. Of particular note was the recommended use of a new code. West Pharmaceutical Services wanted stakeholders to know that it had complied with existing regulations prior to the explosion and that the recommended regulation would have gone beyond the required compliance in 2003. With the investigation completed and the facility operating again, the crisis appears to be over.

Exhibit 13.11   Response to CSB Report

Dr. Donald E. Morel, West's Chairman and Chief Executive Officer, said "West appreciates the importance, magnitude and complexity of the task undertaken by the CSB and the significant effort that it and other agencies have invested in their respective efforts to understand the circumstances of this tragic event.

West has fully cooperated with the state, federal and local agencies that have investigated various aspects of the Kinston accident, including the CSB. The Company has also shared the findings of its own investigation with the CSB with the hope that this information would make each investigation more complete.

The Company, following its own exhaustive, professionally directed investigation, has concluded that this accident was the result of a combination of unforeseen factors. The CSB, rather than explaining the initiation of the event, has focused its analysis and recommendations on two factors: the presence of combustible dust and the application of fire safety codes.

The CSB has criticized West for not complying with a fire code standard that was not applicable to the construction of this facility and it is not clear to West or from the

CSB report that such a change would have prevented the accident. West's procedures for evaluating materials, such as those that might produce combustible dust, are also identified as being inadequate in several respects. That conclusion cannot be reconciled with current manufacturing safety standards and federal regulations, which stipulate that West and its employees can and should rely on the hazard-related labeling of materials by the manufacturers that supply those materials to West. The product that generated the dust at issue was not accompanied by any warning of a potential dust explosion hazard. The material safety data sheet, or MSDS, given to West by the manufacturer said that there were no known hazards. West believes that the CSB's criticisms would be more appropriately directed at those entities that the CSB itself found did not warn West of the potential dust hazards.

The explosion on January 29, 2003 was triggered by a complex series of events which the CSB did not conclusively explain, in spite of all of the time, effort and cooperation devoted to this effort. Investigators may not agree on each event or circumstance that contributed to this tragic accident. However, there is apparent consensus that a central factor in this accident was the unseen accumulation of dust, which proved to be combustible and provided the fuel for the explosion."

Dr. Morel concluded, saying "West has always considered workplace safety and cleanliness a significant priority and has maintained rigorous standards in all of its manufacturing facilities worldwide. The visible work area in Kinston was kept clean and free of dust. In the immediate aftermath of the explosion, West conducted a thorough safety review of all of its facilities, with a particular emphasis on the risks posed by dust. For more than a year, West has been implementing many of the steps now being recommended by the CSB. For example, the Company has carefully reviewed the health and safety procedures in its plants and has implemented procedures, where necessary, to ensure the safety of its plants."

("West Pharmaceutical Comments on Chemical," 2004, para. 2–7)

In general, the community supported West Pharmaceutical after the explosion and hoped they would rebuild. An early headline from nearby news station WRAL read: "Kinston Residents Hope West Pharmaceutical Will Rebuild Plant Destroyed in Fire" ("Kinston," 2003). When the plant reopened, the community and news media had a positive reaction. There was an excitement that the workers that had been temporarily transferred to other West Pharmaceutical facilities out of state were returning. As one story reported, "More than 100 workers were forced to take temporary jobs out of state. Now, those workers are returning home to their old jobs at a new plant" ("Kinston Plant," 2004, para. 1). The joy was mixed with some sadness as people remembered the victims. "The celebration was an emotional one as survivors of the January 2003 plant explosion reunited and shared their experiences and recovery" ("Kinston Pharmaceutical," 2004, para. 3). The community support and positive media stories reflect the economic value West Pharmaceutical has represented to the area. In 2007, the company, with state support, announced an expansion to the new Kinston facility. Kinston City Manager Scott Stevens noted West Pharmaceutical was "a good employer in our community" ("Kinston," 2007, para. 8).

Thirty Kinston workers were part of a class action lawsuit against West Pharmaceutical that was dismissed in 2006 ("Victims," 2004; "Workers," 2006). As Robert Fuller, an employee seriously injured in the blast remarked, "I really get upset about it, you know, to know that someone could have prevented something that is going to affect you for the rest of your life. Every time I look at myself in the mirror, I'm going to know I've been through something" ("Workers," 2006, para. 4). Not everyone considers the crisis to be over. The new Kinston facility has operated without any significant incidents since 2004 until the writing of this case in late 2012.

Reading Guide

1. If this situation is a crisis, what type of crisis is it?

2. What is the problem and the source(s) of the problem in this case?

3. What stakeholders should be interested in this case?

4. What is business continuity?

Discussion Questions

1. How did West Pharmaceutical deal with the need for remembrance and a memorial? Did their efforts hurt or help their reputation? Justify your answer.

2. Why did business continuity play such a prominent role in this case?

3. What effect do you think the dispute over the report had on West Pharmaceutical's crisis communication efforts? Why did the company dispute the report?

4. What role did rebuilding the facility play in this case? Did the rebuild reflect the necessary elements of the discourse of renewal?

5. Which stakeholder groups seemed to be the focus of the West Pharmaceutical messages, and what evidence is there to support your conclusion?

6. How have economic factors affected how some stakeholders reacted to West Pharmaceutical's crisis communication efforts?

Websites

U.S. Chemical Safety Board statement on West Pharmaceutical: http://www.csb.gov/newsroom/detail.aspx?nid=114

U.S. Chemical Safety Board video about dust explosions: http://www.csb.gov/newsroom/detail.aspx?nid=114

West Pharmaceutical: http://www.westpharma.com/en/Pages/Default.aspx (Click on News and Events tab then the Financial Releases tab to view actual news releases)

References

Combustible dusts. (2011). Retrieved from http://www.osha.gov/Publications/3371 combustible-dust.html

Coombs, W. T. (2012). *Ongoing crisis communication: Planning, managing, and responding* (3rd ed.). Thousand Oaks, CA: Sage.

Final report for West Pharmaceutical. (2004). Retrieved from http://www.csb.gov/assets/ document/CSB_WestReport.pdf

Jonsson, P. (2003). Lessons from a factory fire. Retrieved from http://www.csmonitor .com/2003/0203/p02s01-usgn.html.

Kinston pharmaceutical plant back in business after deadly explosion. (2004, August 26). Retrieved from http://www.wral.com/news/local/story/1090645/

Kinston plant to expand years after explosion. (2007). Retrieved from http://www.wral.com/ business/story/1971945/

Kinston plant workers return to old jobs at new plant. (2004, March 17). Retrieved from http://www.wral.com/news/local/story/109481/

Kinston residents hope West Pharmaceuticals will rebuild plant destroyed in fire. (2003, April 3). Retrieved from http://www.wral.com/news/local/story/104759/

Memorial service to be held in honor of survivors and those lost at West Pharmaceutical Services Kinston Plant. (2003, February 14). Retrieved from http://www.westpharma .com/EN/EVENTS/Pages/News.aspx?reqtype=releasetxt&reqdisplay=releasetxt& reqid=382895

Rutledge, C. (2011). Five factors: The combustible dust fire and explosion pentagon. Retrieved from http://www.fsmmag.com/Articles/2009/11/Five%20Factors%20The%20Combustible %20Dust%20Fire%20and%20Explosion%20Pentagon.htm

Victims in Kinston plant explosion file class action lawsuit. (2004). Retrieved from http:// www.wral.com/news/local/story/110513/

West Pharmaceutical Services announces agreement to rebuild molding operations in Lenoir County, North Carolina. (2003, May 16). Retrieved from http://www.westpharma.com/ EN/EVENTS/Pages/News.aspx?reqtype=releasetxt&reqdisplay=releasetxt&reqid=414019

West Pharmaceutical Services announces groundbreaking ceremony for New Lenoir County, North Carolina, facility. (2003, July 1). Retrieved from http://www.westpharma.com/EN/ EVENTS/Pages/News.aspx?reqtype=releasetxt&reqdisplay=releasetxt&reqid=427652

West Pharmaceutical Services announces Kinston plant memorial service and Kinston employee fund. (2003, February 20). Retrieved from http://www.westpharma.com/EN/ EVENTS/Pages/News.aspx?reqtype=releasetxt&reqdisplay=releasetxt&reqid=384381

West Pharmaceutical Services announces official opening of North Carolina facility with ribbon-cutting ceremony. (2004, August 26). Retrieved from http://www.westpharma.com/EN/ EVENTS/Pages/News.aspx?reqtype=releasetxt&reqdisplay=releasetxt&reqid=607321

West Pharmaceutical Services announces temporary relocation of Kinston plant employees (2003, February 21). Retrieved from http://www.westpharma.com/EN/EVENTS/Pages/ News.aspx?reqtype=releasetxt&reqdisplay=releasetxt&reqid=384808

West Pharmaceutical Services comments on Chemical Safety and Hazard Investigation Board presentation. (2004, September 23). Retrieved from http://www.westpharma .com/EN/EVENTS/Pages/News.aspx?reqtype=releasetxt&reqdisplay=releasetxt& reqid=618294

West Pharmaceutical Services comments on plant explosion. (2003, January 29). Retrieved from http://www.westpharma.com/EN/EVENTS/Pages/News.aspx?reqtype=releasetxt &reqdisplay=releasetxt&reqid=376450

West Pharmaceutical Services dedicates memorial to colleagues in new Kinston facility: Private service held today for Kinston employees and family members. (2004, June 9). Retrieved from http://www.westpharma.com/EN/EVENTS/Pages/News.aspx?reqtype= releasetxt&reqdisplay=releasetxt&reqid=580427

West Pharmaceutical Services holds commemorative service: Company observes first anniversary of Kinston, North Carolina plant accident. (2004, January 29). Retrieved from http://www.westpharma.com/EN/EVENTS/Pages/News.aspx?reqtype=releasetxt&reqd isplay=releasetxt&reqid=489726

West Pharmaceutical Services provides update on assessment of manufacturing capabilities. (2003). Retrieved from http://www.westpharma.com/EN/EVENTS/Pages/News.aspx? reqtype=releasetxt&reqdisplay=releasetxt&reqid=381506

West Pharmaceutical Services provides update on Kinston plant status. (2003, February 4). Retrieved from http://www.westpharma.com/EN/EVENTS/Pages/News.aspx?reqtype= releasetxt&reqdisplay=releasetxt&reqid=378795

West Pharmaceutical Services provides update on plant explosion. (2003, January 30). Retrieved from http://www.westpharma.com/EN/EVENTS/Pages/News.aspx?reqtype= releasetxt&reqdisplay=releasetxt&reqid=376849

West Pharmaceutical Services thanks General Assembly and governor for legislation expediting benefits for displaced Kinston workers. (2003, February 28). Retrieved from http://www.westpharma.com/EN/EVENTS/Pages/News.aspx?reqtype=releasetxt&reqd isplay=releasetxt&reqid=387205

West story. (2011). Retrieved from http://www.westpharma.com/en/about/Pages/TheWest Story.aspx

Workers still scarred by West Pharmaceutical explosion. (2006). Retrieved from http://www .wral.com/news/local/story/1088462/

CHAPTER 14

Jensen Farm, Listeria, and Cantaloupe

F ruit is supposed to be good for people's health. A common fruit people eat in the summer and fall is cantaloupe. Cantaloupe is orange, juicy, and sweet. In the fall of 2011, some cantaloupe in the United States were also deadly. On September 2, 2011, the Colorado Department of Public Health and Environment (CDPHE) informed the Centers for Disease Control and Prevention (CDC), the federal office charged with public health safety, that it was investigating seven cases of listeriosis (*Listeria*). On September 6, the CDC's PulseNet identified the same listeriosis strain in patients from two other states. PulseNet is a network of public health laboratories that identify the DNA "fingerprints" of food-borne disease-causing bacteria.

Exhibit 14.1   FDA Recall Information

FDA PRESS RELEASE

For Immediate Release: Sept. 14, 2011

Media Inquiries: [. . .]

Consumer Inquiries: 888-INFO-FDA

FDA warns consumers not to eat Rocky Ford Cantaloupes shipped by Jensen Farms

Jensen Farms recalls Rocky Ford cantaloupe due to potential link to a multi-state outbreak of listeriosis

Fast Facts

- The FDA is warning consumers not to eat Rocky Ford Cantaloupe shipped by Jensen Farms and to throw away recalled product that may still be in their home.

- Jensen Farms is voluntarily recalling Rocky Ford Cantaloupe shipped from July 29 through September 10, 2011, and distributed to at least 17 states with possible further distribution.
- The recalled cantaloupes have the potential to be contaminated with Listeria and may be linked to a multi-state outbreak of listeriosis.
- The CDC reports that at least 22 people in seven states have been infected with the outbreak-associated strains of *Listeria monocytogenes* as of September 14.
- Patients reported eating whole cantaloupes they purchased from grocery stores marketed from the Rocky Ford growing region of Colorado.
- While all people are susceptible to Listeria, older adults, persons with weakened immune systems and pregnant women are at particular risk.

What Is the Problem?

The FDA is warning consumers not to eat Rocky Ford Cantaloupe shipped by Jensen Farms of Granada, Colo. The majority of the patients reported eating cantaloupe marketed from the Rocky Ford growing region. FDA's traceback data from the State of Colorado about their confirmed cases of *Listeria monocytogenes* have identified a common producer of Rocky Ford cantaloupes. That producer is Jensen Farms. Although the investigation is ongoing, no other Rocky Ford cantaloupe producer has been found in common in the Colorado traceback.

Jensen Farms is voluntarily recalling Rocky Ford Cantaloupe. The recalled cantaloupes were shipped from the Rocky Ford growing region of Colorado from July 29 through September 10 and are potentially linked to a multi-state outbreak of listeriosis. The recalled cantaloupes were distributed to at least 17 states with possible further distribution.

What Are the Symptoms of Listeriosis?

Listeriosis is a rare and serious illness caused by eating food contaminated with bacteria called Listeria. Persons who think they might have become ill should consult their doctor. A person with listeriosis usually has fever and muscle aches.

Who Is At Risk?

Listeriosis can be fatal, especially in certain high-risk groups. These groups include older adults, people with compromised immune systems and certain chronic medical conditions (such as cancer), and unborn babies and newborns. In pregnant women, listeriosis can cause miscarriage, stillbirth, and serious illness or death in newborn babies, though the mother herself rarely becomes seriously ill.

What Do Consumers Need To Do?

Consumers should not eat Rocky Ford Cantaloupe shipped by Jensen Farms and should immediately discard the recalled cantaloupes in the trash in a sealed container so that children and animals, such as wildlife, cannot access them. Consumers who are concerned about illness from *Listeria monocytogenes* should consult their healthcare professionals.

What Does the Product Look Like?

The cantaloupe may be labeled: Colorado Grown, Distributed by Frontera Produce, USA, Pesticide Free, Jensenfarms.com, Sweet Rocky Fords.

The cantaloupes are packed in cartons that are labeled: Frontera Produce, www .fronteraproduce.com or with Frontera Produce, Rocky Ford Cantaloupes. Both cartons also include: Grown and packed by Jensen Farms Granada, CO and Shipped by Frontera Produce LTD, Edinburg, Texas.

Not all of the recalled cantaloupes are labeled with a sticker. Consumers should consult the retailer if they have questions about the origin of a cantaloupe.

Where Is it Distributed?

The recalled cantaloupes were distributed to the following states: IL, WY, TN, UT, TX, CO, MN, KS, NM, NC, MO, NE, OK, AZ, NJ, NY, PA. Further distribution is possible.

What Is Being Done About the Problem?

Jensen Farms is working with the FDA and the State of Colorado to remove its Rocky Ford Cantaloupe from the marketplace. The FDA is also working with CDC, the states and other regulatory partners to investigate where in the supply chain the contamination occurred.

This is the first time a *Listeria monocytogenes* outbreak has been reportedly linked to whole cantaloupe. Foods that typically have been associated with foodborne outbreaks of Listeriosis are deli meats, hot dogs, and Mexican-style soft cheeses made with unpasteurized milk. Listeriosis has not often been associated with the consumption of fresh produce with the exception of two foodborne illness outbreaks related to consumption of sprouts in 2009 and fresh-cut celery in 2010.

Because of this unusual circumstance, FDA's newly formed Coordinated Outbreak Response and Evaluation (CORE) Network is working with FDA Districts, CDC, the States and other regulatory partners on a root cause analysis to determine where in the supply chain and what circumstances likely caused the implicated cantaloupe to be contaminated. FDA is exploring whether harvesting and/or postharvest practices may have contributed to this contamination, as well as what could be done differently to prevent future occurrences.

For more information:

CDC Investigation on multi-state listeriosis outbreak:

http://www.cdc.gov/nczved/divisions/dfbmd/diseases/listeriosis/outbreak .htm14

Listeria page on FS.gov: http://www.foodsafety.gov/poisoning/causes/bacteria viruses/listeria/index.htm15

Produce Safety page on FDA: http://www.fda.gov/Food/ResourcesForYou/ Consumers/ucm1142996

Coordinated Outbreak Response and Evaluation (CORE) Network:

http://www.fda.gov/Food/FoodSafety/CORENetwork/default.htm7.

("FDA," 2011)

The CDC has victims of a food-borne illness complete questionnaires to help them locate possible sources of contamination. The CDC's questionnaire research found "Rocky Mountain" cantaloupe to be the common food and likely source of the outbreak. By September 14, 2011, the CDC had located the exact source of the listeriosis, Jensen Farms in Granada, Colorado. The Food and Drug Administration (FDA) announcement for the recall of cantaloupe from Jensen Farms is provided in Exhibit 14.1. Note how the FDA directly told people not to eat cantaloupe from Jensen Farms. On October 19, 2011, the FDA announced it had found the likely sources of the listeriosis contamination at Jensen Farms. The text of the FDA announcement is located in Exhibit 14.2. Of particular interest in the statement are the lines "FDA has issued a warning letter to Jensen Farms based on environmental and cantaloupe samples collected during the inspection. FDA's investigation at Jensen Farms is still considered an open investigation" ("Information," 2011, para. 10). A warning letter denotes safety violations that should be corrected. By November of 2011, 139 people had been infected in 22 different states resulting in 29 deaths and one miscarriage ("Today's Highlights," 2011). This had become one of the worst food-related outbreaks of listeriosis in U.S. history (Cohen, 2011).

Exhibit 14.2   FDA and CDC Recall Announcements

Information on the Recalled Jensen Farms Whole Cantaloupes

Updated October 19, 2011

FDA Publishes Report on Factors Potentially Contributing to the Contamination of Fresh, Whole Cantaloupe Implicated in the Multi-State *Listeria monocytogenes* Foodborne Illness Outbreak

On October 19, 2011, FDA released a document which provides an overview of factors that potentially contributed to the contamination of fresh, whole cantaloupe with the pathogen *Listeria monocytogenes*, which was implicated in a 2011 multi-state outbreak of listeriosis. In early September 2011, the Food and Drug Administration (FDA), in conjunction with the Centers for Disease Control and Prevention (CDC) and state health departments, began to investigate a multi-state outbreak of listeriosis. Early in the investigation, cantaloupes from Jensen Farms in the southwest region of Colorado were implicated in the outbreak.

On September 10, 2011, FDA, along with Colorado state officials, conducted an inspection at Jensen Farms during which FDA collected multiple samples, including whole cantaloupes and environmental (non-product) samples from within the facility, for laboratory culturing to identify the presence of *Listeria monocytogenes*. Of the 39 environmental samples collected from within the facility, 13 were confirmed positive for *Listeria monocytogenes* with pulsed-field gel electrophoresis (PFGE) pattern combinations that were indistinguishable from three of the four outbreak strains collected from affected patients. Cantaloupe collected from the firm's cold storage during the inspection was also confirmed positive for *Listeria monocytogenes* with PFGE pattern combinations that were indistinguishable from two of the four outbreak strains.

As a result of the isolation of outbreak strains of *Listeria monocytogenes* in the environment of the packing facility and whole cantaloupes collected from cold storage, and the fact that this is the first documented listeriosis outbreak associated with fresh, whole cantaloupe in the United States, FDA initiated an environmental assessment in conjunction with Colorado state and local officials. FDA, state, and local officials conducted the environmental assessment at Jensen Farms on September 22–23, 2011. The environmental assessment was conducted to gather more information to assist FDA in identifying the factors that potentially contributed to the introduction, growth, or spread of the *Listeria monocytogenes* strains that contaminated the cantaloupe.

FDA identified the following factors as those that most likely contributed to the introduction, spread, and growth of *Listeria monocytogenes* in the cantaloupes:

Introduction

There could have been low level sporadic *Listeria monocytogenes* in the field where the cantaloupe were grown, which could have been introduced into the packing facility

A truck used to haul culled cantaloupe to a cattle operation was parked adjacent to the packing facility and could have introduced contamination into the facility

Spread

The packing facility's design allowed water to pool on the floor near equipment and employee walkways;

The packing facility floor was constructed in a manner that made it difficult to clean

The packing equipment was not easily cleaned and sanitized; washing and drying equipment used for cantaloupe packing was previously used for postharvest handling of another raw agricultural commodity.

Growth

There was no pre-cooling step to remove field heat from the cantaloupes before cold storage. As the cantaloupes cooled there may have been condensation that promoted the growth of *Listeria monocytogenes*.

FDA's findings regarding this particular outbreak highlight the importance for firms to employ good agricultural and management practices in their packing facilities as well as in growing fields. FDA recommends that firms employ good agricultural and management practices recommended for the growing, harvesting, washing, sorting, packing, storage and transporting of fruits and vegetables sold to consumers in an unprocessed or minimally processed raw form.

FDA has issued a warning letter to Jensen Farms based on environmental and cantaloupe samples collected during the inspection. FDA's investigation at Jensen Farms is still considered an open investigation.

Jensen Farms' Recall

Jensen Farms voluntarily recalled its whole cantaloupes on Sept. 14 in response to the multi-state outbreak of *listeriosis*. Cantaloupes from other farms have not been linked to this outbreak.

FDA has successfully audited the majority of Jensen Farms' direct and secondary accounts. The recalled cantaloupes were produced from the end of July to September 10, 2011. Given that the Jensen Farms' recall has been in effect for more than a month and that the shelf life of a cantaloupe is approximately two weeks, it is expected that all of the recalled whole Jensen Farms cantaloupes have been removed from the marketplace.

FDA has verified that the following states received recalled cantaloupes directly from Jensen Farms: Arizona, Arkansas, Colorado, Idaho, Illinois, Indiana, Kansas, Louisiana, Minnesota, Missouri, Montana, Nebraska, New Jersey, New Mexico, New York, North Dakota, Oklahoma, Pennsylvania, South Dakota, Tennessee, Texas, Utah, Wisconsin and Wyoming. There is no indication of foreign distribution.

Consumer Safety Information

Listeria can grow at refrigerator temperatures, about 40° Fahrenheit (4° Celsius). The longer ready-to-eat refrigerated foods are stored in the refrigerator, the more opportunity *Listeria* has to grow.

It is very important that consumers clean their refrigerators and other food preparation surfaces. Consumers should follow these simple steps:

Wash hands with warm water and soap for at least 20 seconds *before* and *after* handling food.

Wash the inside walls and shelves of the refrigerator, cutting boards and countertops; then sanitize them with a solution of one tablespoon of chlorine bleach to one gallon of hot water; dry with a clean cloth or paper towel that has not been previously used.

Wipe up spills in the refrigerator immediately and clean the refrigerator regularly.

Always wash hands with warm water and soap following the cleaning and sanitization process.

FDA advises consumers not to eat the recalled cantaloupes and to throw them away. Do not try to wash the harmful bacteria off the cantaloupe as contamination may be both on the inside and outside of the cantaloupe. Cutting, slicing and dicing may also transfer harmful bacteria from the fruit's surface to the fruit's flesh.

Listeriosis is rare but can be fatal, especially in certain high-risk groups. These groups include older adults, people with compromised immune systems and unborn babies and newborns. In pregnant women, listeriosis can cause miscarriage, stillbirth, and serious illness or death in newborn babies, though the mother herself rarely becomes seriously ill. A person with listeriosis usually has fever and muscle aches. Persons who think they might have become ill should consult their doctor.

For more information on the epidemiologic investigation, please refer to CDC's Investigation on the Multi-State Listeriosis Outbreak.

("Information," 2011)

Jensen Farms is a small, family owned agricultural company. Here is the company's initial response to the recall:

STATEMENT REGARDING 9/16/11 CANTALOUPE TEST RESULTS FROM COLORADO DEPARTMENT OF PUBLIC HEALTH AND ENVIRONMENT
"We are deeply saddened to learn that cantaloupes grown on our farm have been linked to the current Listeria outbreak. Our hearts go out to those individuals and their families who have been affected by this terrible situation. We have been cooperating fully with public health officials who are trying to

determine the source of the outbreak, and we will continue to do everything we can to assist them in their efforts. We hope that the investigation into the entire supply chain from farm to retail identifies the source of the contamination so that appropriate steps can be taken to prevent such an occurrence from ever happening again."—Eric and Ryan Jensen, Jensen Farms. ("Jensen Farms Recalls," 2011, Company Statement section)

Jensen Farms also has a Facebook page with a small set of fans. People began posting comments to the site after the recall was announced. Most of the statements were positive. Here is a sample of the Facebook page postings:

"Love you guys and hope everything gets cleared up soon!!!"

"I am praying for your family/farm, and will continue to buy your produce!"

"I cant even imagine but you have mine and my families support. . [. .] click on me if you need any help, I'll try and do what ever I can . . . Im really ticked that this happened weather it was planted or just a freak of nature. Im even more ticked that someone is wanting to be greedy and gain from this mess. . [. .] But you do have my support, just ask . . . thats what people do they come together and help."

"As you know, we have enjoyed your produce for 15 years and will continue to do so. Your family farm is amazing to see in operation and I pray that the media will choose to broadcast the true integrity and values that you live by. Hold strong, and know lots of prayers are being sent your way." ("Jensen," 2011)

The vast majority of the posts were supportive of Jensen Farms. Some, such as the third post, even suggest someone might have purposely planted the bacteria to discredit Jensen Farms. The traditional news media reported no links to tampering. Of course, social media is an open environment, and eventually a few critics did appear. However, as the exchange below illustrates, fans of Jensen Farms rose to its defense:

"People have died. That is not to be taken lightly. Someone may accidentally shoot someone when playing around with a gun. They didn't mean to. They are one of the nicest and kindest people you know. But they still shot somebody. They have to pay the price dor [sic] their carelessness. Same with Jensen Farms. They accidentally killed people because of not making sure the equipment was thoroughly cleaned. They now must pay the price for their carelessness."

"But you need to look at the bigger picture, this is an Organic Family run 'Christian' farm who are under attack by the FDA and the Monsanto's. I believe they are innocent and this is an inside job just like 9/11. Not for a moment do I believe this Farm is responsible, Monsanto wants all family run Organic Farm finished and especially the Christian ones. I pray for those hurt in this attack by the enemy just like I pray for the ones who died in 9/11, it is end times and it will only get worse till we are all slaves of the FDA, drugs, Chemtrails, food additives, Monsanto, mafia, vaccines that kill our children, that contain human fetus's. check it out." ("Jensen," 2011)

The Facebook page had become another channel for Jensen Farms's crisis communication. Jensen Farms took the opportunity to thank their supporters on Facebook:

We want to reach out and thank everyone for supporting us through this terrible time in the history of our beloved farm. Your messages and wall posts are helping us stay motivated, and optimistic about our future. Thank you. ("Jensen," 2011)

Facebook also served as a place for the company to update information. Here are two company posts related to the FDA investigation and report on Facebook:

Jensen Farms—Rocky Ford Cantaloupe
   With test results pending, and the FDA's investigation into this outbreak ongoing, our counsel has advised us to refrain from answering any questions or becoming involved in any discussions at this time. We do, however, feel that it is important to show our supporters that we remain focused.
   As our research continues, we thought to share the following video (Fox 31 Denver) highlighting the work of Dr. Mansour, with whom we have been consulting over the past few weeks. His experience yields insight that we have found to be very helpful in deepening our understanding of the science behind food borne illness—and listeria specifically. His lab has researched numerous US outbreaks, and is respected throughout the industry for its comprehensive and accurate testing methods.
   We eagerly await results from both Mansour and the FDA, and hope to post once they become available.
   Again a huge thanks to all those in continued support of our Family Farm.
   Very Truly, our hearts go out to anyone with loss to this outbreak.— The Jensen Family

Jensen Farms—Rocky Ford Cantaloupe
   Jensen Farms has just been provided with a copy of the report issued today by the FDA. We will give it our careful review. We also awaiting receipt of additional information from the agency. Our operations will not resume until we are completely satisfied that we have done everything within our power to insure [sic] the safety of our products. We continue to cooperate fully with the FDA and other government agencies and extend our deepest concerns to any and all members of the public who have been effected by this outbreak. ("Jensen," 2011)

The Facebook page was used in conjunction with the company website to update the situation. Here is the October 21, 2011 statement from the website:

Jensen Farms has just been provided with a copy of the report issued today by the FDA. We will give it our careful review. We are also awaiting receipt of additional information from the agency. Our operations will not resume until we are completely satisfied that we have done everything within our power to insure [*sic*] the safety of our products. We continue to cooperate fully with the FDA and other government agencies and extend our deepest concerns to any and all members of the public who have been effected by this outbreak. ("Jensen," 2011)

As you can see, the messages are identical. Multiple online channels were being used to update stakeholders about the crisis.

The Jensen family gave one interview about the crisis to the local 7 News in Denver, Colorado. The interview occurred after Charles Palmer, a 71-year-old Colorado Springs man, filed a lawsuit against Jensen Farms after he contracted listerosis from its cantaloupe. The food-borne illness had required hospitalization for Palmer. Here are statements made by Eric Jensen that were reported in the story:

"We're sadden[ed] that there's a possibility that our family's cantaloupe could have gotten somebody sick."

"Our first priority is the public's health and safety."

"We're still in shock. We're completely focused on our recall efforts right now."

"We'll definitely be back."

When asked about the source of the contamination, Eric Jensen indicated he did not know the source but said it might be found "on the retail end." (Stanley & Nguyen, 2011)

Jensen Farms was closed, and its crop destroyed. However, other cantaloupe growers suffered as well. The uncertainty created problems for all cantaloupe growers. People became fearful of the product and avoided all cantaloupe. People just knew cantaloupe was dangerous and avoided it. Little effort was made to determine the source of the cantaloupe that people might eat. Even the CDC recommended not eating cantaloupe if you did not know its source (Chan, 2011). The recall was devastating to the other cantaloupe farmers in the Rocky Ford area of Colorado.

A similar situation transpired in 1991 when Texas cantaloupe was associated with a salmonella outbreak. California cantaloupe growers experienced a drop in sales too as customers just knew "cantaloupe" was dangerous and were not differentiating between Texas and California cantaloupe. In 1992, the Cantaloupe Advisory Board in California reduced its promotional spending, believing a low profile would help people to forgive and forget the health scare from 1991 (Puzo, 1992). Other crises have created industry-wide effects. The wreck of the cruise ship

Costa Concordia in 2012 created a temporary decline in cruise ship bookings. This decline was for the entire industry and not just Carnival Cruise Lines, the owner of the sunken ship (Martin, 2012). The drop in bookings was a result of questions about cruise ship safety raised by the crisis (LaPosta & Lister, 2012).

Colorado farmers were the first to voice their fears because Jensen Farms is located in Colorado (Slevin, 2011). In 2012, the Colorado Department of Agriculture worked with farmers to make media and customers aware of their efforts to promote food safety in the cantaloupe industry. Colorado Commissioner of Agriculture John Salazar noted, "It was one isolated incident with one isolated farm that has given this area a black eye" (Rittiman, 2012, para. 7). That is why his department was now certifying cantaloupe through farm inspections with the label "Good Agricultural Practices" (Rittiman, 2012).

California felt the pain again in 2011 as the sales of California cantaloupe dropped sharply. As Rodney Van Bebber, sales manager for Mendota-based Pappas Produce Company noted, "We can't sell the fruit. . . . Retail stores are taking cantaloupes off the shelves, and growers are disking in their fruit because people are afraid to eat them" (Wozniacka, 2011, para. 5). There was a general fear of cantaloupe. The U.S. government said not to eat Jensen Farms's cantaloupe but many people just heard "don't eat cantaloupe." Any time one company in a food industry has a food-borne illness, there is the risk of people generalizing the crisis to the entire industry. Such was the fate of cantaloupe in 2011.

In 2012, Jensen Farms was still facing a number of lawsuits from victims of the listerosis. The FDA investigation indicated the outbreak was preventable, placing Jensen Farms at greater risk. The company filed for bankruptcy protection in 2012 and planted no crop in 2012 while the lawsuits were being addressed (Flener, 2012). As of November of 2012, the lawsuits had not been settled.

Reading Guide

1. If this situation is a crisis, what type of crisis is it?

2. What is the problem and the source(s) of the problem in this case?

3. What stakeholders should be interested in this case?

4. What was the food-borne illness in this case?

5. How did this food-borne illness compare in size to others in the United States?

6. What was the collateral damage in this case?

Discussion Questions

1. What were the unintended consequences of the FDA announcement? Could they have been avoided? Why or why not?

2. What role did social media play in the crisis?

3. What role did customers of Jensen Farms play in the crisis?

4. What role did risk intolerance play in the crisis?

5. What is the value of a low profile during a crisis?

6. How might the lawsuits have influenced the crisis communication by Jensen Farms?

7. Why might an industry association need to become involved in a crisis? How would that alter the rhetorical arena for the crisis?

Websites

Jensen Farms home page: http://jensenfarms.com/

Jensen Farms Facebook page: http://www.facebook.com/#!/pages/Jensen-Farms-Rocky-Ford-Cantaloupe/159818224031339

FDA recall announcement: http://www.fda.gov/Safety/Recalls/ucm271879.htm

References

Chan, A. (2011). Listeria outbreak in cantaloupe: What are the symptoms and dangers? Retrieved from http://www.huffingtonpost.com/2011/09/29/listeria-symptoms-cantaloupe-recall_n_987125.html

Cohen, T. (2011). FDA cites sanitation issues in listeria outbreak. Retrieved from http://www.cnn.com/2011/10/19/us/med-cantaloupe-deaths/index.html?eref=mrss_igoogle_cnn

FDA warns consumers not to eat Rocky Ford cantaloupes shipped by Jensen Farms. (2011). Retrieved from http://www.fda.gov/NewsEvents/Newsroom/PressAnnouncements/ucm271899.htm

Flener, M. (2012). Jensen Farms idle during listeria settlement process. Retrieved from http://www.9news.com/news/article/271559/339/Jensen-Farms-idle-during-listeria-settlement

Information on the Jensen Farms whole cantaloupes. (2011). Retrieved from http://www.fda.gov/Food/FoodSafety/CORENetwork/ucm272372.htm

Jensen Farms. (2011). Retrieved from http://www.facebook.com/#!/pages/Jensen-Farms-Rocky-Ford-Cantaloupe/159818224031339

Jensen Farms recalls cantaloupe due to possible health risk. (2011, September 14). Retrieved from http://prstrategyandapplication.wordpress.com/tag/jensen-farms/

LaPosta, D., & Lister, T. (2012). Concordia disaster focuses attention on how cruise industry operates. Retrieved from http://articles.cnn.com/2012–07–04/world/world_europe_costa-concordia_1_concordia-disaster-cruise-industry-cruise-ship-disaster?_s=PM:EUROPE

Martin, H. (2012). Cruise ship industry rebounding after disaster. Retrieved from http://www.seacoastonline.com/articles/20120924-BIZ-209240321

Puzo, D. P. (1992). Cantaloupe growers want to put health scare in the past. Retrieved from http://articles.orlandosentinel.com/1992–07–30/lifestyle/9207280149_1_cantaloupe-melons-wash-fruit

Rittiman, B. (2012). Cantaloupe famers promote safety after last season's listeria outbreak. Retrieved from http://www.9news.com/news/story.aspx?storyid=264091&catid=222

Slevin, C. (2011). Colorado cantaloupe farmers fear outbreak fallout. Retrieved from http://www.denverpost.com/breakingnews/ci_19148230?source=pkg

Stanley, D., & Nguyen, K. (2011). Exclusive: Jensen Farms reacts to lawsuit, recall. Retrieved from http://www.thedenverchannel.com/news/29191856/detail.html

Today's highlights (2011, November). Retrieved from http://www.cdc.gov/listeria/outbreaks/cantaloupes-jensen-farms/index.html

Wozniacka, G. (2011). Listeria outbreak devastates California cantaloupes. Retrieved from http://www.denverpost.com/breakingnews/ci_19111581?source=pkg

CHAPTER 15

Chick-fil-A and the Dangers of Social Issues

S ocial issues are political concerns that involve people's personal lives. Social issues are highly controversial and include some of the most divisive concerns in a society. In the United States, same-sex marriage is a highly charged social issue. Social issues always have at least two sides. On one side of the same-sex marriage issue are those who choose to define marriage as limited to between one male and one female. There are 38 states in the United States that have laws defining marriage as between one man and one woman. On the other side are those who support same-sex marriage. They choose to broaden the definition of marriage to include one male and one male or one female and one female. As of the spring of 2013, nine states permitted same-sex marriage. Same-sex marriage is a concern because same-sex partners can be denied many legal rights afforded to married couples. Examples include health care benefits and adoptions. The health care benefit illustrates how economic factors can be associated with social issues as well. Social issues are minefields for organizations. Taking any side on a social issue is guaranteed to upset the other sides. Chick-fil-A Restaurants entered the same-sex marriage social issue arena in 2012.

Truett Cathy began what became Chick-fil-A Restaurants in 1946 in the town of Hapeville, Georgia. The original restaurant was called The Dwarf Grill. Cathy had a strong commitment to his spiritual beliefs. For that reason, his restaurant was closed on Sundays to allow employees to spend time with their families and worship if they so desired ("Why," n.d.). To this day, Chick-fil-A Restaurants are closed on Sunday, remaining a day for God and family (Kuchinsky, 2007). The name Chick-fil-A was born in 1967 ("Company," n.d.). Even with a new name, the company retained its commitment to its original values.

Chick-fil-A is active in community relations, involved in a variety of programs for children including scholarships and placement in foster homes. The company has used a private foundation to support religious organizations. The giving to religious activities includes Focus on Family, Veggie Tales (faith-based toys),

Financial Peace for Kids (books), Adventures in Odyssey (radio), and programs such as Athletes in Action and Family First (Kuchinsky, 2007). Many patrons are aware of Chick-fil-A's strong religious values and commitment. Off and on there had been minor concerns expressed by some stakeholders about where Chick-fil-A stood on some social issues. However, the company's position of social issues had not been a serious problem until 2012 when President Dan Cathy expressed support for defense of opposite-sex marriage—those who oppose same-sex marriage. The message was delivered during an interview with the *Baptist Press* when he said, "very much supportive of the family—the biblical definition of the family unit" (Talty, 2012, para. 1).

Chick-fil-A had entered the minefield of same-sex marriage amid a swirling storm of traditional or legacy and digital media coverage on July 16, 2012. Facebook and Twitter provided the firestorm of digital media coverage for Chick-fil-A. Twitter was used by critics, including some customers, to condemn Chick-fil-A. Actor Ed Helms even called for a boycott of the chain. Chick-fil-A posted the following message to its official Facebook page that Thursday:

> The Chick-Fil-A culture and service tradition in our restaurants is to treat every person with honor, dignity and respect—regardless of their belief, race, creed, sexual orientation or gender. ("Chick-fil-A," 2012)

In a few hours, the post generated over 10,000 comments and 47,000 likes (Laird, 2012). This single statement served as the company's initial response to the crisis. The 10,000 plus comments were a mix of support for Chick-fil-A and anger at its opposition to same-sex marriage.

Part of the Facebook discussion involved the removal of toys created by the Jim Henson Company. The Jim Henson Company claimed it severed ties with Chick-fil-A over their opposition to same-sex marriage, while Chick-fil-A argued the toys were removed for safety reasons (Wong, 2012). On Facebook, the Jim Henson Company posted the following message:

> The Jim Henson Company has celebrated and embraced diversity and inclusiveness for over fifty years and we have notified Chick-Fil-A that we do not wish to partner with them on any future endeavors. Lisa Henson, our CEO is personally a strong supporter of gay marriage and has directed us to donate the payment we received from Chick-Fil-A to GLAAD. (Burra, 2012)

Tiffany Greenway, a spokesperson for Chick-fil-A, indicated the removal of the toys was "for the protection of our customers" (Wong, 2012).

One Facebook poster, Abby Farely, was activity supporting Chick-fil-A's position on the toys. Her post argued the decision to remove the toys came weeks before the statement by Cathy. Abby Farely then became the story when an investigation proved the account was fake. The Facebook account had been created recently, and Abby's photo was a stock photo available online. This led to charges that Chick-fil-A was behind the fake, supportive "poster" (Hill, 2012). Tiffany Greenway reported, "I can confirm that Chick-fil-A has not created any false Facebook page, account, or persona of any kind. Our official corporate Facebook page continues to be our only one" (Hill, 2012, para. 4). The official Facebook statement from Chick-fil-A read:

> Hey Fans, thanks for being supportive. There is a lot of misinformation out there. The latest is we have been accused of impersonating a teenager with a fake Facebook profile. We want you to know we would never do anything like that and this claim is 100% false. Please share this with your friends. (Hill, 2012)

Over 56,000 people liked the post and over 8,000 did share it with others.

Chick-fil-A encountered reactions from politicians as well that drew traditional or legacy media coverage (Foust, 2012). Local politicians in both Boston and Chicago condemned Chick-fil-A. Boston Mayor Thomas Menino said the company did not belong in Boston because it is discriminatory while Chicago Mayor Rahm Emanuel claimed Chick-fil-A did not reflect Chicago's values (Talty, 2012). There were supportive politicians too, such as Mike Huckabee, who helped to organize and to promote August 1st 2012 as Chick-fil-A Appreciation Day. Here is Huckabee's statement about the event on Facebook:

> I have been incensed at the vitriolic assaults on the Chick Fil-A company because the CEO, Dan Cathy, made comments recently in which he affirmed his view that the Biblical view of marriage should be upheld. The Cathy family, led by Chick Fil-A founder Truett Cathy, are a wonderful Christian family who are committed to operating the company with Biblical principles and whose story is the true American success story. . . .
>
> I ask you to join me in speaking out on Wednesday, August 1 "Chick Fil-A Appreciation Day." No one is being asked to make signs, speeches, or openly demonstrate. The goal is simple: Let's affirm a business that operates on Christian principles and whose executives are willing to stand for the Godly values we espouse by simply showing up and eating at Chick Fil-A on Wednesday, August 1. Too often, those on the left make corporate statements to show support for same sex marriage, abortion, or profanity, but if Christians affirm traditional values, we're considered homophobic, fundamentalists, hate-mongers, and intolerant. This effort is not being launched by the Chick Fil-A company and no one from the company or family is involved in promoting it.
>
> There's no need for anyone to be angry or engage in a verbal battle. Simply affirm appreciation for a company run by Christian principles by showing up on Wednesday, August 1 or by participating online—tweeting your support or sending a message on Facebook. (Huckabee, 2012, para. 1, 3–4)

It was estimated that over half a million people ate at Chick-fil-A restaurants on August 1 (Barrick, 2012). Chick-fil-A's reaction to the appreciation day effort is provided in Exhibit 15.1. In reaction to Huckabee's efforts, a "Same Sex Kiss-in Day" was planned for Chick-fil-A on August 3rd (Palmer, 2012). The turnout was much smaller for this pro-same-sex marriage event. On Facebook, over 600,000 supported the "Chick Fil-A Appreciation Day" compared to 16,000 for "Same Sex Kiss-in Day." There are no exact figures for who appeared for each event, but the anecdotal evidence is similar ("Chick-fil-A Supporters" 2012).

Exhibit 15.1 Appreciation Day Statement

Aug. 02, 2012 Statement Following Chick-fil-A Appreciation Day.

Attribute to: Steve Robinson, Executive Vice President, Marketing, Chick-fil-A Inc.

We are very grateful and humbled by the incredible turnout of loyal Chick-fil-A customers on August 1 at Chick-fil-A restaurants around the country. Chick-fil-A Appreciation Day was not a company promotion; it was initiated by others.

We congratulate local Chick-fil-A Owner/Operators and their team members for striving to serve each and every customer with genuine hospitality.

While we don't release exact sales numbers, it was an unprecedented day.

(Bingham, 2012)

It should be noted that Dan Cathy did not speak for the entire organization in his interview. The official statement about the controversy appears in Exhibit 15.2 and is dated July 31. The company position is one of tolerance and inclusion. However, the company has contributed money to groups that actively campaign against same-sex marriages through funds given to the WinShape Foundation. The WinShape Foundation was created by the Cathys and is funded primarily through money from Chick-fil-A ("Post-Crisis," 2012). The company's actions are taken as support for Dan Cathy's words about defending traditional marriage.

Exhibit 15.2 Chick-fil-A Response to Recent Controversy

Attribute to: Steve Robinson, Executive Vice President Marketing

Chick-fil-A is a family-owned and family-led company serving the communities in which it operates. From the day Truett Cathy started the company, he began applying biblically-based principles to managing his business. For example, we believe that closing on Sundays, operating debt-free and devoting a percentage of our profits back to our communities are what make us a stronger company and Chick-fil-A family. The Chick-fil-A culture and service tradition in our restaurants is to treat every person with honor, dignity and respect—regardless of their belief, race, creed, sexual orientation or gender. We will continue this tradition in the over 1,600 Restaurants run by independent Owner/Operators. Going forward, our intent is to leave the policy debate over same-sex marriage to the government and political arena. Our mission is simple: to serve great food, provide genuine hospitality and have a positive influence on all who come in contact with Chick-fil-A.

("Chick-fil-A Response to Recent Controversy," 2012)

The case was re-energized in September of 2012 because Chicago Alderman Joe Moreno sought to block Chick-fil-A restaurants from being built in his district. Moreno said after negotiating with Chick-fil-A that he was satisfied they were no longer supportive of anti-same-sex marriage groups (Barrow, 2012). Moreno's comments stirred up social media action as supporters of Chick-fil-A were upset the company was reversing its position (Barrow, 2012). Exhibits 15.3 and 15.4 contain the two announcements Chick-fil-A made concerning Moreno's comments (Sept. 30 and Oct. 3). Even by October of 2012, Chick-fil-A was not finished with the same-sex marriage crisis. The name Chick-fil-A was now a part of a U.S. social-issue debate.

Exhibit 15.3   Chick-fil-A Statements From September 2012

Sep. 20, 2012 Chick-fil-A: Who We Are. A Response to Recent Controversy

For many months now, Chick-fil-A's corporate giving has been mischaracterized. And while our sincere intent has been to remain out of this political and social debate, events from Chicago this week have once again resulted in questions around our giving. For that reason, we want to provide some context and clarity around who we are, what we believe and our priorities in relation to corporate giving.

A part of our corporate commitment is to be responsible stewards of all that God has entrusted to us. Because of this commitment, Chick-fil-A's giving heritage is focused on programs that educate youth, strengthen families and enrich marriages, and support communities. We will continue to focus our giving in those areas. Our intent is not to support political or social agendas.

As we have stated, the Chick-fil-A culture and service tradition in our restaurants is to treat every person with honor, dignity and respect—regardless of their belief, race, creed, sexual orientation or gender. We will continue this tradition in the over 1,600 restaurants run by independent Owner/Operators.

For better understanding of our corporate giving, please download the PDF document titled "Chick-fil-A: Who We Are."

("Chick-fil-A: Who We Are," 2012)

Exhibit 15.4   Chick-fil-A Statement From October 2012

Oct. 03, 2012 Chick-fil-A Statement

Chick-fil-A is a family-owned and family-led company dedicated to serving the communities in which we operate. From the day Truett Cathy started the company, he began applying biblically-based principles to managing his business.

For example, we believe that we are stronger because of such principles as closing on Sundays, going the extra mile in service, treating others as we want to be treated, and devoting a percentage of profits back to our communities. Those same principles have been applied throughout the history of Chick-fil-A and still apply today.

The Chick-fil-A culture and 66-year service tradition in our locally owned and operated restaurants is to treat every person with honor, dignity and respect—regardless of their beliefs, race, creed, sexual orientation or gender. We are a restaurant company focused on food, service and hospitality; our intent is not to engage in political or social debates.

("Chick-fil-A Statement," 2012)

Reading Guide

1. If this situation is a crisis, what type of crisis is it?

2. What is the problem and the source(s) of the problem in this case?

3. What stakeholders should be interested in this case?

4. How did the crisis begin?

5. What is the importance of a social issue?

6. What was the social issue in this case?

7. Why did Chick-fil-A get involved with this social issue?

8. Why were stakeholders so divided?

Discussion Questions

1. Why do social issues make a crisis situation so volatile?

2. How well can stakeholders separate the CEO's seemingly discrepant, or conflicting, words and actions about the company he or she represents? Why is this so important in this case?

3. How might the rhetorical arena be used to plot the crisis communication in this case?

4. How much responsibility lies with the CEO and how much with activists? Justify your distribution of responsibility.

5. How would you judge the effectiveness of Chick-fil-A's corporate response to the crisis?

6. Why did the fake Facebook support become such a concern in the case?

7. What role did the Muppet promotion play in the case? Was it significant? Why or why not?

Websites

Chick-fil-A Company FAQs: http://www.chick-fil-a.com/Company/Highlights-Fact-Sheets

Chick-fil-A news releases: http://www.chick-fil-a.com/Pressroom/Press-Releases

How the crisis was related to social media: http://mashable.com/2012/07/19/chick-fil-a-gay-marriage/

News story about mixing religion and business: http://www.businessweek.com/articles/2012–07–26/god-and-gay-marriage-what-chick-fil-a-could-learn-from-marriott

References

Barrick, A. (2012). Chick-fil-A Appreciation Day: Half a million to show up at restaurants. Retrieved from http://www.christianpost.com/news/chick-fil-a-appreciation-day-half-a-million-to-show-up-at-restaurants-79237/

Barrow, B. (2012). Chick-fil-A hit with another PR uproar. Retrieved from http://lubbock online.com/national-news/2012–09–21/chick-fil-hit-another-pr-uproar%23.UFycKmA1ZQ5

Bingham, A. (2012). Chick-fil-A has "record-setting" sales on Appreciation Day. Retrieved from http://abcnews.go.com/Politics/OTUS/chick-fil-record-setting-sales-appreciation-day/story?id=16912978

Burra, K. (2012). Jim Henson Company and Chick-Fil-A: "Muppets" makers sever ties with anti-gay fast food chain. Retrieved from http://www.huffingtonpost.com/2012/07/23/jim-henson-company-chick-fil-a-anti-gay_n_1694809.html

Chick-fil-A (2012, July 19). Facebook. Retrieved from https://www.facebook.com/ChickfilA/posts/10151226208515101

Chick-fil-A response to recent controversy. (2012). Retrieved from http://www.chick-fil-a.com/Media/PDF/LGBT-statement.pdf

Chick-fil-A statement. (2012). Retrieved from http://www.chick-fil-a.com/Pressroom/Press Releases/cfa-statement#?release=cfa-statement

Chick-fil-A supporters throng to Walnut store. (2012). Retrieved from http://www.pasadena starnews.com/news/ci_21213507/chick-fil-supporters-throng-walnut-store?source=rss#ixzz22ZnFngsu

Chick-fil-A: Who we are. (2012). Retrieved from http://www.chick-fil-a.com/Pressroom/Press-Releases/who-we-are#?release=who-we-are

Company fact sheet. (n.d.). Retrieved from http://www.chick-fil-a.com/Company/Highlights-Fact-Sheets

Foust, M. (2012). Chick-fil-A, in nat'l media storm, swims against cultural tide. Retrieved from http://www.bpnews.net/BPnews.asp?ID=38301

Hill, K. (2012). Chick-fil-A has completely lost control of its Facebook page. Retrieved from http://www.forbes.com/sites/kashmirhill/2012/07/25/chick-fil-a-has-completely-lost-control-of-its-facebook-page/

Huckabee, M. (2012). Chick-fil-A Appreciation Day. Retrieved from https://www.facebook.com/events/266281243473841/

Kuchinsky, C. (2007). Chick-fil-A company history: Even the cows agree it's time to eat more chicken. Retrieved from http://voices.yahoo.com/chick-fil-company-history-405537.html?cat=22

Laird, S. (2012). Chick-Fil-A faces gay marriage backlash on Twitter, Facebook. Retrieved from http://mashable.com/2012/07/19/chick-fil-a-gay-marriage/

Palmer, K. (2012). Chick-fil-A hit by "kiss-in" protests in gay marriage flap. Retrieved from http://www.reuters.com/article/2012/08/03/us-usa-gaymarriage-chickfila-idUSBRE 8720XP20120803

Post-crisis evaluation: After igniting a gay-rights firestorm with CEO's comments last month, Chick-fil-A fine-tunes its PR. (2012, September 20). Retrieved from http:// www.bulldogreporter.com/dailydog/article/post-crisis-evaluation-after-igniting-gay -rights-firestorm-ceos-comments-last-month

Talty, J. (2012). Chick-fil-A battles PR nightmare over same-sex marriage stance. Retrieved from http://www.ibtimes.com/articles/366793/20120725/chick-fil-anti-gay-marriage -stance.htm

Why we're closed on Sunday. (n.d.). http://www.chick-fil-a.com/Company/Highlights -Sunday

Wong, C. M. (2012). Chick-fil-A recalling Jim Henson kids' meal toys as partnership severed over anti-gay donations. Retrieved from http://www.huffingtonpost.com/2012/07/24/ chick-fil-a-jim-henson-toy-recall-gay_n_1699597.html

CHAPTER 16

The Bhopal Tragedy

On December 3, 1984, the Union Carbide facility in Bhopal, India, released a massive cloud of methyl isocyanate gas (MIC). The gas cloud killed over 3,500 people and injured over 500,000 more. Bhopal remains one of the worst industrial accidents in world history (Broughton, 2005). Dow Chemical purchased Union Carbide in 2001. Unfortunately for Dow Chemical, the purchase included the Bhopal situation. In December of 2011, I received the following e-mail message.

In 1984, an industrial plant in Bhopal, India leaked 27 tons of toxic gas. Thousands of people in the local area were killed and half a million exposed—making it one of the world's worst industrial catastrophes.

Twenty-seven years later, the situation remains a humanitarian and environmental crisis. The company now in charge of the site has been accused of neglecting their duties to clean up the area, continuing to place thousands of people at risk of death by exposure. **That company is Dow Chemical—a major partner of the London 2012 Olympics.**

London resident Lorraine Close knows the horror of the health crisis in Bhopal—she served as a nurse there for six months this year. She was so appalled to learn about the Olympics' partnership with Dow that she started **a petition on Change.org to get London 2012 to distance itself from the chemical company. Will you sign Lorraine's petition calling on the London Olympic Games Organizing Committee to drop Dow Chemical from its list of sponsors?**

The people in Bhopal have lost their family members and watched their children be born with horrendous congenital birth defects. They've endured years of suffering, long court battles, injustice and a lack of recognition from the company responsible for their suffering. **Instead of addressing this, Dow Chemical are pouring their money into Olympics sponsorship.**

Lorraine's campaign is making progress—her petition was delivered to the Indian Olympic Association, which called for London 2012 to drop Dow in response. And Dow just announced that its name and logo will not appear on the Olympic stadium in an attempt to quiet the global outcry. But this isn't enough. Unless you help stop it, Dow's name and its toxic legacy in Bhopal will be synonymous with the 2012 Olympics.

Please stand with Lorraine and the victims of the Bhopal disaster. Sign Lorraine's petition to get Dow Chemical dropped as a sponsor of the London Olympics in 2012.

Lorraine is a firm believer in the power of small groups to create big change—exactly what we see on Change.org every day as thousands of people start campaigns for social change. As Lorraine says: "Living amongst the people in Bhopal taught me that the power of the human voice can be heard. I watched them rally, and fight and refuse to accept what they have been dealt by those who hold power. That's why I started this petition on Change.org, because we should all use our voices to fight for what's right."

Thanks for being a change-maker.

—Weldon and the Change.org team. (W. Kennedy, personal communication, Dec. 20, 2011)

Over 27 years later, the Bhopal tragedy was still having a negative effect upon the corporation associated with the crisis. Dow, the corporation that purchased Union Carbide assets, experienced protests over its 2012 Summer Olympic sponsorship, a reputation building effort, due to Bhopal.

The Union Carbide facility in Bhopal manufactured the pesticide Sevin, a product still available today. Methyl isocyanate (MIC) was used in the manufacturing of Sevin at the Union Carbide facilities in Bhopal, India, and Institute, a community in West Virginia, in the United States. Union Carbide closed its facility in the United States for over 4 months after the Bhopal disaster due to concerns over methyl isocyanate. However, Union Carbide's final report on Bhopal noted that the U.S. facility had more safeguards and proper operations compared to the facility in Bhopal. The final report indicated that the trigger for the disaster was large amounts of water entering the three storage tanks for the methyl isocyanate. Methyl isocyanate expands when mixed with water. A description of MIC can be found in Exhibit 16.1. Union Carbide noted a number of procedural violations and operating errors as the cause of the water mixing with methyl isocyanate. The report placed responsibility for the poor operations on local management, not top management at Union Carbide headquarters (Diamond, 1985).

Exhibit 16.1	**Environmental Protection Agency's Description of Methyl Isocyanate**

Methyl Isocyanate

624-83-9

Hazard Summary-Created in April 1992; Revised in January 2000

Methyl isocyanate is used to produce carbamate pesticides. Methyl isocyanate is extremely toxic to humans from acute (short-term) exposure. In Bhopal, India, accidental acute inhalation exposure to methyl isocyanate resulted in the deaths of about 3,800 people and adverse health effects in greater than 170,000 survivors. Pulmonary edema was the probable cause of death in most cases, with many deaths resulting from secondary respiratory infections. Survivors continue to exhibit damage to the lungs and eyes. Reproductive effects and increased number of stillbirths and spontaneous abortions were noted in the survivors of the Bhopal, India accident. EPA has classified methyl isocyanate as a Group D, not classifiable as to human carcinogenicity.

Please Note: The main sources of information for this fact sheet are EPA's Health and Environmental Effects Profile for Methyl Isocyanate and the California Environmental Protection Agency's (CalEPA's) Technical Support Document for the Determination of Noncancer Chronic Reference Exposure Levels.

Uses

- Methyl isocyanate is used as a chemical intermediate for the production of carbamate insecticides and herbicides.

Sources and Potential Exposure

- No information is available on the levels of methyl isocyanate is [*sic*] ambient air or water.
- Occupational exposure to methyl isocyanate may occur for those workers who use insecticides and herbicides produced from methyl isocyanate. Few known exposures to the general public have occurred.
- Methyl isocyanate has been detected in cigarette smoke.

Assessing Personal Exposure

- No information is available on the assessment of personal exposure to methyl isocyanate.

Health Hazard Information

Acute Effects:

- In 1984, in Bhopal, India, an accidental Union Carbide gas leak of methyl isocyanate resulted in the deaths of more than 2,000 people and adverse health effects in greater than 170,000 survivors. Pulmonary edema was the cause of death in most cases, with many deaths resulting from secondary respiratory infections such as bronchitis and bronchial pneumonia.
- Other effects noted from acute inhalation exposure to methyl isocyanate in humans are respiratory tract irritation, difficulty breathing, blindness, nausea, gastritis, sweating, fever, chills, and liver and kidney damage. Survivors continue to exhibit damage to the lungs (e.g., bronchoalveolar lesions and decreased lung function) and the eyes (e.g., loss of vision, loss of visual acuity, and cataracts).

- Animal studies have reported pulmonary edema, upper respiratory tract irritation, respiratory lesions, and weight loss from acute inhalation exposure to methyl isocyanate.
- Acute animal tests in rats have shown methyl isocyanate to have extreme acute toxicity from inhalation exposure and high acute toxicity from oral exposure.

Chronic Effects (Noncancer):

- No information is available on the chronic (long-term) effects of methyl isocyanate in humans or animals.
- EPA has not established a Reference Concentration (RfC) or a Reference Dose (RfD) for methyl isocyanate. (5)
- CalEPA has calculated a chronic inhalation reference exposure level of 0.001 milligrams per cubic meter (mg/m^3) based on lung and body weight effects in rats. The CalEPA reference exposure level is a concentration at or below which adverse health effects are not likely to occur. It is not a direct estimator of risk but rather a reference point to gauge the potential effects. At lifetime exposures increasingly greater than the reference exposure level, the potential for adverse health effects increases.

Reproductive/Developmental Effects:

- After the Bhopal, India, accident, an unusually high percentage of survivors had disorders of the reproductive system, including leukorrhea, pelvic inflammatory disease, excessive menstrual bleeding, and suppression of lactation. Other adverse effects included increases in the number of stillbirths, spontaneous abortions, and increased infant mortality.
- Animal studies have reported increased incidence of fetal deaths and decreased fertility, live litter size, fetal body weight, and neonatal survival following inhalation exposure to methyl isocyanate during pregnancy.

Cancer Risk:

- No information is available on the carcinogenic effects of methyl isocyanate in humans.
- In a study in which animals were exposed once by inhalation, no tumors were significantly associated with methyl isocyanate exposure in mice and female rats; male rats had marginally increased rates of tumors of the pancreas.
- EPA has classified methyl isocyanate as a Group D, not classifiable as to human carcinogenicity.

Physical Properties

- Methyl isocyanate is a colorless liquid that has a sharp odor.
- The odor threshold for methyl isocyanate is 2.1 parts per million (ppm).

- The chemical formula for methyl isocyanate is C^2H^3NO, and the molecular weight is 57.05 g/mol.
- The vapor pressure for methyl isocyanate is 348 mm Hg at 20 °C.

(Environmental Protection Agency [EPA], n.d.)

While Union Carbide's final report noted procedural and operational errors, the corporation maintained that the Bhopal tragedy was a result of employee sabotage. Union Carbide argued that an employee purposely introduced the water in to the methyl isocyanate (Sissell, 2004). Union Carbide hired Arthur M. Little Inc. to investigate Bhopal. The Little report supported Union Carbide's claim of sabotage. Allegedly, an employee hooked a rubber hose to a methyl isocyanate tank in order to add water to the tank ("Disaster," 1988). Union Carbide claimed to have altered logs and other documents to support their position (Weisman & Hazarika, 1987). No group or individual outside of Union Carbide and Little has found support for the sabotage theory for Bhopal.

Ronald Wishert, Union Carbide's vice president for Federal Government Relations, said, "No words can describe the sorrow felt by employees of the Union Carbide Corporation for the people of Bhopal" (Shabecoff, 1984, p. A-10). Here are excerpts from Union Carbide's official statement on the Bhopal Tragedy:

The 1984 gas leak in Bhopal was a terrible tragedy that understandably continues to evoke strong emotions even 27 years later. In the wake of the gas release, Union Carbide Corporation, and then chairman Warren Anderson, worked diligently to provide aid to the victims and set up a process to resolve their claims. All claims arising out of the release were settled 20 years ago at the explicit direction of and with the approval of the Supreme Court of India.

Shortly after the gas release, Union Carbide launched an aggressive effort to identify the cause. Engineering consulting firm, Arthur D. Little, Inc., conducted a thorough investigation. Its conclusion: The gas leak could only have been caused by deliberate sabotage. Someone purposely put water in the gas storage tank, and this caused a massive chemical reaction. Process safety systems had been put in place that would have kept the water from entering into the tank by accident. ("Statement," n.d., para. 1, 4)

Other excerpts come from "The Incident, Response, and Settlement":

Union Carbide launched an immediate investigation into the Bhopal disaster and took the following actions:

- Immediately provided approximately $2 million in aid to the Prime Minister's Relief Fund
- Immediately and continuously provided medical equipment and supplies

- Sent an international team of medical experts to Bhopal to provide expertise and assistance
- Openly shared all its information on methylisocyanate (MIC) with the Government of India, including all published and unpublished toxicity studies available at the time
- Dispatched a team of technical MIC experts to Bhopal on the day after the tragedy, which carried MIC studies that were widely shared with medical and scientific personnel in Bhopal
- Funded the attendance by Indian medical experts at special meetings on research and treatment for victims
- Provided a $2.2 million grant to Arizona State University to establish a vocational-technical center in Bhopal, which was constructed and opened, but was later closed and leveled by the government
- Offered an initial $10 million to build a hospital in Bhopal; the offer was declined
- Provided an additional $5 million to the Indian Red Cross
- Established an independent charitable trust for a Bhopal hospital and provided initial funding of approximately $20 million
- Upon the sale of its interest in UCIL, and pursuant to a court order, provided approximately $90 million to the charitable trust for the hospital. ("Incident," n.d., para. 3, 5)

In the 1980s, it was a common crisis communication recommendation to have the CEO go to the site of the crisis. The idea is that the presence of the CEO shows that the organization is taking the crisis seriously. Then-Union Carbide CEO Warren Anderson flew to India to be on site. Anderson arrived in India 4 days after the disaster and was promptly arrested by Indian authorities when he left his plane (Kidwai, 2010). Anderson was charged with culpable homicide. The U.S. government helped to persuade the Indian government to release Anderson on bail. Anderson signed a bond that said he would cooperate with the investigation and return if required to do so. Anderson never returned to India despite governmental attempts to bring him back to face charges. In 1987, Anderson was formally charged and a summons issued for his return. In 1998, an arrest warrant was issued for Anderson. In 2003, the Indian government formally requested his extradition from the United States, but the request was denied ("Anderson," 2010).

Other investigations have noted the lax safety standards and general lack of maintenance as the cause for the Bhopal tragedy. Here is a list of the safety problems that existed at Bhopal prior to the disaster:

- Various temperature and pressure gauges, including those on the MIC storage tanks, were so unreliable that workers ignored any warning signs from them
- The refrigeration unit used to keep the MIC at low temperatures and prevent expansion had been shut off for over six months

- The gas scrubber used to neutralize any escaping MIC had been shut off for maintenance and was inadequate for the amount of MIC even when it worked
- The flare tower that was supposed to burn off MIC escaping from the scrubber was shut down because it needed a replacement pipe and was inadequate for the amount of MIC as well
- The water curtain that was supposed to neutralize any remaining gas was too short to reach the top of the flare tower
- The alarm on the storage tank failed to signal the increase in temperature during the disaster
- MIC storage tank number 610 had been filled beyond recommended capacity ("Learning," 2007, para. 3–10)

The existing safety procedures were inadequate when they were functional and were not even operational the night of the disaster.

Some viewed Bhopal as a negative example of the effects of globalization. A transnational corporation (Union Carbide) was exploiting lax safety and environmental regulations for profit. Union Carbide admitted its U.S. facility was safer than the one in Bhopal. The U.S. facility utilized more manual systems for safety control rather than the automated systems in Bhopal (Shabecoff, 1984). In fact, Union Carbide's own documents stated that the safety technology at Bhopal was untested ("Bhopal," n.d.). Moreover, the list of safety equipment that was not operational and the general state of poor maintenance at Bhopal added to the view that Union Carbide had a different operating standard in Bhopal than in the United States. Here are some of the public statements reflecting the Bhopal disaster as the result of exploitation:

> Internal documents that have come to light during the discovery process in the US courts in the contamination case over the last few years clearly indicate that UCC (*a*) transferred unproven technology to UCIL; (*b*) did everything it could to ensure that it maintained a majority stake of over 50% in UCIL; (*c*) was aware of the possibility of a potential runaway reaction that triggered the MIC leak in Bhopal; (*d*) had far lower safety standards in place in Bhopal than it did in the USA; and (*e*) was aware right from 1982 that the Bhopal plant suffered from serious safety problems. (Nagaraj & Raman, n.d., para. 2)

> UCC did not export the same standards of safety in design or operations to Bhopal as it had in place in the USA. In particular, UCC failed to set up any comprehensive emergency plan or system in Bhopal to warn local communities about leaks, even though it had such a plan in place in the USA. As early as 1982, UCC was aware that there were major safety concerns regarding the Bhopal plant. Months before the accident, UCC was warned of the possibility of a reaction similar to the one that caused the eventual leak in Bhopal. ("Clouds," 2004, p. 39)

> The tragedy in the Indian town of Bhopal is far from the only example of what happens when Western monopolies lord it unceremoniously in the countries of the so-called Third World. (Pasko, 1984)

While there are documented differences between the Bhopal and Institute facilities, Union Carbide's motives behind the differences remain a matter of speculation and interpretation.

In 1984, James Gustave Speth, head of World Resources Institute and chairman of the Council on Environmental Quality in the Carter Administration, observed,

> It is likely that Bhopal will become the chemical industry's Three Mile Island—an international symbol deeply imprinted on public consciousness. Just as Three Mile Island spurred a thorough assessment of the safety of nuclear power, Bhopal will bring justifiable demands that hazardous facilities in the chemical industry be designed, sited and operated so that nothing even close to Bhopal can ever happen again. (Shabecoff, 1984, p. A-10)

His observation was prophetic. Governments and industry had to respond to the grand scope of the Bhopal disaster—changes needed to be made to reassure stakeholders.

Industry responded in 1985 with the creation of the Center for Chemical Process Safety (CCPS). The CCPS was created by the American Institute for Chemical Engineers, an industry group. The CCPS, what was later to become the American Chemistry Council (ACC), created a new emergency response program for its members. This initial effort would become the Responsible Care program in 1988 (Sissell, 2004). These two actions were measures taken by the private sector to improve chemical safety. Exhibit 16.2 provides an explanation of the ACC and Responsible Care. The chemical industry was taking steps to improve safety. It also changed how the chemical industry thought about safety. Prior to Bhopal, the industry's safety focus was on the facility, not beyond the fence line. Bhopal forced the chemical industry to rethink the scope of its safety concerns to place greater emphasis on those living outside of the facility (Sissell, 2004).

Exhibit 16.2 Responsible Care and the American Chemistry Council

Responsible Care

For more than 20 years, the Responsible Care program has helped American Chemistry Council (ACC) member companies significantly enhance their performance, discover new business opportunities, and improve employee safety and the health of the communities in which they operate and the environment as a whole, moving us toward a safer, more sustainable future.

("History," 2011, para. 1)

American Chemistry Council

The American Chemistry Council's (ACC's) mission is to deliver business value through exceptional advocacy using best-in-class member performance, political engagement, communications and scientific research. We are committed to sustainable development by fostering progress in our economy, environment and society.

ACC is America's oldest trade association of its kind, representing companies engaged in the business of chemistry—an innovative, $720 billion enterprise that is helping solve the biggest challenges facing our nation and the world.

("About ACC," 2011, para. 1–2)

In the United States, the government made significant changes to safety regulations for chemical facilities. The most prominent change was the Environmental Protection Agency's (EPA's) 1986 Emergency Planning and Community Right-to-Know Act. According to the EPA:

The objective of the Emergency Planning and Community Right-To-Know Act (EPCRA) is to: (1) allow state and local planning for chemical emergencies, (2) provide for notification of emergency releases of chemicals, and (3) address communities' right-to-know about toxic and hazardous chemicals. (Emergency, 2011, para. 1)

Here is another overview of EPCRA:

The Superfund Amendments and Reauthorization Act (SARA) of 1986 created EPCRA, also known as SARA Title III, a statute designed to improve community access to information about chemical hazards and to facilitate the development of chemical emergency response plans by state/tribe and local governments. EPCRA required the establishment of state/tribe emergency response commissions (SERCs/TERCs), responsible for coordinating certain emergency response activities and for appointing local emergency planning committees (LEPCs). ("Emergency," 2011, para. 2)

The EPCRA required companies and communities to work together in private-public partnership to improve chemical safety with a focus on planning and communication. In essence, EPCRA catapulted risk communication onto the national stage as companies needed to discuss their hazardous materials and safety measures with those living near the facilities. This change has issued in a revolution in risk communication as it has evolved into a rather sophisticated communication discipline (Palenchar, 2005).

The lawsuits spawned by Bhopal helped to create a continuing traditional or legacy news media presence for the crisis and created a digital footprint for the crisis. Union Carbide was sued by a variety of entities within days of the disaster. The highest profile lawsuit was the one brought by the Government of India, or

Union Government. Union Carbide settled with the Union Government in 1989 for $470 million (Sissell, 2004). A number of groups still have claims against Dow, the heirs to Union Carbide, for continuing problems stemming from toxic chemicals remaining in Bhopal's environment (Bidwai, 2010). On some level, the crisis does remain. An illustration of the continuing nature of the Bhopal crisis is a 2010 court case related to the event.

In 2010, seven former Union Carbide managers were convicted for the Bhopal tragedy. There had been an eighth manager charged, but he died prior to a final judgment. Moreover, Warren Anderson refused extradition attempts and escaped judgment. The penalty was very minor, similar to the penalty for a car accident that caused a fatality. The penalty for the managers was 2 years in jail and a fine of 100,000 rupees. The court case had lasted for over 25 years, and the decision returned attention to the crisis. The decision was met with anger from protestors still seeking justice for the Bhopal disaster. Satyanath Sarangi, president of the Bhopal Group for Information and Action said, "In fact, it will encourage hazardous corporations to kill more people and maim them because they can do it so easily because a disaster like Bhopal can be converted into something like a traffic accident" (Page, 2010, para. 11). The case shows there was continuing interest and anger over Bhopal—the crisis lingers.

One final unique aspect of the Bhopal disaster is the way digital media keeps the crisis alive through websites. Some of the websites, such as Bhopal.net, are trying to pressure Dow into a site cleanup, while others just want the world to remember this horrific event. The Bhopal Memory Project is an example of efforts to remember the event. Here is how the site describes itself:

> The Bhopal Memory Project is dedicated to documenting the Bhopal gas disaster as well as providing education resources and updates on its political progress. ("Memory," n.d., para. 1)

> To "remember Bhopal" today means not just collecting and understanding information about the disaster and its aftermath, but also critiquing it, teaching it, and using it in creative ways. The way that we remember Bhopal *should* be different. Through this work of memory and advocacy, we, in solidarity with those struggling for health, survival and justice in Bhopal, are working for a future memory of Bhopal that is *not* part of a continuing tragedy. ("Memory," n.d., para. 4)

Of course even a memory site has political overtones as groups seek to support various sides of the issue. Memories can be contested as different sides present their version of events that they hope become part of the collective memory (Roediger & Wertsch, 2008). The Memory Project promotes the images about the continuing health problems of people living in Bhopal and the need to finally clean up the site. Union Carbide even has its statements and account of the events of Bhopal online—their version of memories of Bhopal. It is interesting that the Union Carbide site remains active even after it became part of Dow. The Bhopal crisis lingers as it is very much alive in the digital media.

Reading Guide

1. If this situation is a crisis, what type of crisis is it?

2. What is the problem and the source(s) of the problem in this case?

3. What stakeholders should be interested in this case?

4. How does the crisis continue to linger?

5. What is the Bhopal Memory Project?

Discussion Questions

1. What does the Bhopal disaster say about the dangers of globalization?

2. What is the danger of Union Carbide using its sabotage claim? How credible is that claim?

3. What effect did Bhopal have on risk communication and crisis communication?

4. Why could the argument be made that the Bhopal crisis has not ended?

5. What issues have been created by the Bhopal disaster?

6. Is it fair that an organization "buys" a crisis when it buys a company? Why or why not?

7. Why do you think the CEO should or should not have returned to face charges in India? What impact would that have had on the crisis communication effort?

Websites

Bhopal Memory Project home page: http://bhopal.bard.edu/
Union Carbide Information about Bhopal: http://www.bhopal.com/
Medical review of Bhopal's effects: http://www.ncbi.nlm.nih.gov/pmc/articles/PMC1142333/

References

About ACC. (2011). http://www.americanchemistry.com/About

Anderson: The man who got away. (2010). Retrieved from http://indiatoday.intoday.in/story/anderson-the-man-who-got-away/1/100622.html

Bhopal, India (n.d). Retrieved from http://www.chemicalindustryarchives.org/dirtysecrets/bhopal/index.asp

Bidwai, P. (2010). Bhopal still waits for justice. Retrieved from http://www.prafulbidwai.org/index.php?post/2010/06/28/Bhopal-still-waits-for-justice

Broughton, E. (2005, May 10). The Bhopal disaster and its aftermath: A review. *Environmental Health, 4.* doi: 10.1186/1476–069X-4–6

Clouds of injustice: Bhopal disaster 20 years on. (2004). Retrieved from http://amnesty.org/en/library/info/ASA20/015/2004

Diamond, S. (1985, March 21). Union Carbide's inquiry indicates error led to India plant disaster. *The New York Times,* p. A-1.

Disaster in Bhopal laid to sabotage: Study blames worker at Carbide facility. (1988, May 11). *Los Angeles Times.* Retrieved from http://articles.latimes.com/1988-05-11/business/fi-2522_1_carbide-disaster-bhopal

Emergency Planning and Community Right-to-Know Act (EPCRA). (2011). Retrieved from http://www.epa.gov/agriculture/lcra.html

Environmental Protection Agency (EPA). (n.d.). Methyl isocyanate. Retrieved from http://www.epa.gov/ttnatw01/hlthef/methylis.html

History of excellence. (2011). Retrieved from http://responsiblecare.americanchemistry.com/

Incident, response, settlement. (n.d). Retrieved from http://www.bhopal.com/incident-response-and-settlement

Kidwai, R. (2010). Cops saw off Warren with salutes: Pilot. Retrieved from http://www.telegraphindia.com/1100610/jsp/frontpage/story_12549314.jsp

Learning from major accidents. (2007). Retrieved from http://www.erris.org/accidents/majaccidents/bhopal.html

Memory Project (n.d.). Retrieved from http://bhopal.bard.edu/about/project.shtml

Nagaraj, V. K., & Raman, N. V. (n.d.). Are we prepared for another Bhopal? Retrieved from http://www.india-seminar.com/2004/544/544%20nagaraj,%20raman.htm

Page, J. (2010, June 8). Seven Union Carbide employees convicted over 1984 Bhopal gas disaster. Retrieved from http://www.timesonline.co.uk/tol/news/world/asia/article7145106.ece

Palenchar, M. J. (2005). Risk communication. In R. L. Heath (Ed.), *Encyclopedia of public relations: Volume 2* (pp. 752–755). Thousand Oaks, CA: Sage.

Pasko, V. (Interviewer). (1984, December 8). [Interview with Pavel Kasparov]. International Diary [Radio Broadcast]. Moscow, Russia: BBC.

Roediger, H. L., & Wertsch, J. V. (2008). Memory studies: Creating a new discipline of memory studies. *Memory Studies, 1*(1), 9–22.

Shabecoff, P. (1984, December 13). Officials tell a House hearing that plant in West Virginia is safe. *The New York Times,* p. A-10.

Sissell, K. (2004, December 15). 20 years after: Charting progress in plant safety. *Chemical Week,* 19.

Statement of Union Carbide Corporation regarding the Bhopal tragedy. (n.d.). Retrieved from http://www.bhopal.com/union-carbide-statements

Weisman S. R., & Hazarika, S. (1987, June 23). Theory of Bhopal sabotage is offered. Retrieved from http://www.nytimes.com/1987/06/23/world/theory-of-bhopal-sabotage-is-offered.html

CHAPTER 17

Odwalla and E. Coli

When you drink milk or fruit juice, you probably do not think too much about food safety. You assume that what comes out of the bottle is safe to drink, if the bottle has been properly stored and not past the expiration date. Your confidence is based upon years of trust in pasteurization. Pasteurization is a process developed by scientist Louis Pasteur that heats a liquid to kill the deadly bacteria that can be in the liquid. Using pasteurization protects people from an array of bacteria including *Escherichia coli (E. coli)*. There are some drinks that are not pasteurized, such as some apple cider, but most are. In the 1980s and early 1990s, a few U.S. juice makers chose not to pasteurize as a way to preserve the taste and quality of their juices. Inherently, this was a dangerous choice that required strict safety monitoring to prevent a food-borne illness outbreak, such as *E. coli*.

Odwalla was one of the U.S. juice manufacturers that chose not to pasteurize. Odwalla was founded in 1980 in Santa Cruz, California. It moved its headquarters to Half Moon Bay, California, and began to experience strong growth after it incorporated in 1985. During most of these years, it was growing at a 30% rate. What was started by Greg Steltenpohl, Gerry Percy, and Bonnie Bassett using a $200 hand juicer to make orange juice had become a multimillion dollar enterprise. The Odwalla brand differentiated itself from competitors by being "conscious." At its core, Odwalla was health conscious. The product was natural and healthy, due in part to not pasteurizing (Baker, n.d.). Odwalla was considered socially conscious as well on a par with companies like The Body Shop and Ben & Jerry's. Greg Steltenpohl, the founder, would talk about his respect for the fruit and respect for people. He was very popular when speaking to socially responsible investing groups. Analysts believed the messages from Steltenpohl and lauded the quality and responsibility of Odwalla. Through this consciousness, Odwalla was developing into a successful brand that was breeding a cult-like following of loyal consumers (Entine, 1999). Odwalla's fortunes took a sudden, negative turn in 1996.

In October of 1996, health officials in the Seattle-King County Health Department were tracking an *E. coli* outbreak. The initial evidence pointed to Odwalla apple juice. Officials decided to take action immediately and not wait for further lab tests because it was the day before Halloween, a day when apple juice and cider are very popular. Odwalla management immediately recalled the product in question. The Seattle-King County Health Department officials had made the correct call: Odwalla apple juice was the source of the *E. coli*. The officials were praised for their quick actions (Burros, 1996). The event was the beginning of a serious crisis that posed problems for Odwalla in 1996 and 1998.

In October of 1996, Odwalla was at the center of a product harm crisis. Its apple juice was linked to about 70 illnesses and one death from *E. coli* poisoning, *E. coli* 0157:H7 to be more precise. *E. coli* food poisoning is unpleasant, with vomiting and diarrhea. But it can become deadly, especially for children and those in poor health. Children are at greater risk because of their small body mass. Sixteen children were hospitalized and 16-month-old Anna Gimmestad of Denver, Colorado, died from this *E. coli* outbreak. It was speculated that a fallen apple, known in the business as a *grounder*, was the source of the contamination. By touching the ground, the apple could have been exposed to *E. coli*. Without pasteurization, the *E. coli* could then enter the juice. Odwalla's policy for suppliers specified that shipments should contain no grounders. The crisis for Odwalla was intense, its product made people ill and had killed a child. Not surprisingly, there was an immediate 90% drop in Odwalla sales, its stock price dropped 34%, more than 20 personal injury lawsuits were filed against Odwalla, and some key employees considered leaving the company (Layne, 2001). People expect their healthy drinks to be safe and not to endanger their lives—this was a serious expectation violation.

Odwalla used crisis communication effectively to bounce back from the *E. coli* crisis and regain its previous sales. Edelman Public Relations was hired to help Odwalla craft its crisis response. As in any product harm, the first step is the recall. A *recall* is a form of instructing information that tells stakeholders how to protect themselves from harm—do not use the product, and return it. Odwalla management acted immediately to recall its products after being warned by health officials of the possible link. Odwalla management could have demanded more evidence and waited for the additional lab tests being performed in Washington State. Instead, they acted on the early warning with a fast recall. The products had been recalled within 48 hours at a cost of $6.5 million. The quick action portrays Odwalla in a positive light. Stakeholders feel an organization really cares about their safety when they are willing to initiate a recall so quickly. Edelman entered the crisis during its early hours.

A key factor in product harm is the organization's responsibility for the product defect. Stakeholders assess whether or not management could have prevented the crisis. Technical errors, such as process or equipment failures, are difficult to control, and the organization is attributed moderate crisis responsibility. But human error or knowingly allowing a defective product to reach consumers both creates attributions of strong crisis responsibility and is a greater reputational threat to an organization. Odwalla's messages cultivated a technical-error perspective by describing the organization as a victim in this crisis as well. One question people asked was why Odwalla did not test for *E. coli* when it was not using pasteurization.

Odwalla's founder George Steltenpohl stated: "We didn't test for E. coli because we believed evidence showed it was not found at that acid level" (Entine, 1998, Growing Up section). Odwalla's position was that there was no need to test because of the industry belief that acidic juices would not grow E. coli. Therefore, Odwalla was a victim of industry thinking rather than negligent for not testing for *E. coli*.

Odwalla management was quick to express sympathy and regret too. In media interviews, CEO Stephen Williamson frequently expressed concern for the victims and said Odwalla would cover all of their medical costs (Baker, n.d.). Such statements and actions created the impression that Odwalla was taking, not ducking, responsibility for the crisis. Odwalla, guided by Edelman, was saying and doing the right things to create a positive, postcrisis impression among its stakeholders.

Odwalla's crisis communication was a comprehensive effort to reach internal and external stakeholders. Employees are often overlooked and under informed during a crisis. But CEO Williamson began daily conference calls with employees. The calls were designed to keep employees updated and to allow employees to ask questions about the crisis. The employees were kept abreast of Odwalla's crisis management efforts.

The most unique aspect of the Odwalla crisis response was the use of the Internet to keep external stakeholders informed. This was Odwalla's first use of a website. Within the first 49 hours, the website received over 20,000 visitors. The website traffic numbers suggest it was useful in providing information to stakeholders. Odwalla would update the site as the situation evolved thereby keeping external stakeholders up to date on the crisis management efforts. Here are some statements made about Edelman's pioneering use of the Internet for crisis management:

> Edelman found that the site enabled Odwalla to present its case and reassure customers in a manner that was more timely and more manageable than holding news conferences and sending news releases. Odwalla survived the crisis and is still in business. Meanwhile, the experience was a turning point for Edelman in terms of the company's attitude toward the Internet.
>
> "Suddenly, we realized the value of the Web in crisis management," said the firm's president, Richard Edelman. "From that point on, we began to think of it as the predominant way to release information in situations like that." (Berger, 2000, p. 2, para. 1–2)

During a product harm crisis, customers want and will seek additional information. It is logical that Internet savvy customers will search online for crisis-related information. While that seems obvious today, in the early stages of Internet usage, it was a revelation. Edelman created the site in one day and included information they anticipated stakeholders would want about the crisis. The website (a) included questions and answers about the situation, (b) asked visitors to submit questions, and (c) provided links to the two government agencies involved in food-borne illness recalls, the Centers for Disease Control and Prevention and the Food and Drug Administration for information (Thomsen & Rawson, 1998).

Odwalla was providing additional information designed to help stakeholders cope with the product harm crisis.

When people have been injured, a common concern among stakeholders is whether it will happen again. Stakeholders worry that a repeat of the incident could place them at risk again. Odwalla sales dropped because customers feared consuming the juice might expose them to *E. coli*. Odwalla management addressed concerns over the repeat of an *E. coli* outbreak by explaining how it was looking to prevent a repeat of this problem. This part of the news release addresses the need for better prevention:

> Odwalla pledged to lead the industry in solving the complex E. coli 0157:H7 issue as it relates to fresh apple juice. To that end the company has created the Odwalla Nourishment and Food Safety Advisory Council, of which two members, Dr. "Nick" Nickelson and Dr. Michael Doyle, participated in the briefing. Nickelson is founder and president of Red Mesa Microbiology, a consulting company specializing in food quality and safety programs. Doyle is professor of food microbiology and director of the University of Georgia's Department of Food Science and Technology.
>
> With their guidance, Odwalla will be developing the first Hazard Analysis Critical Control Points (HACCP) program in the fresh apple juice industry, which has become a regulatory standard in the beef, poultry and seafood industries. "We now know that E. coli 0157:H7 is a hazard in fresh apple juice," said Nickelson. "We are not looking for a single step, we're looking for a process. Odwalla's program should serve as a model for the entire fresh apple juice industry."
>
> Finally, among other methods, the company is considering some form of heat treatment to kill bacteria while maintaining integrity and optimal nutritional content of the fresh apple juice, producing a safe product that is in keeping with the company's vision of producing nourishing beverages. "Our core values are based around the idea of optimal nutrition," said Greg Steltenpohl, chairman of Odwalla. "It may be possible to heat treat and still maintain the primary nutritional content of our apple juice. We're researching that now and when we have all the information we'll make a decision and share our findings with the industry and the public." Until that time, the company has stopped production of all fresh apple juice and encouraged other producers of fresh apple juice to do the same. ("FDA Report," 1996, para. 3–5)

Odwalla planned to lead the fresh juice industry (a smaller segment of the larger juice market) in *E. coli* safety. The effort to build a better safety system was designed to reassure customers that Odwalla juices were now safe.

In December of 1996, Odwalla instituted "flash pasteurization" as a final solution for preventing *E. coli* in their juices. The move was an admission that not using pasteurization was a failure. Odwalla had policies for growers that said fruit had to be tree-picked and not have touched the ground. Not pasteurizing was a defining element of Odwalla's original identity because it was supposed to enhance taste and nutrients. However, Odwalla could not risk another *E. coli* outbreak. The flash pasteurization showed a commitment to customer health and safety (Layne, 2001). The flash pasteurization was a wise move by Odwalla because the following year the Food and Drug Administration (FDA) asked juice makers that did not pasteurize their products to place warning labels on their products. The label would warn consumers that the product was not pasteurized and contained microorganisms that could cause disease ("FDA Warning," 1997). By the end of 1997, the non-pasteurized juice market in the United States was nonexistent because the risk was considered too great by manufacturers and consumers. However, Odwalla was rebounding, and sales were returning throughout 1997. Their crisis communication has been effective in restoring the organization's reputation and consumer purchasing.

As noted at the start, the *E. coli* incident was a crisis in 1996 and in 1998. It was in 1998 that some of the legal cases over the product harm were settled. Information disclosed during the trial was harmful to Odwalla, hence, represent residual effects from the 1996 crisis. This section will detail some of the harmful disclosures that suggest the 1996 crisis was avoidable.

An essential element of crisis management is prevention. Managers scan for warning signs of a crisis and take action designed to prevent those warning signs from becoming a crisis. For Odwalla, warning signs would include indicators that its juices could be contaminated and were not as safe as its management thought. The U.S. Army had rejected a proposal by Odwalla to sell its juice at army commissaries. Army officials felt the risk of contamination was too great. The rejection suggests the government had doubts about the safety of Odwalla's non-pasteurization process. When this issue was raised in court, Odwalla management denied the incident had occurred. However, army documents proved that the story was true (Entine, 1999).

Odwalla's head of quality assurance, David Stevenson, recommended changing from an acid wash to a chlorine wash for the fruit. The change was recommended because a Florida orange juice contamination case proved that bacteria could survive in drinks with a high acid level. The company that supplied the acid wash recommended it be used with chlorine because the acid wash is only about 8% effective at killing dangerous bacteria (Entine, 1999). This contradicts statements by Odwalla management that it did not know *E. coli* could survive in its juices. Essentially, two clear warning signs existed prior to the 1996 *E. coli* outbreak, and no action was taken to reduce the risk. Moreover, Odwalla management appeared to lie about knowing about the existence of the risk. The failed warning information would suggest the crisis was now human error. Odwalla management knew there was a risk with the non-pasteurization process but did not alter the process. It is even possible to make the case, as lawyers did, that Odwalla purposely placed its customers at risk. Odwalla settled the lawsuits for more than the plaintiffs requested, and the company continued its rebound from the 1996 recall (Entine, 1999).

Food recalls due to risks of food poisoning are rather commonplace. In September of 2012, Trader Joe's recalled its Creamy Salted Valencia Peanut Butter.

The Food and Drug Administration (FDA) and Centers for Disease Control (CDC) had linked the peanut butter to a *Salmonella* outbreak in 18 states (Jalonick, 2012). The recall was expanded when Sunland Inc., the makers of the peanut butter, voluntarily recalled all of its almond butter and peanut butter products. Sunland made the following statement:

> There is nothing more important to us than the health and safety of our customers, particularly the many families who enjoy our peanut butter everyday. While FDA, CDC, and State Health Agencies investigate to confirm the cause of illnesses reported, as a precautionary step, we have decided to voluntarily recall our Almond Butter and Peanut Butter products manufactured between May 1, 2012 and September 24, 2012. If you purchased these products, do not eat them. Please return the product to your supermarket for a full refund or dispose of it. ("Peanut Butter Recall Expands," 2012, para. 4)

Sunland makes organic peanut butter. The recall raised concerns about the long-term viability of organic peanut butter ("Peanut Butter Recall Affects," 2012). Again, a crisis in a supposedly healthy food was raising bigger questions about the industry.

Reading Guide

1. If this situation is a crisis, what type of crisis is it?

2. What is the problem and the source(s) of the problem in this case?

3. What stakeholders should be interested in this case?

4. Why were lawsuits filed?

5. What public relations agency was involved in the crisis?

Discussion Questions

1. Why was the Internet relevant to this crisis?

2. Why can an argument be made that the crisis was avoidable?

3. How did Odwalla benefit from information about its safety record coming out after the crisis passed?

4. Why does public interest fade after a crisis appears to be resolved?

5. Did the lawsuits seem to extend the crisis? Why or why not?

6. How does the case illustrate the unintended crisis consequences for foods intended to be organic and/or healthy?

7. What effect does the crisis being an industry problem have on the crisis communication effort?

8. Why might food-borne illnesses create more intensive crises for organic food suppliers than other types of food suppliers?

Websites

Odwalla home page: http://www.odwalla.com/

Mallen Baker's analysis of the Odwalla case: http://www.mallenbaker.net/csr/crisis05.html

References

Baker, M. (n.d.). Odwalla and the E. coli outbreak. Retrieved from http://www.mallenbaker .net/csr/CSRfiles/crisis05.html

Berger, W. (2000). Spinners' web weapons: T-chips and dark sites. Retrieved from http:// www.nytimes.com/2000/10/25/business/marketing-spinners-web-weapons-t-chips -and-dark-sites.html?src=pm

Burros, M. (1996). Opting for an early warning when E. coli is suspected. Retrieved from http://www.nytimes.com/1996/11/20/garden/opting-for-an-early-warning-when-e-coli -is-suspected.html

Entine, J. (1998, September/October). Intoxicated by success: How to protect your company from inevitable corporate screw-ups. Retrieved October 7, 2010, from http://www .jonentine.com/ethical_corporation/corp_screwups.htm

Entine, J. (1999, January/February). The Odwalla affair: Reassessing corporate social responsibility. Retrieved from http://www.jonentine.com/articles/odwalla.htm

FDA report indicates no E. coli 0157:H7 found at Dinuba plant. (1996, November 18). Retrieved from http://www.kidsource.com/kidsource/content2/ecoli/odwalla.11.23.html

FDA warning labels only impact unpasteurized apple juices. (1997). Retrieved from http://www .kidsource.com/kidsource/products/motts.juice.a11.1.html

Jalonick, M. C. (2012). Chain pulls item after 29 salmonella illnesses in 18 states. Retrieved from http://www.huffingtonpost.com/2012/09/22/trader-joes-peanut-butter -recall_n_1906645.html

Layne, A. (2001). How to make your company more resilient. Retrieved from http://www .fastcompany.com/articles/2001/03/odwalla.html

Peanut butter recall affects country's major retailers. (2012). Retrieved from http://www .oregonlive.com/business/index.ssf/2012/10/peanut_butter_recall_affects_c.html

Peanut butter recall expands beyond Trader Joe's. (2012). Retrieved from http://www.food safetynews.com/2012/09/peanut-butter-recall-expands-beyond-trader-joes/

Thomsen, S., & Rawson, B. (1998, Fall). Purifying a tainted image: Odwalla's response to an E. coli poisoning. *Public Relations Quarterly, 43,* 35–45.

CHAPTER 18

ValuJet Flight 592 and the End of a Brand

When the U.S. government deregulated the airline industry, new airlines appeared to challenge the established order with an emphasis on low prices. The first of these new, low-cost airlines appeared in the 1980s but most of them disappeared. In the 1990s, a stronger class of low-cost airlines emerged, including Southwest, ValuJet, and Air Tran. ValuJet no longer exists as a brand name but was a darling of the airline industry in the early 1990s. ValuJet, headquartered in Atlanta, Georgia, had two planes in 1994. By 1996, it had 51 planes. To keep costs low, ValuJet purchased old DC-9s for its fleet and outsourced its maintenance to a number of private contractors. In total, ValuJet used 56 different maintenance contractors, including one named SabreTech (Ray, 1999). In 1997, the future looked bright for ValuJet, the company with the smiling plane logo known as "the Critter."

Everything changed for ValuJet on May 11, 1996. ValuJet Flight 592 took off from Miami at 2:30 p.m., headed for Atlanta's Hartsfield International Airport. The flight never arrived in Atlanta. Ten minutes after departure, Flight 592 crashed into the swamps of the Everglades. There were no survivors. Investigating the crash was difficult. The Everglades is a very wild and dangerous swamp. It is home to large alligators and poisonous snakes. The people searching for bodies and wreckage were guarded by sharpshooters. The sharpshooters were there to defend the searchers from the alligators and snakes. Add to that mix the heat, the bugs, and the very rough saw grass and you have an extremely tough recovery task. But the flight data recorder, the cockpit voice recorder, and 75% of the plane were recovered (Ray, 1999).

Any crash is a serious crisis for an airline. Two critical and related questions emerge: (a) What caused the crash? and (b) is it safe to fly the airline? It is difficult to view an airline as safe until you know the problem and whether or not the airline has acted to prevent a repeat of that problem. The National Transportation Safety Board (NTSB) investigates airline crashes. Until the NTSB released its report, ValuJet would remain in a crisis because the shadow of doubt about safety would remain.

Louis Jordan, the ValuJet president, became the voice for ValuJet during the crisis. The initial ValuJet statement on the crash was delivered at a press conference by Mr. Jordan. His opening statement, ValuJet's initial response to the crisis, can be found in Exhibit 18.1.

Exhibit 18.1   Louis Jordan's Initial Statement

I would ask that each of you recognize there are a number of other people in this room. Please try to be considerate of everybody here. Our first thoughts, obviously, go to the families, friends and loved ones of the people who were on board the airplane. I want to point out to you that, as president of this company and as a founder of ValuJet Airlines, I have the responsibility for whatever has happened here. We are actively participating in the investigation. We will fully cooperate with the NTSB and the FAA.

As I think most of you know, the way the process works, the NTSB has the responsibility for conducting the investigation. As the investigation goes forward, the NTSB will hold press briefings and they will be actually giving out information, as information is learned. ValuJet will follow the practice of coming forward to talk to the press at any time new information comes forward that makes it appropriate for us to speak. At other times, we will refrain and leave that in the hands of the NTSB.

In anticipation of a couple of your questions, I want to tell you that the media has repeatedly asked about the age of the aircraft. I want to tell you that if ValuJet Airlines had any reason to believe that any one of our aircraft was not safe, we would voluntarily ground it. I can assure you that the FAA, if it had any reason to believe that any one of our aircraft was not safe, they would ground it and we would certainly cooperate in that regard.

We have all experienced a tragedy. The people on board that airplane who lost their lives are obviously the victims of something that we don't understand at this point. It is important to all of us that we investigate as promptly as we can to learn anything we can about that. Not only did we have our customers on board, but we had members of the ValuJet team, our crew members, who understand and know on a daily basis that we put safety at the very highest level of responsibility.

ValuJet is a relatively new carrier. We began service in October of 1993. There's been a lot reported that the FAA has been conducting in-depth inspections of ValuJet Airlines, as a result of the fact that we have been a rapidly-growing airline and that we have been highly visible and that we had some incidents that occurred back in the January-February time frame that, so far as we can tell, were all unrelated.

I believe the FAA will confirm to you that they completed a seven-day in-depth inspection in the February time frame. They were continuing with a 120-day analysis of the data they collected during that period of time to determine if there were any patterns or trends that would tell us there's anything else that we need to do. And, to be very candid and very blunt with you, at this time, we are probably better off that we have been working with the FAA hand-in-hand as our partners in safety throughout these in-depth inspections than if those had not been going on because as of this moment, both the FAA and the Secretary of Transportation have confirmed that they have been looking intently at ValuJet's operations and have found nothing that would be cause for concern.

In fact, Secretary Pena said this morning on national television that he was very surprised about this particular accident because of the fact that they have been looking so closely at ValuJet and found us to be not only in compliance with the law, but in many cases exceeding the requirements of the FAA regulations and to be very, very cooperative at all times.

(O'Brien, 1996, para. 4–10)

Crises are often referred to as information vacuums. People want to know information, but accurate information can be hard to find at the start of a crisis. One essential piece of information for airline crashes is the list of people on the flight. By U.S. law, each victim's family must be contacted before that list of passengers is released. Unfortunately for ValuJet, there were some errors with the passenger manifest. Here is the ValuJet statement related to the manifest confusion:

> The National Transportation Safety Board reported yesterday that, in addition to the 109 customers on ValuJet flight 592, there was an infant traveling with her parents. ValuJet has determined that there was a previously unidentified child who boarded as a child-in-arms with Mahamad Darbor and Saeeda Alihassan Darbor of Atlanta.
>
> ATLANTA, May 15. The child has been identified as Daniel Darbor.
>
> According to the child's grandparents, her age was four years, which would conflict with the representation made at check-in. The age discrepancy and whether there was a violation of regulations are under investigation.
>
> In addition, ValuJet has learned that a person listed on the flight manifest as George Wilson of Fayetteville, Georgia, was apparently traveling under an assumed name. Through family inquiries made to ValuJet, it was learned the customer's name was Jimmy H. Lewis of Atlanta. ("ValuJet Issues," 1996, para. 1–4)

This is a poor start to the crisis management effort when a name is missing from the list of people who died in the crash and there is uncertainty about the name of another passenger on the flight. Accuracy is highly prized in crisis management, and ValuJet had inaccurate information about an essential point for an airline crash.

ValueJet moved quickly to reassure customers and potential customers about its safety practices. The company began an aggressive review of its safety and maintenance procedures immediately after the accident. Of course, ValueJet did not want the actions to raise concerns so they stated: "It is our belief that our operations are completely safe," said Lewis Jordan, ValuJet's president and chief operating officer (COO). "The measures we are announcing today go well beyond the current FAA inspection to reassure our customers that we share their insistence on the utmost safety" ("ValueJet Announces," 1996, para. 2). The centerpiece of the safety reform was the appointment of General James D. Davis to be their safety czar. The ValuJet announcement of the safety czar appointment can be found in Exhibit 18.2.

Exhibit 18.2   Safety Czar Appointment

ValuJet Airlines (Nasdaq-NMM: VJET) has named General James B. Davis (USAF–Ret.), as its "safety czar" to conduct a thorough inspection of the airline's maintenance and safety people, policies and procedures. General Davis recently concluded a 35-year career with the U.S. Air Force as chief of staff Supreme Headquarters, Allied Powers Europe (NATO). He will report directly to ValuJet President Lewis Jordan and conduct his inspections with the full authority of the president's office.

"General Davis has impeccable credentials and the highest respect of major figures in air transportation throughout the world," said Mr. Jordan. "He brings outstanding experience, knowledge and common sense to this position, and his presence adds yet another measure of assurance that ValuJet puts safety above all other considerations."

During his career, General Davis also served as commander, Pacific Air Forces; commander, U.S. Forces-Japan and 5th Air Forces, and commander, U.S. Air Force Military Personnel Center. He has been director and programmer of the U.S. Air Force's personnel and training, and deputy chief of staff for Operations and Intelligence, Pacific Air Forces. Since his recent retirement from the Air Force, General Davis has joined The Spectrum Group, a Washington, D.C.-based consultancy.

General Davis is assembling senior experts in maintenance, training and other fields, and appointed as his chief of staff, Colonel Paul E. McManus (USAF-Ret.) chief executive officer of The Spectrum Group, who has exhaustive credentials in the area of special operations, personnel and other important fields.

Colonel McManus will begin immediately to set up operations for the review, and General Davis will join the inspection and review in early June.

ATLANTA, May 17.

("ValuJet Names," 1996, para 1, 3–6)

On the positive side, ValuJet was praised for the quick notification of family members and the kindness they provided to the victims' families. ValuJet provided grief counselors along with the traditional covering of funeral costs and the arranging and paying for families to visit the site of the crash. Moreover, ValuJet had mentioned to victims' families that it planned to build a memorial near the crash site (Adair, 1996).

As the news media began to examine ValuJet more closely, negative information began to emerge. The first piece of negative information was that ValuJet, at the time of the accident, was under close watch by the Federal Aviation Administration (FAA), following reports of a number of safety problems for the airline. Those problems included a landing gear collapse, a hard landing that damaged the plane, a plane getting stuck in the mud, and a plane sliding off a runway ("ValuJet Had," 1996). Research has shown that past crises intensify the negative effects from a current crisis (Coombs, 2004). Though the past incidents involved no fatalities, they raised additional questions about the safety of ValuJet.

The next piece of negative information was a report that the crash was avoidable—
it should have been prevented. Early speculation about the cause identified improperly stored oxygen generators that should not have been in the plane's cargo hold.
Lewis Jordan, president of ValuJet, defended ValuJet when the information about
improper transportation of oxygen generators began to emerge. Here is an excerpt
from the statement Mr. Jordan made at a news conference:

> Since last Saturday, and since last Sunday, it appears that the entire focus has
> shifted away from aging aircraft and maintenance practices and training and
> experience levels, again, all of which we can talk about. And as of today, and,
> in fact, late yesterday, the focus seems to have been the report that ValuJet
> Airlines was illegally carrying hazardous materials which it is not authorized
> to do on its airplane, and that these hazardous materials may have resulted in
> an explosion that may have caused this crash. Now, I put in a number of
> "mays" there, but it's not very hard to find examples where it was a little more
> direct than that, indicating that this, in fact, was the case. It is wrong for
> ValuJet Airlines, for Lewis Jordan as an individual, for the NTSB, the FAA, the
> DOT, or any of you to prematurely judge the cause. And it is specifically,
> I think, irresponsible and unfair to the traveling public to send a signal that
> this accident may have been caused by something quite apart from what may
> in the end be the real cause.
>
> You have, perhaps, seen reports today, one in particular in the Washington
> Post has indicated that ValuJet was tendered for delivery some canisters, and
> I would emphasize canisters, is what was on the shipping ticket. You've read
> about oxygen generators, which are, in fact, the canister when filled with
> chemicals designed to conduct a chemical reaction to generate oxygen on
> board airplanes. The shipping ticket we have indicates that we received boxes
> of canisters that were noted specifically on the shipping ticket as empty. I have
> no way to know whether that information is accurate at this time, and I don't
> think anyone here does. If, in fact, those canisters were empty as marked on
> the shipping ticket, then we have nothing more than empty metal cans that are
> perfectly legal for ValuJet Airlines to transport from Miami to Atlanta in the
> belly of its airplanes.
>
> I think you can understand why, as we look at that shipping ticket, we
> believe that it is entirely possible that the people of ValuJet Airlines who relied
> upon that information, may have been performing their duties without any
> fault. But I can't speculate on that, and I can't confirm that. That's the job of the
> investigating authorities. And we will determine exactly what the facts are. But
> it seems to me, for the millions of people who are making their choices every
> day as to whether or not to fly an airline like ValuJet or any of the other start-
> up carriers, it is extremely important that they have factual representation for
> what has gone on. (Battista, 1996, para. 5–7)

The stream of negative information continued to flow for ValuJet. First, the
NTSB did rule the oxygen generators were the cause of the crash.

The oxygen generators quickly emerged as the cause of the crash. Oxygen generators are at the other end of the mask that drops down in an airplane if it loses pressure. When oxygen generators activate, they generate heat. Improperly packed oxygen generators had activated in the cargo hold on Flight 592. The heat from the oxygen generators created a fire in the cargo area that caused the plane to crash. Here is one summary of the NTSB's findings for the crash of ValuJet 592:

> A fire begun and nourished by oxygen generators was the cause of the crash of a Valujet plane in the Everglades 15 months ago, but ultimately the accident, which killed all 110 people aboard, occurred because of supervisory failures by the airline and by the Federal Aviation Administration, the National Transportation Safety Board said today. (Wald, 1996, p. A-16)

ValuJet management did not agree with the NTSB findings. Instead, the company argued that the crash was the sole responsibility of SabreTech. The claim was that SabreTech had improperly prepared the oxygen generators for shipping. The NTSB felt ValuJet had an obligation to oversee the transport of the oxygen generators; therefore, ValueJet had some responsibility for the crisis as well as the FAA itself because it should have had better oversight of the entire process. ValuJet argued that its personnel did oversee SabreTech but that SabreTech had lied to them about the oxygen generators. Moreover, it called the report "political grandstanding" by NTSB member John Goglia ("ValuJet Accuses," 1997). A ValuJet statement said: "It is a serious miscarriage of justice that Goglia once again chose to interject his personal views, which have been demonstrably anti-ValuJet" (Adair, 1997, p. A-1). Here is part of the ValuJet statement presenting its claims against SabreTech:

> The tragic accident involving flight 592 on May 11, 1996, happened because SabreTech failed to fulfill its legal and moral obligations as a federally-licensed aircraft maintenance company. They caused an unmarked bomb (mislabeled and deceptively packaged boxes of oxygen generators) to be put on our plane, and as a direct result, 110 innocent people lost their lives. The airline believes that the maintenance company or its employees may also be guilty of an on-going conspiracy to hide evidence of its wrongdoing from investigators.

How SabreTech Caused the Accident

> 1. failed to follow clear written instructions in the McDonnell-Douglas maintenance manual, requiring the installation of safety caps over the firing pins of the oxygen generators, and then falsified maintenance work records to reflect that safety caps were installed (an illegal practice called "pencil-whipping," where work not done is signed off on as completed by a federally licensed mechanic);

> 2. ignored at least three specific warnings from ValuJet supervisory personnel that the removed generators were extremely dangerous and should be disposed of as hazardous waste;

3. failed to comply with numerous hazardous materials handling regulations of the Department of Transportation (DOT), Occupational Health and Safety Administration (OSHA), Resource Conservation and Recovery Act (RCRA) and Environmental Protection Agency (EPA);

4. completed an inaccurate and misleading shipping ticket, on which the full oxygen generators were described as "oxy canisters—empty"; 5. packaged the generators illegally, using unapproved cartons, arrangement and packing materials, failing to mark the packages with a proper shipping name and UN identification number and DOT-required "yellow-diamond" hazard warning label;

6. delivered the cartons directly to a ValuJet aircraft with verbal instructions to load them aboard flight 592 to Atlanta, without disclosing to the airline's employees the dangerous contents of the sealed and unmarked cartons; and

7. contravened ValuJet's policy prohibiting carriage of such materials aboard its flights ("ValuJet," 1997, para. 1–2; 4–10).

Of course SabreTech defended its actions and claimed there was no deception on their part, calling the ValuJet accusations "yet another sad attempt by ValuJet to put up a smokescreen to cover up their own ineptitude that contributed to this tragedy" (Adair, 1997, p. A-1). The public record stated the crash was avoidable and that ValuJet was partially responsible for the tragic event.

Second, the FAA grounded all ValuJet flights in June of 1996. The FAA investigation raised serious safety questions that needed to be addressed. The grounding lasted 15 weeks, during which time ValuJet worked on improving safety with a focus on better oversight of its maintenance activities (Ray, 1999). ValuJet was upset by the FAA decision to ground its fleet. Here is a segment of President Lewis Jordan's statement on the grounding of ValuJet:

Yesterday afternoon, we learned that it was in the best interest of ValuJet Airlines in our ongoing spirit of cooperation with the FAA, that we voluntarily cease operations as of midnight last night. The alternative would have been a less desirable one for ValuJet Airlines, and we chose not to put the FAA in a position of having to forcefully ground ValuJet. It has been our spirit and our commitment from day one that we always cooperate 100 percent with the FAA. They have a tough job to do. Their oversight as regulators in our industry is a very important one. We do not agree with everything they do. We do not agree with every decision they make, but we always go forward with a spirit of cooperation. As of midnight last night, all revenue operations were ceased temporarily at ValuJet Airlines . . . In the meanwhile, with ValuJet having reached an agreement with the FAA to cease operations on a temporary basis, our focus and emphasis have shifted. We have been working on a consent order, a document that we expect to sign later today, that will outline the terms and conditions under which ValuJet's stand down will continue over the next few days and weeks, and what we hope will outline the policies, procedures, practices that we will need to follow in order to return ValuJet Airlines to service. We hope in approximately 30 days, but I must hasten to add that that is beyond my control and beyond the control of the people of ValuJet. I can only tell you that if spirit, energy, dedication, professionalism, and hard work count, we'll be back up and running soon and very strong. Now the FAA has indicated that we will have a limited number of airplanes that we will be able to operate initially, and that will all be part of the consent order, and we will be able to divulge more details on that once it's signed and agreed to. . . .

We would not have chosen to be grounded as of today if everything had gone our way, but everything hasn't gone our way for quite some time, and we will work back from this. We also have the ability to be optimistic because, three years ago, nobody had any idea what a ValuJet might be. And yet, if you look at the little history book we've written in the last three years or close to that, you see the most successful little airline that ever started, the one that grew fast, the one that created jobs for fine professionals, the one that made a lot of money for investors and shareholders, the one that was profitable from the first day it ever operated, by paying attention to and avoiding any waste, and by always doing the things that were right, to serve our customer in a market where hundreds of thousands of people told us they wanted an alternative to high airfares. They wanted the ability to afford to travel and be with their loved ones on holidays. They wanted the ability to send their child from one state to another if there was a divorce. They wanted the ability to take a vacation on short notice, or take a long weekend with the family without having to take out a loan. They wanted the ability to travel on business, and occasionally be able to afford to take their family members and loved ones with them. And in short, over the last month, as we faced this terrible tragedy and the aftermath of it, the hundreds and hundreds and hundreds of letters and cards and phone calls that have come thanking ValuJet for what we have done has heartened us, given us strength, and given us resolve. (Rook, 1996, para. 6, 8, 10)

ValuJet would survive the crisis as a company but not as a brand. In July of 1997, ValuJet essentially merged with the Orlando-based, low-cost carrier AirTran with a stock swap. The "new" airline would operate under the name AirTran. The "Critter" was gone, but ValuJet lived on under another name. ValuJet was rebranded into AirTran. Rebranding involves an organization changing some combination of its name, logo, or slogan. Rebranding is risky because the organization is severing connections with an established brand that has generated sales and market share. Rebranding is costly as well because the organization must promote the new brand and replace all uses of the current brand, for example, websites, building signage, and so on (Stuart & Muzellec, 2004). ValuJet changed its name, logo, and slogan when it became AirTran. Common reasons for rebranding include mergers and acquisitions, shifts in the marketplace created by new competitors, changes in legal conditions, an outdated brand, creation of a new vision for the organization, or separation of an organization from "social or moral baggage"(Stuart & Muzellec, 2004, p. 474). ValuJet could argue the name change was a function of its merger. However, commentators noted that ValuJet had engaged in extreme rebranding to escape the stigma created by the crash of Flight 592 (Kaplan, 1997). AirTran was acquired by Southwest in 2010.

There is a memorial for the 110 victims in the Everglades consisting of 110 concrete pillars located just north of Tamiami Trail, about 11 miles west of Krome Avenue in Dade County, Florida, and it points to the location of the actual crash site 8 miles to the north. It has been over 15 years since the crash, but the memories linger. Here is a statement from one of the victim's family members on the 15th anniversary: "For Marilyn Chamberlin, whose daughter, Capt. Candalyn Kubkeck, was the plane's pilot, the memory of that day still stings. 'Fifteen years, you never get closure,' Chamberlin said. 'I don't care what they say, it's always an open wound. So you just live the best you can'" (Mcardle, 2011, para. 3–4).

Reading Guide

1. If this situation is a crisis, what type of crisis is it?

2. What is the problem and the source(s) of the problem in this case?

3. What stakeholders should be interested in this case?

4. Why did ValuJet have problems with the actions taken by the NTSB and its report?

5. How were the victims of the crash memorialized?

Discussion Questions

1. What case can be made that the crisis was avoidable?

2. Did ValuJet's efforts to blame SabreTech help or hurt its crisis communication efforts? Justify your answer.

3. Did ValuJet's efforts to attack the NTSB's findings help or hurt its crisis communication efforts? Justify your answer.

4. What were the benefits and harms created by grounding the ValuJet fleet?

5. How would you evaluate the ethicality of ValuJet's rebranding?

6. What role does the memorial play in the crisis?

7. What are the risks and rewards in crisis communication when an organization is as aggressive as ValuJet in disputing crash investigations and decisions by Federal regulatory agencies like the FAA?

Websites

YouTube video of a news story including an eyewitness account: http://www.youtube.com/watch?v=N4BSkNNr4zQ

YouTube video of the graphics used in the ValuJet trial: http://www.youtube.com/watch?v=3k_Mcg6TSHM

News story about 15 year anniversary of the crash: http://articles.sun-sentinel.com/2011–05–11/news/fl-valujet-crash-anniversary-20110511_1_valujet-crash-crash-site-fiery-crash

Images of the memorial to the victims of ValuJet Flight 592: http://www.waymarking.com/waymarks/WM6HNC_ValuJet_Flight_592_Memorial_Everglades_National_Park

References

Adair, B. (1996, June 26). ValuJet contends crash was someone else's fault. *St. Petersburg Times,* p. A-1.

Adair, B. (1997, August 23). ValuJet blasts back after crash ruling. *St. Petersburg Times,* p. A-1.

Battista, B. (1996, May 16). Text of ValuJet news conference. CNN: http://www.cnn.com/search/

Coombs, W. T. (2004). Impact of past crises on current crisis communications: Insights from situational crisis communication theory. *Journal of Business Communication, 41,* 265–289.

Kaplan, P. (1997, July 11). ValuJet to shed name in merger: Will fly as AirTran Airlines, hopes image woes are over. *The Washington Post,* p. A-1.

McArdle, J. (2011). Indicted in 1996 ValuJet crash, airline mechanic still on EPA's most wanted list. Retrieved from http://www.nytimes.com/gwire/2011/05/11/11greenwire-indicted-in-1996-valujet-crash-airline-mechanic-771.html?pagewanted=all

O'Brien, M. (1996, May 12). ValuJet president takes full responsibility for crash. CNN: http://www.cnn.com/search/

Ray, S. J. (1999). *Strategic communication in crisis management: Lessons from the airline industry.* Westport, CT: Quorom Books.

Rook, S. (1996, June 18). Text of ValuJet news conference. CNN: http://www.cnn.com/search/

ValuJet. (1996). ValueJet President Louis Jordan testifies before Congress. PR Newswire: http://www.prnewswire.com/

ValuJet. (1997, August 19). ValuJet releases statement in response to NTSB final report on flight 592 airline traces accident cause, points to possible SabreTech cover-up. PR Newswire: http://www.prnewswire.com/

ValuJet accuses NTSB's Goglia of "political grandstanding." (1997). *Aviation Daily, 329*(37), 329.

ValueJet announces aggressive safety and maintenance review. (1996, May 17). PR Newswire: http://www.prnewswire.com/

ValuJet had been under FAA scrutiny. (1996, May 12). *San Jose Mercury News,* p. A-22.

ValuJet issues statement on Flight 592 fatalities. (1996, May 16). PR Newswire: http://www.prnewswire.com/

ValuJet names General James B Davis (USAF-Ret) as safety czar. (1996, May 17). PR Newswire: http://www.prnewswire.com/

Wald, M. L. (1996, August 20). Safety board faults airline and F.A.A. in Valujet crash. *The New York Times,* p. A-16.

CHAPTER 19

Greenpeace Pressures H&M to Detox the Garment Industry

Globalization has been increasing rapidly over the past decade. World markets and businesses are becoming increasing interconnected. To see globalization for yourself, check the tags on your clothes to see what country they claim as their point of origin or assembly. Examples of globalization include the spread of international retailers and the common usage of long, international supply chains. Globalization is a contested development. There are pro-globalization forces that argue for free trade and anti-globalization forces that argue it harms certain groups. The reality is that globalization does permeate our lives and complicates the world for many corporations. Globalization is a complication for corporations because they must contend with an ever-increasing number and variety of stakeholders as their global footprint expands. The Detox Campaign organized by Greenpeace is an excellent example of the complexity globalization creates for organizations.

The international garment industry has wrestled with a number of labor issues, including child labor, forced labor, and sweatshops. The Detox Campaign addressed a different problem in the garment industry, water pollution. The Detox Campaign began in July of 2011 with the goal of preventing human suffering from the water pollution created by certain practices in the garment industry. Greenpeace published the results of their examination of water pollution in China related to the garment industry in their "Dirty Laundry" report. The report examined pollution in the Yangtze and Pearl River deltas. Here is how Greenpeace described the findings:

> Alkylphenols (including nonylphenol) were found in wastewater samples from both factories, and perfluorinated chemicals (PFCs) were present in the wastewater from the Youngor Textile Complex. These findings come despite the presence of a modern wastewater treatment plant at the Youngor facility.

The alkylphenols and PFCs found in the samples are a cause for serious concern, as these chemicals are known hormone disruptors and can be hazardous even at very low levels. Both groups of chemicals are man-made substances that persist in the environment and can have potentially devastating effects as they accumulate up the food chain.

Many hazardous chemicals can also be transported in our oceans, atmosphere and food chains and accumulate in places far away from their original source. They have been found to build up in the bodies of animals including birds, fish, whales, polar bears and even human breast milk. ("Detox Campaign," 2011, para 7-9)

The key point was that the textile industry, a supplier to the garment industry, was polluting waterways with toxins that were harmful to humans, wildlife, and the environment. What makes the situation so troubling is that water is fundamental to life.

The follow-up report, "Dirty Laundry 2," moved the danger closer to home for consumers. The second report studied how the toxins remained in the clothes. The chemicals could have a direct impact on consumers by wearing them as well as entering the water supplies far from their points of origin when the clothes were washed. Here is a short segment from Dirty Laundry 2.

Further investigations by Greenpeace revealed that shoppers around the world are buying contaminated clothing and unwittingly spreading water pollution when they wash their new garments. Of the 78 articles analysed for Greenpeace's Dirty Laundry 2 report2, 52 tested positive for the presence of Nonylphenol ethoxylates (NPEs) above the detection limit of 1 milligram NPE per kilogram of material (mg/kg). Clothing from all but one of the fifteen brands tested (GAP, two samples) contained NPEs above the detection limit. The clothes sampled were purchased from shops in eighteen countries. (as quoted in "Detox Campaign," 2011, para 11).

Note how Greenpeace worked to tie the problem to specific brands. The garment or textile industries are vague entities for people. Who are they?What are their products?Greenpeace made the problem more personal and precise by identifying specific brands being supplied by the textile facilities creating the dangerous water pollution. People would know the brands and whether or not their purchases supported this irresponsible behavior.

Greenpeace is a major non-governmental organization (NGO) with operations around the world and has almost 3 million supporters ("About," n.d.). Greenpeace describes itself as "the leading independent campaigning organization that uses peaceful protest and creative communication to expose global environmental problems and to promote solutions that are essential to a green and peaceful future" ("About," n.d., para. 1). For over four decades, Greenpeace has utilized a variety of public relations techniques and tools as part of its "creative communication." That creative communication is part of its effort to pressure organizations into changing their operations. Detox is a current creative communication effort by Greenpeace designed to improve the environment.

Detox began with a petition action, which is a request for change. This means that Greenpeace sent letters to each of the companies that use the polluting facilities and asked them to stop sourcing from such destructive facilities. The companies declined to address Greenpeace's concerns for a number of reasons. Exhibit 19.1 lists the companies that Greenpeace contacted. Greenpeace then placed the corporate responses on the website that became the central organizing point for the Detox Campaign. Once the petition action was rejected, Greenpeace took the Detox Campaign to the consumers. The idea was to pressure the name brands into changing their practices by creating potentially negative perceptions among their consumers. Greenpeace would threaten reputational assets by revealing the irresponsible practices of the brands. Since most of the brand name owners portray themselves as responsible corporate citizens, the Detox Campaign was a threat to their corporate social responsibility (CSR) legitimacy, reputations, and ultimately their sales.

Exhibit 19.1   Original List of Companies That Responded Negatively to the Greenpeace Petition
Lacoste
Peerless
Adidas
American Eagle
Nike
Puma
Abercrombie & Fitch
GAP
Bauer Hockey
Lining
Metersbonwe
Youngor
H&M

("Letters," 2011)

The Detox Campaign utilized a variety of tactics to spread the word about harmful chemicals in the apparel industry. The name "Detox" is also the solution—stop sourcing from factories using toxic chemicals in their production. PUMA became the first major garment corporation to agree to Detox. PUMA's 2011 statement describing their support for the "Zero Discharge" advocated by Greenpeace can be found in Exhibit 19.2.

Exhibit 19.2   Puma Compliance Statement

PUMA Roadmap Towards Zero Discharge of Hazardous Chemicals

PUMA is fully committed to the Joint Industry Roadmap toward Zero Discharge of Hazardous Chemicals released by the adidas group, C&A, H&M, Li Ning, Nike and PUMA on November 18th.

The individual PUMA Roadmap as outlined below reflects PUMA's additional contributions to achieving the target of Zero Discharges by 2020.

PUMA's efforts to remove hazardous chemicals from products and production date back to 1999, when the first PUMA Handbook for Product Related Environmental Standards was established. In the meantime, this handbook has been superseded by the PUMA. Safe Handbook on Environmental Standards which is legally binding for PUMA suppliers and publicly available on the PUMA website at: http://safe.puma .com/us/en/category/workplace/

Since 1999, PUMA has worked intensively with its suppliers to ensure compliance to our Restricted Substances List (RSL) which is regularly updated to reflect new scientific developments.

As part of these efforts, PUMA eliminated PVC from its entire product range as early as 2003. PUMA also collaborated with Greenpeace on Chemicals Management in 2005 as part of the "Cleaning up our Chemical Homes" campaign.

Frequently updated information on hazardous chemicals through PUMA's membership in the AFIRM working group on restricted substances (http://www.afirm-group.com/), the Sustainable Apparel Coalition (www.apparelcoalition.org) and the Leather Working Group (http://www.leatherworkinggroup.com/) is being distributed into PUMA's supply chain through meetings and trainings.

PUMA's Approach towards Reaching our Zero Discharge Goals by 2020

In addition to the "Joint Roadmap Towards Zero Discharge of Hazardous Chemicals" PUMA will initiate the following brand specific actions:

- Update the current PUMA Restricted Substances List (RSL) and implement a Manufacturing Restricted Substances List (MRSL) until the end of 2011;
- Update the PUMA Safe Handbook on Environmental Standards with respect to the elimination of chemical groups classified as persistent, bio-accumulative and toxic (PBT); very persistent and very bio-accumulative (vPvB); carcinogenic, mutagenic and toxic for reproduction (CMR); endocrine disruptors (ED); or equivalent concern until mid 2012 (following consultation with stakeholders including Greenpeace);
- Support PUMA's efforts to phase out hazardous chemicals through the cooperation with organizations specialized in chemical management and evaluation (starting 2011);
- Encourage Strategic PUMA Suppliers to disclose their chemicals management systems regularly within their own Sustainability Reports (starting 2012) as part of the existing PUMA GANTSCh Initiative (http://safe.puma.com/us/en/2010/05/ puma-commits-its-strategic-suppliers-to-sustainability-reporting/#more-705)

- Raise awareness among PUMA Suppliers through capacity building measures on chemical management
- Integrate the phasing out of hazardous chemicals in the supply chain as an additional element of the existing PUMA sustainability scorecard 2015.
- Report frequently on the ongoing results of PUMA's activities in relation to phasing out hazardous chemicals in PUMA's Annual Financial and Sustainability Report.

This ambitious approach can only be realized through a cooperation of internal and external stakeholders and partners. PUMA looks forward to working with our industry peers, our suppliers as well as the Chemical Industry to achieve this paradigm shift in Chemicals Management.

("PUMA," 2011)

Exhibit 19.3   Adidas Compliance Statement

Adidas Group's Commitment to Zero Discharge of hazardous chemicals

Herzogenaurach, August 26, 2011

Context

Since July 2011 Greenpeace International has been campaigning to drive change in our industry. They are calling for the zero discharge of all hazardous and persistent chemicals at all points in global supply chains: from the cotton fields, to the mills and dye houses that make the fabric and the garment production. In China alone, there are an estimated 50,000 textile mills and hundreds of chemicals suppliers. To put this in context, the adidas Group buys fabric from 10 key textile mills and dye houses in China. These materials suppliers follow some of the strictest standards in the industry.

Greenpeace has directed its campaign towards sporting goods companies in the belief that they can act as a catalyst for change for the whole industry. Why? Because sporting goods companies, such as the adidas Group, are already widely recognised for their leadership when it comes to environmental sustainability. The adidas Group has one of the most stringent restricted substances policies of any consumer goods company operating in the apparel sector. We have been working successfully on the reduction and progressive elimination of hazardous chemicals in our supply chain for more than 15 years.

Greenpeace's Detox campaign has been characterised as a competition among brands. The simple truth, however, is that there can be no "winners" unless the industry acts together. With that objective in mind, the adidas Group has together with other brands been working tirelessly in recent weeks to bring the industry together in a forum to develop a roadmap that will address the "zero discharge" challenge that Greenpeace has posed. That forum is planned to be held at the end of September in Amsterdam.

The following statement is our commitment to deliver change.

Our statement to Greenpeace

The adidas Group is committed to the goal of zero discharge of hazardous chemicals from our supply chain via all pathways, with a 2020 timeline.

The scale and complexity of this endeavour make this a very challenging task, which we will work on through an open and informed dialogue with all stakeholders.

If we are to deliver lasting solutions, our actions need to be guided by transparency, fact-based decision-making and based on a preventative, precautionary and integrated approach to chemicals management.

Within seven weeks, we will develop a roadmap specifically for the adidas Group and our entire supply chain, which will include programmes and actions that we commit to, including actions concerning disclosure. In addition, we will develop and disclose a joint roadmap to detail specific programmes and actions that we can take collectively with other brands to drive our industry towards the goal of zero discharge of hazardous chemicals.

This goal demands the collective action of industry, regulators and other stakeholders. We believe that the elimination of hazardous chemicals needs not only collaboration and partnership with our industry peers, but also a holistic and integrated approach. We will apply value-chain as well as life-cycle thinking and innovation throughout this process and to our approach for Integrated Chemicals Management.

Further, we recognise that to achieve the goal of zero discharge of hazardous chemicals, mechanisms for disclosure and transparency about the hazardous chemicals used in our global supply chains are important and necessary, in line with the "right to know principle." A set of actions to be executed by the adidas Group within the period of these seven weeks will be:

- Re-emphasising to our suppliers, T1 and nominated T2, the strict standards of our Environmental Guidelines and our Restricted Substances List (RSL).
- Request information from our suppliers in relation to the use of NPEs in the manufacturing processes and request that they require of their sub-suppliers to avoid the intentional use of NPEs.
- Request information from our T2 suppliers about their chemicals suppliers.
- Give renewed notice to our suppliers that they must eliminate and replace hazardous substances that have been banned from use, with a non-hazardous chemical.
- Increase the focus on chemicals management and wastewater treatment practices in our regular, comprehensive, environmental audit programme, with specific attention given to the T2 suppliers.
- Begin developing a workshop approach for designers and product developers, where the understanding and knowledge of the colour choice consequences will be enhanced, as well as screening support is delivered. This work will be supported by our target-in-progress to reduce the number of colours used.
- Continue our dialogue with peers to develop a joint roadmap.
- Engage with other brands and associations to increase the leverage of such a joint roadmap. . . .

Furthermore, we foresee that the joint roadmap would contain activities, research and decision milestones related to the following, specific aspects:

- Application of a value-chain approach with a set of priorities and a phased approach.
- Drive the implementation of a Globally Harmonised System of Classification and Labelling of Chemicals.

- Develop or apply an approach to structure inventories of hazardous chemicals.
- Apply a rigorous and transparent verification procedure.
- Develop a joint generic environmental audit approach, with specific attention to, but not narrowly focussed on, chemicals management. The additional purpose will be to begin sharing audit experiences and results between brands with the ultimate aim to improve environmental audit coverage and reduce duplication.
- Develop a single standard of good environmental practices for dye houses. This will include sound chemicals management. The development will be done in wide consultation.
- Work with chemicals suppliers to develop screening, selection criteria and prioritisation approaches to drive the elimination of hazardous chemicals and the substitution with less harmful chemicals.
- Strive to define timelines for the phase-out of the prioritised hazardous substances.
- Assess the need for inclusion of additional chemicals to the RSL.
- Assess the need for inclusion of additional chemicals on lists of banned (from the manufacturing) chemicals.
- Develop mechanisms to transfer experiences with banned, phased-out chemicals from region to region and promote the global implementation of bans that have already been successfully executed in one region.
- Enter into a dialogue with scientists and regulators in different regions with the purpose of influencing the pace of regulation of hazardous chemicals and the diffusion of a global approach to regulation. . . .

Many of these activities build on programmes and initiatives which the adidas Group is already committed to, through our existing industry collaborations, such as the Sustainable Apparel Coalition, the OIA (Outdoor Industry Association) Working Group on Toxics and AFIRM.

("adidas," 2011)

Exhibit 19.4   Nike Statement

NIKE, Inc. Commitment on Zero Discharge of Hazardous Chemicals

17 August, 2011

In support of the principles of prevention and precaution, and in line with our overall commitment to water stewardship, NIKE, Inc. supports the goal of systemic change to achieve zero discharge of hazardous chemicals associated with supply chains and the lifecycles of products within one generation or less.

NIKE, Inc. is committed to the goal of zero discharge of hazardous chemicals by 2020.

To make this a reality, NIKE, Inc. will continue phasing out hazardous chemicals in our supply chain and we will accelerate the phase out of the highest priority hazardous chemicals. NIKE, Inc. will continue to work with brands, material suppliers, the broader chemical industry, NGOs and other stakeholders to achieve this goal. We will drive towards innovative solutions for transparency in chemical management disclosure.

We recognize the path to reaching this goal must be through innovation, the application of green chemistry, and broad industry and regulatory collaboration and engagement. NIKE, Inc.'s commitment and investment towards this goal and the dedication to system change is unwavering.

We will work tirelessly to affect system change across the industry towards this goal. This commitment includes sustained investment in moving industry, government, science and technology to deliver on systemic change.

We commit to continue to share what we learn, our approaches and tools and work with others in finding new solutions and removing existing barriers, and to report progress towards comprehensive chemicals management.

Within eight weeks, NIKE, Inc. will announce its action plan for the goal of eliminating hazardous chemicals within our supply chain addressing transparency, chemical management, including how we will address the need for industry disclosure in line with right to know principles and a timeline for the elimination of the highest priority hazardous chemicals. Due to the highly complex and shared nature of supply chains, we invite others in our industry to co-create a broader action plan for the industry, as collaboration is critical to drive progress.

("Nike," 2011)

One of the first tactics to be employed was a video challenge posted to YouTube, calling on garment industry giants Nike and adidas to Detox. The challenge video was followed by protests at Nike and adidas retail outlets around the world. Protestors danced and stripped in front of the stores. Videos of the protests were then edited for a second video, calling on Nike and adidas to Detox. Both corporations did agree to Detox, and their statements can be found in Exhibit 19.3. Greenpeace was slowly gaining corporate acceptance for Detox. Greenpeace reflected on its progress:

"Now the market leaders have blazed a trail for the industry to follow, we'll be making sure the pack maintain the pace as they race towards zero. All around the world, the consumers of both their products and their pollution deserve nothing less than full transparency and a total detox," added Greenpeace UK campaigner Tamara Stark ("Impossible," 2011, para 7).

Following the release of the Dirty Laundry reports it appears that "Detoxing" is back in fashion, with a number of other clothing brands publicly engaging in the "Detox" challenge, including Lacoste (9), G-Star Raw (10), Uniqlo (11) and Chinese sports brand Li Ning. Greenpeace will be talking with all of these brands in the coming weeks to turn their initial engagement into strong individual commitments for a toxic-free future. ("Impossible," 2011, para. 5).

It is interesting how Greenpeace acknowledges the strategy of targeting the industry leaders first as a way to build pressure on other brands. Also, the range of brand leaders agreeing to Detox reflects a very global collection.

The effort to target H&M is one of the best illustrations of the mix of tactics and global reach of the Detox Campaign. H&M is a Swedish retailer with a strong European brand and growing global presence. Greenpeace made H&M a priority target because it is the largest clothing company appearing in its Dirty Laundry reports. Again, the belief is that if the largest among a group of companies agrees to change, the smaller ones will follow. In September of 2011, H&M was the focus of internationally coordinated pressure that used a mix of in-person and online communication tactics. Public relations was being used to pressure H&M by increasing stakeholder awareness of their use of toxic chemicals. Here is the core message Greenpeace was communicating:

> There's a skeleton in H&M's closet. The fast-fashion retailer sells clothes made with chemicals which cause hazardous water pollution around the world, and the only way to stop this water pollution is to come clean and stop using such chemicals for good. As one of the largest clothing groups in the world, an H&M committed to a toxic-free future would set the trend for the rest of the fashion industry to follow. ("Will," 2011, para 1).

The H&M element of the Detox Campaign fused in-person and online tactics. The in-person tactics involved people in 12 different nations, placing stickers on the windows at H&M stores that said "Detox our future" and "Detox our water." The sticker protests helped to attract traditional or legacy media attention and to raise awareness among customers at those stores. This was an international, in-person effort. The online tactics included Twitter and Facebook. These two social media channels had strategic value because H&M utilizes these channels to reach customers. H&M has over 6 million people who "like" it on Facebook and uses Twitter to disseminate brand information. Greenpeace started a petition on Twitter about H&M and Detox. The petition reached over 635,000 Twitter users and was retweeted over 1,200 times. On Facebook, people began posting questions and comments about the Detox Campaign, and others where indicating they liked the Detox postings. As Greepeace observed about H&M, "Its reputation as a sustainability leader was on the line" ("Clickers," 2011, para 7). Within a few days of this concentrated effort, H&M met with Greenpeace and agreed to Detox. Here is part of the announcement from H&M:

> Greenpeace International is calling for zero discharge of all hazardous chemicals in the global textile supply chain. H&M shares this goal with Greenpeace; since 1995 H&M has been working practically to reduce the use and impact of hazardous chemicals using an approach based on the Precautionary Principle. This is a continuous process depending on development of science and technology and revisions will therefore be necessary in future, not limited to the period up to 2020. ("H&M," 2011, para 1)

Through public relations efforts, Greenpeace has successfully moved a number of companies to act on Detox after those companies declined the original petition for Detox. The H&M segment of the campaign highlights the international dimension and multichannel of Greenpeace's efforts to pressure corporations into Detoxing.

The Detox Campaign keeps progressing. In December of 2011, C&A (a leading fashion retailer originating from Germany) and Li-Ning (China's largest sportswear company) agreed to be toxin free by 2010. In October of 2012, Marks & Spencer (a major British clothing retailer) agreed to Detox as well. The companies have all agreed to what is called the *joint roadmap*. The joint roadmap is a plan to move toward zero discharge of hazardous chemicals (ZDHC) in the supply chain by 2020. Greenpeace defined zero discharge:

> **Zero discharge:** Elimination of all releases, via all pathways of release, i.e. discharges, emissions and losses, from our supply chains and our products. In light of the increasing sophistication of analytical tools and methods, references to "elimination" or "zero" must be understood as "not above background concentration" rather than "not detectable." ("Joint," 2011, p. 4, section 1.2)

Each company that agrees to Detox is accepting the joint roadmap.

While Greenpeace is excited about the progress, the organization feels there is still much to be done to Detox the world. First, there are other organizations in the garment industry that need to agree to the joint roadmap. Global brand groups including Abercrombie & Fitch, Ralph Lauren, and G-Star are still contributing to pollution through their supply chains ("Detox Timeline," 2012). Second, Greenpeace would like to see greater commitment to the joint roadmap by those who have agreed to it. Greenpeace feels there is a need for "concrete and measurable deliverables and timelines" by most of the signees ("Progress," 2012, para. 7). Greenpeace is pushing signees to do more, including disclosing on company websites the pollution released by suppliers ("Progress," 2012). The Detox Campaign continues as Greenpeace targets new organizations and pressures those that have agreed to Detox to prove they are taking concrete steps toward zero discharge.

Reading Guide

1. If this situation is a crisis, what type of crisis is it?

2. What is the problem and the source(s) of the problem in this case?

3. What stakeholders should be interested in this case?

4. What strategies did Greenpeace use in its Detox Campaign?

5. What company was the first to take action on Detox?

6. Why did H&M become a target?

7. Why is combining online and real-world actions so powerful?

8. How can paracrisis be used to explain some aspects of this case?

Discussion Questions

1. What is the ethicality of "forcing" companies to become more socially responsible? Explain your answer.

2. Why does a challenge become more powerful when it combines online and real-world activities?

3. What was the role of social media in this case?

4. How does this case illustrate the effects of globalization on corporations and NGOs?

5. Why should corporations give into protests similar to Detox? Why should they not? Justify your answer.

6. What are the differences and similarities between the compliance statements of Puma, adidas, and Nike? What are the possible reasons for these differences, and how do they relate to crisis communication?

7. What effect might past successes in the Detox Campaign have on new targets for the Greenpeace campaign?

Websites

Detox Campaign: http://www.greenpeace.org/international/en/campaigns/toxics/water/detox/

Dirty Laundry reports: http://www.greenpeace.org/international/en/publications/reports/Dirty-Laundry/

YouTube video of a Detox protest in Germany: http://www.greenpeace.org/international/en/publications/reports/Dirty-Laundry/

Story about H&M bowing to pressure: http://www.greenconduct.com/news/2011/09/23/nike-and-hm-bow-to-greenpeaces-detox-challenge/

References

About. (n.d.). (2011). Retrieved from http://www.adidas-group.com/en/sustainability/News/2011/Commitment_to_Zero_Discharge_Aug_2011.aspx

Clickers and stickers make H&M detox. (2011). Retrieved from http://www.greenpeace.org/international/en/news/features/Clickers-and-Stickers-Make-HM-Detox/

Detox Campaign. (2011). Retrieved from http://www.greenpeace.org/international/en/campaigns/toxics/water/detox/intro/

Detox timeline. (2012). Retrieved from http://www.greenpeace.org/international/en/campaigns/toxics/water/detox/Detox-Timeline/

Dirty laundry 2: Hung out to dry. (2011). Greenpeace International. Retrieved from http://www.greenpeace.org/international/Global/international/publications/toxics/Water%202011/dirty-laundry-report-2.pdf

H&M engages with Greenpeace. (2011). Retrieved from http://activacorp.net/nano/new/

Impossible is nothing as adidas join Nike and Puma in cleaning up their supply chain. (2011). Retrieved fromhttp://www.greenpeace.org/international/en/press/releases/Impossible-is-nothing-as-Adidas-join-Nike-and-Puma-in-cleaning-up-their-supply-chain-/

Joint roadmap: Toward zero discharge of hazardous chemicals. (2011). Retrieved from http://www.roadmaptozero.com/pdf/Joint_Roadmap_November_2011.pdf

Letters received from the companies. (2011, July 11). Retrieved from http://www.greenpeace.org/international/en/campaigns/toxics/water/nike-adidas-detox/Letters-received-from-the-companies/

Nike, Inc. commitment to zero discharge of hazardous chemicals. (2011). Retrieved from http://nikeinc.com/news/nike-inc-commitment-on-zero-discharge-of-hazardous-chemicals

Progress and hurdles on the road to detox. (2012). Retrieved from http://www.greenpeace.org/international/en/campaigns/toxics/water/detox/intro/Progress-and-hurdles-on-the-road-to-Detox/

PUMA Roadmap towards Zero Discharge of Hazardous Chemicals. (2011). Retrieved from http://about.puma.com/wp-content/themes/aboutPUMA_theme/media/pdf/2011/pumaroadmap.pdf

Will H&M make "detox" the new must have? (2011). Retrieved from http://tweetbuzz.us/entry/68200175/www.greenpeace.org/international/en/news/features/hm-detox/

Index

About the Author

W. Timothy Coombs, PhD, Purdue University, is a full professor in the Nicholson School of Communication at the University of Central Florida. He is the 2002 recipient of the Jackson Jackson & Wagner Behavioral Science Prize from the Public Relations Society of America for his crisis research, which led to the development and testing of the situational crisis communication theory (SCCT). SCCT provides recommendations about how crisis managers should respond to crises by evaluating key elements of the crisis situation. Dr. Coombs has published widely in the areas of crisis management and preparedness, including a number of journal articles and book chapters. His research includes the award-winning book *Ongoing Crisis Communication* as well as *Code Red in the Boardroom: Crisis Management as Organizational DNA*. He is coauthor of a number of books, including *It's Not Just PR* and *Public Relations Strategy and Application: Managing Influence* with Sherry Holladay and *Today's Public Relations* with Robert Heath. He has edited *The Handbook of Business Security* and coedited *The Handbook of Crisis Communication* with Sherry Holladay. He was part of the Darden School of Management Batten Institute's "Defining Leadership: A Forum to Discuss Crisis Leadership Competency" and has a chapter in the related publication, *Executive Briefing on Crisis Leadership*. Dr. Coombs has lectured on the subject of crisis management at various venues in the United States, Denmark, Norway, Sweden, Belgium, the United Kingdom, Hong Kong, and Australia. He has also consulted with companies in the petrochemical and health care industries on crisis-related topics.

⑤SAGE research**methods**

The essential online tool for researchers from the world's leading methods publisher

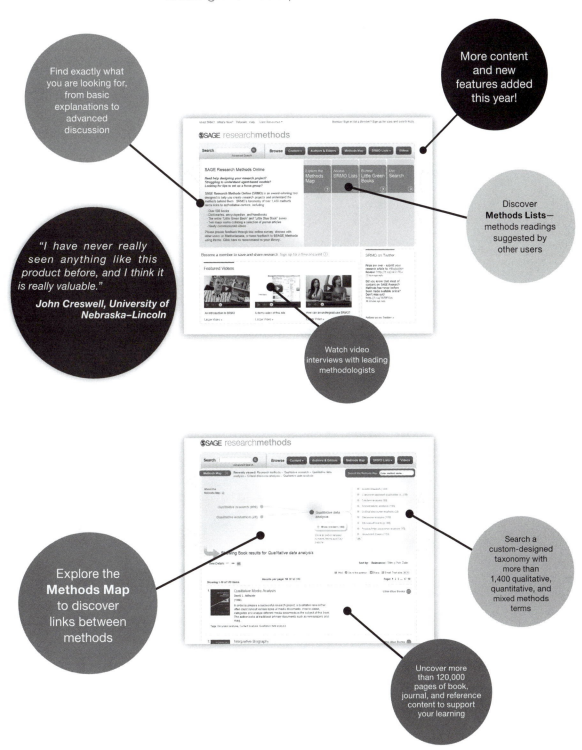

Find exactly what you are looking for, from basic explanations to advanced discussion

More content and new features added this year!

Discover **Methods Lists**— methods readings suggested by other users

"I have never really seen anything like this product before, and I think it is really valuable."

John Creswell, University of Nebraska–Lincoln

Watch video interviews with leading methodologists

Explore the **Methods Map** to discover links between methods

Search a custom-designed taxonomy with more than 1,400 qualitative, quantitative, and mixed methods terms

Uncover more than 120,000 pages of book, journal, and reference content to support your learning

Find out more at
www.sageresearchmethods.com